Implementing Program Management

Templates and Forms Aligned with the *Standard for Program Management* – Second Edition (2008)

Ginger Levin, PMP, PgMP
Allen R. Green, PMP, PgMP

CRC Press
Taylor & Francis Group
Boca Raton London New York

CRC Press is an imprint of the
Taylor & Francis Group, an **informa** business

AN AUERBACH BOOK

CRC Press
Taylor & Francis Group
6000 Broken Sound Parkway NW, Suite 300
Boca Raton, FL 33487-2742

© 2010 by Taylor and Francis Group, LLC
CRC Press is an imprint of Taylor & Francis Group, an Informa business

No claim to original U.S. Government works

Printed in the United States of America on acid-free paper
10 9 8 7 6 5 4 3 2 1

International Standard Book Number: 978-1-4398-1605-9 (Hardback)

This book contains information obtained from authentic and highly regarded sources. Reasonable efforts have been made to publish reliable data and information, but the author and publisher cannot assume responsibility for the validity of all materials or the consequences of their use. The authors and publishers have attempted to trace the copyright holders of all material reproduced in this publication and apologize to copyright holders if permission to publish in this form has not been obtained. If any copyright material has not been acknowledged please write and let us know so we may rectify in any future reprint.

Except as permitted under U.S. Copyright Law, no part of this book may be reprinted, reproduced, transmitted, or utilized in any form by any electronic, mechanical, or other means, now known or hereafter invented, including photocopying, microfilming, and recording, or in any information storage or retrieval system, without written permission from the publishers.

For permission to photocopy or use material electronically from this work, please access www.copyright.com (http://www.copyright.com/) or contact the Copyright Clearance Center, Inc. (CCC), 222 Rosewood Drive, Danvers, MA 01923, 978-750-8400. CCC is a not-for-profit organization that provides licenses and registration for a variety of users. For organizations that have been granted a photocopy license by the CCC, a separate system of payment has been arranged.

Trademark Notice: Product or corporate names may be trademarks or registered trademarks, and are used only for identification and explanation without intent to infringe.

Library of Congress Cataloging-in-Publication Data

Levin, Ginger.
   Implementing program management : templates and forms aligned with the standard for program management / Ginger Levin, Allen R. Green.
      p. cm.
   Includes bibliographical references and index.
   ISBN 978-1-4398-1605-9 (hardcover : alk. paper)
   1. Project management. I. Green, Allen R. II. Title.

HD69.P75.L483 2009
658.4'04--dc22   2009031666

Visit the Taylor & Francis Web site at
http://www.taylorandfrancis.com

and the CRC Press Web site at
http://www.crcpress.com

Personal Property of Cynthia Self

Dedication

To my husband, Morris, for his continuing support and love.

—Ginger Levin

To my loving wife, Cindy, who somehow manages to love me back even when I work too much.

—Allen Green

Contents

Foreword xi
Preface xiii
About the Authors xv
Acronyms xvii

1 Introduction 1
   About Program Management 2

2 Getting Started 3
   Why So Many Plans? 3
   First Steps 4

3 The Pre-Program Preparations Phase 5
   Program Benefits Statement 5
      Program Benefits Statement Instructions 6
   Initial Stakeholder Identification 6
      Initial Stakeholder Identification Instructions 7
   Program Business Case 10
      Program Business Case Instructions 10
   Program Brief 14
      Program Brief Instructions 14

4 The Program Initiation Phase 21
   Program Charter 21
      Program Charter Instructions 22
   Program Road Map 27
      Program Road Map Instructions 28

5 The Program Setup Phase 33
   Benefits Realization Plan 33
      Benefits Realization Plan Instructions 34
   Program Governance Plan 40
      Program Governance Plan Instructions 40

Phase Gate Review Agenda 46
    Phase Gate Review Agenda Instructions 46
Program Review Agenda 48
    Program Review Agenda Instructions 48
Issue Escalation Process 50
    Issue Escalation Process Instructions 50
Audit Plan 53
    Audit Plan Instructions 53
Change Management Plan 57
    Change Management Plan Instructions 58
Program Scope Management Plan 63
    Program Scope Management Plan Instructions 63
Program Scope Statement 67
    Program Scope Statement Instructions 68
Program Stakeholder Management Plan 72
    Program Stakeholder Management Plan Instructions 72
    Considerations 77
    Steps to Consider in Preparing the Plan 77
Component Stakeholder Management Guidelines 78
    Component Stakeholder Management Guidelines Instructions 78
Stakeholder Register 80
    Stakeholder Register Instructions 80
Stakeholder Inventory 82
    Stakeholder Inventory Instructions 83
Stakeholder Management Strategy 87
    Stakeholder Management Strategy Instructions 87
Program Communications Management Plan 91
    Program Communications Management Plan Instructions 91
Communications Log 97
    Communications Log Instructions 98
Communications Strategy 99
    Communications Strategy Instructions 99
Program Resource Plan 103
    Program Resource Plan Instructions 103
Program Requirements Document 107
    Program Requirements Document Instructions 107
Program Architecture Plan—Baseline 112
    Program Architecture Plan—Baseline Instructions 112
Task Responsibility Matrix 116
Program WBS 116
Work Breakdown Structure Matrix 116

Quality Management Plan 117
    Quality Management Plan Instructions 117
Risk Management Planning Meeting Agenda 121
    Risk Management Planning Meeting Agenda Instructions 121
Lessons Learned Review Agenda 123
    Lessons Learned Review Agenda Instructions 123
Lessons Learned Database 124
    Lessons Learned Database Instructions 125
Program Risk Management Plan 127
    Program Risk Management Plan Instructions 127
Program Risk Register 133
    Program Risk Register Instructions 133
    Probability/Impact Matrix 136
Contingency Plan 137
    Contingency Plan Instructions 137
Change Request Form 140
    Change Request Form Instructions 140
Schedule Management Plan 141
    Schedule Management Plan Instructions 142
Program Financial Plan 145
    Program Financial Plan Instructions 145
Financial Metrics 150
Procurement Management Plan 150
    Procurement Management Plan Instructions 151
Contracts Management Plan 156
    Contracts Management Plan Instructions 156
Interface Management Plan 163
    Interface Management Plan Instructions 164
Staffing Management Plan 168
    Staffing Management Plan Instructions 168
Program Transition Plan 173
    Program Transition Plan Instructions 173
Program Management Plan 176
    Program Management Plan Instructions 178
Knowledge Management Plan 185
    Knowledge Management Plan Instructions 185

6 The Delivery of Program Benefits Phase: Executing 191
Team Charter 191
    Team Charter Instructions 192
Audit Report 198
    Audit Report Instructions 198

Decision Log...202
    Decision Log Instructions...203
Component Initiation Request...205
    Component Initiation Request Instructions 205
Component Transition Request 209
    Component Transition Request Instructions................................210
Program Issues Register 214
    Program Issues Register Instructions 214
Change Request Log...218
    Change Request Log Instructions..218
Component Charter 223
    Component Charter Instructions 223

7 The Delivery of Program Benefits Phase: Monitoring and Controlling...227
Impact Analysis 227
    Impact Analysis Instructions 228
Benefits Realization Report..231
    Benefits Realization Report Instructions......................................231
Governance Decision Register 235
    Governance Decision Register Instructions 235
Program Performance Report 237
    Program Performance Report Instructions 237
Program Closure Recommendation 244
    Program Closure Recommendation Instructions 245
Risk Audit Report..249
    Risk Audit Report Instructions...249

8 The Program Closure Phase 255
Contract Closure Procedure...255
    Contract Closure Procedure Instructions.....................................256
Program Final Report..258
    Program Final Report Instructions...258
Knowledge Transition... 266
    Knowledge Transition Report Instructions................................. 266
Supplier Performance Review 271
    Supplier Performance Review Agenda Instructions.....................271
Procurement Performance Report...273
    Procurement Performance Report Instructions..........................273
Component Termination Request...278
    Component Termination Request Instructions...........................278

References 283
Index 285

Foreword

This year marks the fortieth anniversary of Project Management Institute (PMI®). In 1984, PMI launched the Project Management Professional (PMP®) credential designed for PM Professionals. By the early 1990s there were still less than a thousand credentialed PMPs. The publication of the 1996 Project Management Body of Knowledge (PMBOK®) guide marked the beginning of the future. Still, at that time there were less than seven thousand PMPs worldwide. Because of the year 2000 scare, the PMP® credential became very popular with IT professionals. During this time, AT&T decided to get all their project managers certified as PMPs in hopes of developing a competitive advantage. Sprint and MCI quickly followed suit. Today there are more than 325,000 PMPs worldwide. With the increased interest and focus for organizations and businesses to perform work using project management, it was only natural that emphasis also needed to be placed on program management. In early 2007, PMI piloted the Program Management Professional (PgMP®) credential and launched it publicly in October of the same year. To date, approximately 300 people have obtained this difficult credential, with Ginger, Allen, and me being a lucky three that have. While the number of PMP®-credentialed PMs gains by over a thousand per month, the number of PgMPs increases by only ten per month because of the difficulty in the requirements and completing the process of obtaining it. However, with the growing interest in program management as a profession unto itself, we should see an exponential increase in PgMPs over the coming years.

I first met Dr. Ginger Levin at the 2007 PMI Congress, as she was also one of the thirty-one successful pilot participants to receive the PgMP® credential. She has been a leader in the field of program management education ever since, developing and teaching a PgMP® boot camp class. Now Ginger has teamed up with Allen Green, another respected PgMP®, to write this first-ever complete reference book specifically for program managers. This book will most certainly be an excellent source of information for the new to the most experienced program manager. It is well thought out and provides a detailed step-by-step methodology for managing a program from initiation to closure. Having received an early copy, mine is now dog-eared and filled with small yellow Post-its on the edge to mark references. No doubt, you will make at least one change or improvement to your program by using this book, so consider the purchase a good small investment.

With that said, I'm honored to write the foreword for their book. Enjoy!

Jeffrey G. Hodgkinson, PMP®, PgMP®
PMO/Program Manager at Intel

Preface

> Let our advance worrying become advance thinking and planning.
> —**Winston Churchill**

Many of the most successful organizations worldwide have specific program management templates that they treat as carefully guarded trade secrets and consider critical to their consistent success. At this writing, it is difficult to find examples of many of the myriad documents referenced in the Project Management Institute's (PMI®) *Standard for Program Management*—Second Edition (2008), released December 2008. When we do find roughly comparable documents here and there, they overlap or are intended for specific situations or even atypical definitions of project or program management. What is a practitioner supposed to do? What is supposed to be in the various documents? How do they complement rather than overlap each other?

This book is an attempt to lift the shroud of obscurity surrounding such documents. The templates and forms herein are examples to consider for making your next programmatic adventure a little less reminiscent of a sequel to *Raiders of the Lost Ark*. We want this book to be a liberating breath of fresh air that breaks the writer's block so commonly encountered in the program management process. We feel it will also be extremely valuable to students of program management, who forever request "go-by" templates for their work, and rightfully so.

The professions (and we dare say arts) of project and program management are moving toward maturity and standards. PMI's *A Guide to the Project Management Body of Knowledge*—Fourth Edition (2008) and the *Standard for Program Management*—Second Edition (2008) are already standards of the American National Standards Institute (ANSI). Further, as we write, a current International Organization for Standardization (ISO) effort is establishing a global standard for project management knowledge and processes. PMI is playing a very active role in that effort. Various organizations worldwide will likely position themselves as consistent with that ISO standard. Program and portfolio management are not currently on the ISO radar screen, but their standardization would seem a natural next step. We have chosen to align this book as much as possible with PMI's *Standard for Program Management* —Second Edition (2008). Included are details on many of the elements referenced in that standard and a few additional items complementary to those elements. It is critical to realize that, as an industry-agnostic work, the *Standard for Program Management* —Second Edition (2008) must be adapted in multiple ways when used on any specific program:

1. For the given industry and industry segment
2. For the culture and practices of a given organization
3. For the preferences of the program manager and program team
4. For the target program and its environment, considering its purpose and scale

That is a lot of adaptation! Program documents are a little like a covered dish supper at Grandma's house in that each planner has unique tastes. So it is that the *Standard for Program Management*—Second Edition (2008) is a backbone of best practices, which must be considered and tailored for each situation.

As just one illustration, consider the *Defense Acquisition Guidebook*[1] published by the U.S. Department of Defense. Accommodating multi-billion-dollar programs and having complex stakeholder relationships, many consider that program management discipline to be completely different. In fact, it has much in common with the *Standard for Program Management* —Second Edition (2008) at its core, and several plans herein are valuable elaborations of its prescribed documents.

Many program practitioners may already have commercial off-the-shelf or homegrown systems in place that implement some of the concepts we illustrate here. We hope this book spurs ideas for improvement of those systems as well.

So it is that your documents will likely look quite different. Bravo!

Ginger Levin, PMP®, PgMP®
Lighthouse Point, Florida

Allen R. Green, PMP®, PgMP®
Huntsville, Alabama

About the Authors

Ginger Levin, Ph.D., is a senior consultant and educator in project management. Her specialty areas are portfolio management, program management, the project management office, metrics, and maturity assessments. She is certified as a PMP®, PgMP®, and *OPM3* (Organizational Project Management Maturity Model) assessor and consultant.

In addition, Dr. Levin is an adjunct professor in project management for the University of Wisconsin–Platteville and for Esc Lille University, France, in its project management program at the master's and doctoral levels. Also, she is a visiting professor for RMIT in Melbourne, Australia, and a registered examiner for UTS in Sydney, Australia.

In consulting, she has served as project manager in numerous efforts for Fortune 500 and public sector clients, including Bank One, UPS, Citibank, the Food and Drug Administration, General Electric, SAP, EADS, John Deere, Schreiber Foods, TRW, New York City Transit Authority, and the U.S. Department of Agriculture. Prior to her work in consulting, she held positions of increasing responsibility with the U.S. government, including the Federal Aviation Administration, the Office of Personnel Management, and the General Accounting Office.

She is the co-author of *Project Portfolio Management*, *Metrics for Project Management*, *Achieving Project Management Success with Virtual Teams*, *Advanced Project Management Office: A Comprehensive Look at Function and Implementation*, *People Skills for Project Managers*, *Essential People Skills for Project Managers*, *The Business Development Capability Maturity Model*, and ESI's *PMP® Challenge!*, *PMP® Study Guide*, and *PgMP® Study Guide*.

Dr. Levin received her doctorate in information systems technology and public administration from The George Washington University, and received the

Outstanding Dissertation Award for her research on large organizations. She also received her master of science in business administration from Wake Forest University.

Allen R. Green, MS, PMP®, PgMP®, of Science Applications International Corporation, is currently president-elect of Project Management Institute's North Alabama Chapter. As the chapter's professional development vice president he organized and participated in the training of hundreds of Project Management Professional (PMP®) and Program Management Professional (PgMP®) candidates. He has broad and extensive leadership experience in the commercial, military, National Aeronautics and Space Administration, civil service, civic, local government, and academic sectors.

He led software development projects at Capability Maturity Model Integrated (CMMI) levels II through V for twelve years, including the earliest delivered applications for the U.S. Army's Future Combat System. His additional training experience included tours as president and management development vice president of the Alabama Junior Chamber of Commerce, metropolitan vice president of the U.S. Junior Chamber of Commerce, and president of the Alabama Junior Chamber of Commerce Foundation, with responsibility for training of project planners. As vice chairman of the Madison County Emergency Communications (E-911) Board, he chaired the effort to establish a unified central call center in Madison County, Alabama. In the commercial sector, he led the development program for the first shrink-wrapped electronic software distribution suite for industry standard microcomputers.

His current focus is on process improvement, operations, and planning for large defense programs. He received PMI's PgMP® credential in August 2008 and his bachelor of electrical engineering and master of science in electrical engineering degrees from Auburn University.

Acronyms

DoD	U.S. Department of Defense
KM	Knowledge management
MIL-HDBK	Military Standard
PWBS	Program work breakdown structure
PMBOK®	Project Management Body of Knowledge
PMI®	Project Management Institute
RAM	Responsibility assignment matrix
RACI	Responsible, accountable, consult, inform

Chapter 1

Introduction

> Discipline is the bridge between goals and accomplishment.
>
> —Jim Rohn

This book is a workbook for successful program management. Success in program management requires discipline—the kind of discipline that results in repeatability of success. It requires appropriately complete plans, well-run meetings with meaningful agendas, accurate record keeping, and general adherence to global best practices. Toward those ends, this book is a compendium of plans, forms, agendas, registers, and procedures.

This work is specifically designed to be compatible with and in a few cases supplementary to the Project Management Institute's (PMI®) *Standard for Program Management*—Second Edition (2008). Starting out to produce artifact prototypes for all the documents mentioned therein, we found that the task proved a bit more elusive than expected. Some artifacts have slightly different names at different locations in the standard. Some documents are explicitly enumerated in the *Standard for Program Management*—Second Edition (2008), and others are more implicit—so we have made judgments as to what to include. We have included almost all of the identifiable documents referenced in the *Standard for Program Management*—Second Edition (2008). We have also kept some useful ones from prior editions (including the Second Edition's Exposure Draft) that are now omitted. We also added some of our own. In a couple of instances, the *Standard for Program Management*—Second Edition (2008) defers to PMI's *A Guide to the Project Management Body of Knowledge*—Fourth Edition (PMBOK®), and so do we.

This work is not intended to be a complete guide to program management. Nor will it be useful as a supplementary study for PMI's Program Management

Professional (PgMP®) credential examination. You will need the *Standard for Program Management*—Second Edition (2008) and perhaps some of the other available texts on program management. We make no assumptions about your level of experience in program management but accept the fact that you may or may not be new to the discipline.

Our focus is on two heretofore neglected agendas: (1) helping you apply the *Standard for Program Management*—Second Edition (2008) in the successful execution of your program on a daily basis, and (2) meeting the needs of undergraduate and graduate students at the university level and those in short courses in program management who may require guidance in their planning and execution exercises.

About Program Management

Although projects have been under way since the time of the pyramids, and project management emerged as a profession in the late 1950s and early 1960s, we now work in a project-oriented society. However, rather than having only one or two large projects under way, organizations have hundreds of projects of various sizes and complexities. Organizations view projects as assets and are practicing management by projects.

The emphasis, though, now has shifted to program management.

If projects, and other ongoing work, can be grouped into a program because they share common attributes, the organization can then realize more benefits than if the projects were managed in a stand-alone fashion, resources can be coordinated across projects, customer relationship management is improved, as well as supply chain management, and greater effectiveness and efficiencies can result.

Recognizing the increasing use of programs, in 2006, PMI issued a standard on program management, which was then updated at the end of 2008. This standard describes best practices in program management and contains a common set of terms to best communicate globally among the various program stakeholders. These best practices are of enormous value, as they show the importance of key documents to initiate a program, plan it, execute and monitor and control it, and close it.

Let's get to work!

Chapter 2

Getting Started

> In preparing for battle I have always found that plans are useless, but *planning is indispensable.*
>
> —Dwight D. Eisenhower

Planning is woefully implemented in some programs. On the other hand, in certain cultures, planning is almost an (endless) end in itself—sort of like the infamous "paralysis by analysis." Your world needs to be somewhere in between.

An important take-home message here is that, given natural and often turbulent change in a program's environment, planning in too much detail can be a counterproductive drain on your time. Planning in too little detail, however, can cause you to overlook things that need to be at least thought through in advance. One of the most important program manager skills is the ability to do just the right amount of all the right things and at the right time.

If the documents we describe are new to your organization, almost certainly the first application will be the most difficult. Major parts of your work will become what the Project Management Institute (PMI®) refers to as organizational process assets. So if you are in that situation, you will be a pioneer. As they say about pioneers, they are the ones with the arrows in their back. That's sort of like us perhaps, in even daring such a work as this.

Why So Many Plans?

The seeming paradox that leads off this chapter actually makes sense! How?

During the often furious pace of a program's lifetime, indeed things do change. And unmanaged change is your enemy, while considered and managed change is your friend. When it occurs, your prior planning work has provided you with an understanding of the program and proves invaluable in defining and implementing the necessary changes.

In numerous templates that follow, organized by program management phase, we begin in each case with a brief statement of its value, followed by a detailed description of its contents, and then a template, ready to tailor and use.

First Steps

As in all endeavors, it is best to take advantage of preexisting assets. As pointed out in the preface, your organization is unique. In some cases, you will need only to reference existing standard documents for your organization. In other cases, you may need to prepare extensive documents using ours as a starting point. And in yet other cases, you might only need to include a paragraph as part of another document, indicating how due consideration has been given to the matter at hand.

First, consult with your program management office, if available, or senior management to get electronic access to any templates, forms, and standards for program, quality, financial management, etc., and other plans that you can adapt for your program. Depending on the program and project management maturity of your organization, these items may be fairly easily obtained. If all else fails, you may be able to locate suitable plans for similar programs in the past, or just begin with the templates we provide. In some cases, you will be able to refer to external standards by reference, so long as they are appropriately archived in your program repository.

Next, where applicable, gather program-unique standards that your customer requires. Being able to refer to these items may make your writing experience considerably easier.

Chapter 3

The Pre-Program Preparations Phase

> Luck is what happens when preparation meets opportunity.
>
> —Seneca

In this phase there is as yet no program—that is, a program charter does not yet exist. In fact, the purpose of this phase is to justify or provide the business case for the program. A description of the benefits to be achieved, a high-level business case, the highest-level milestones, and a plan for initiation are produced here in order to convince the organization's program selection process to accept the effort at all, and then as a program rather than a project.

Let's take a look at the artifacts produced in the pre-program preparations phase.

Program Benefits Statement

The benefits statement for the program is the seminal work. Without a practical and useful statement, there is no reason to have a program or to bother preparing a business case for it.

Program Benefits Statement Instructions

The program benefits statement includes the following:

Purpose: A brief introductory statement defining the purpose of the benefits statement, such as:

> The program benefits statement defines the benefits for pursuing a program by documenting exactly what will be accomplished.
>
> Its purpose is to address the value and organizational impact of the program. It is an iterative document prepared early in the program life cycle that can be further refined as the program progresses throughout the life cycle. It is used to initiate the program, develop the program management plan, and monitor and control program work processes.

Objectives and success criteria: This section formalizes the benefits to be realized by the program, both tangible and intangible.

Assumptions: This section lists and describes the specific program assumptions associated with the program benefits and the potential impact of the assumptions should they prove to be false.

Constraints: This section lists and describes the specific program constraints associated with the program benefits that limit the team's options.

Interdependencies between projects in the program: This section identifies interdependencies between the benefits in the various projects that comprise the program, as one project may produce benefits that then are used by another project later in the program.

Changes: This section identifies the potential impact of program changes on benefit outcomes.

Approvals: This section contains the written approval of the program benefits statement by the program sponsor, the program management office, members of the governance board, and other stakeholders.

Initial Stakeholder Identification

To be successful, you must identify in a timely fashion all those people who can help, hurt, or perhaps even kill your program before or after its birth. You must ultimately deal with each appropriately. Skip this step at your peril.

This is an initial cut in the list of stakeholders. It is actually referenced later in the *Standard for Program Management*—Second Edition (2008) as the stakeholder inventory, but we include it here because it is so important at program inception. We expand this document later in this book with our stakeholder inventory template.

Initial Stakeholder Identification Instructions

The initial stakeholder identification document includes the following:

Purpose: A brief introductory statement defining the purpose of the initial stakeholder identification, such as:

Stakeholder management is a key theme in program management. It is necessary to identify the stakeholders who will have an interest in or involvement with the program as early as possible to build support for the program and to show with whom communication is required.

Different stakeholders will have an interest in or influence over the program at different times. During the pre-program preparations phase in the life cycle, stakeholder identification begins. It then is used to support the program brief and the business case, as it helps to build support for the program and assists in the development of the program stakeholder management plan and the stakeholder inventory. It also assists in the development of the overall program management plan and the stakeholder register.

At times, programs are established because a number of the organization's projects involve the same stakeholders. Stakeholder involvement is a prerequisite for program success.

Stakeholder definition: Different organizations will define stakeholders in different ways; a standard definition may be provided by a program management office. This section states what is meant by a stakeholder, as a clear definition is required to determine whether the relevant stakeholders are identified. Note that the definition may be a person or group with an interest in the program, involvement (passive or active) in the program, or influence over the program, or that provides information to the program or is otherwise affected by the program. Stakeholders may be internal or external to the program.

Stakeholder roles: This section defines the various roles of program stakeholders, noting the importance of involving those stakeholders who are expected to be more active than others throughout the program life cycle. Roles can be based on functions to be performed, such as making program decisions, having responsibility for a program package, providing funding, providing resources, providing expert advice and consultation as appropriate, defining benefits and outcomes, ensuring that customer or user requirements are met, or contributing to the outcomes. This section states the names or groups involved in each identified role and provides contact information as appropriate.

Phases of the program life cycle: This section shows the roles, specific stakeholders, and their expected levels of involvement in the various phases of the program life cycle. A classification system such as high, medium, or low; active versus passive; or positive versus negative may be used.

Stakeholder communication methods: This section provides initial information as to methods to communicate with each of the identified stakeholders to obtain their support for the program. It will be further elaborated in the program stakeholder management plan and the communications management plan. It is included to engage those key stakeholders in initial support for the program.

Approvals: This section contains the written approval of the initial stakeholder identification by the program sponsor and others as appropriate.

Initial Stakeholder Identification Template

<Insert Program Name>
Initial Stakeholder Identification

Program name:	
Program sponsor:	
Proposed start date:	
Proposed end date:	
Prepared by:	
Revision history:	
Business unit:	

A. PURPOSE

A brief introductory statement defining the purpose of initial stakeholder identification, such as:

> Stakeholder management is a key theme in program management. It is necessary to identify the stakeholders who will have an interest in or involvement with the program as early as possible to build support for the program and to show with whom communication is required.

_____
_____
_____

B. STAKEHOLDER DEFINITION

This section states what is meant by a stakeholder of the program, as a clear definition is required to determine whether the relevant stakeholders are identified.

C. STAKEHOLDER ROLES

This section defines the various roles of program stakeholders, noting the importance of involving those stakeholders who are expected to be more active than others throughout the program's life cycle. It states the names or groups involved in each identified role and provides contact information as appropriate.

D. PHASES IN THE PROGRAM LIFE CYCLE

This section shows the role of specific stakeholders and their expected levels of involvement in the various phases of the program life cycle.

E. STAKEHOLDER COMMUNICATIONS METHODS

This section provides initial information as to methods to communicate with each of the identified stakeholders to obtain their support for the program.

F. APPROVALS

This section contains the approval of the initial stakeholder identification template by the program sponsor and others as required.

SIGNATURES AND DATE APPROVAL OBTAINED

Program sponsor _____
Person 1   _____
Person 2   _____
Person N   _____

Program Business Case

The program business case (Figure 3.1) is an input to the program from an external source. It describes, among other things, the program's cost-benefit justification. Quite naturally, this information is important in many processes within the program. The business case is an input to the initiate program process in the *Standard for Program Management*—Second Edition (2008).

Program Business Case Instructions

Purpose: A brief introductory statement defining the purpose of the program business case, such as:

The program business case describes the need, feasibility, and justification for the program.

Typically, this document is prepared by the program sponsor with input from other key stakeholders. It may be provided by the client or the funding organization. It serves as the mandate for the program, and it is prepared before the program is approved, as it is the key document used in selecting the

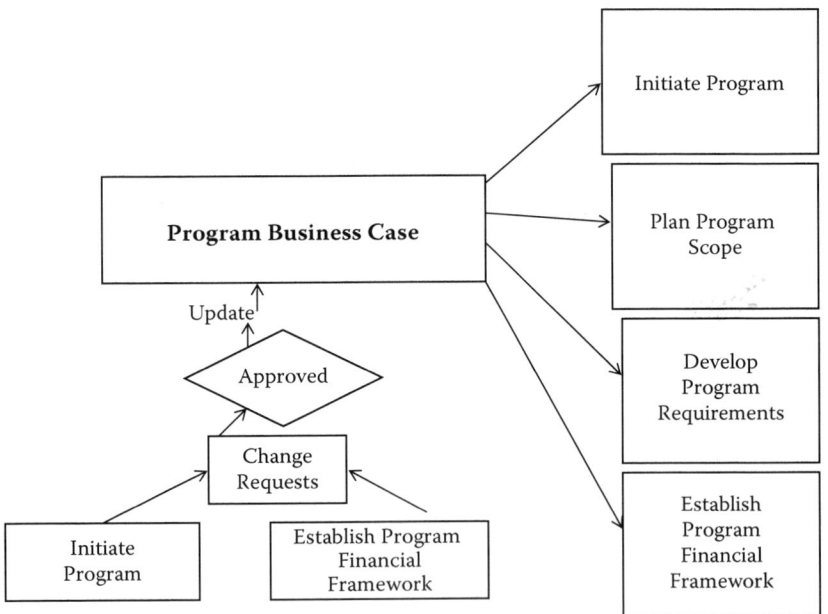

Figure 3.1 Program business case.

program for approval by the organization's portfolio review board or other decision-making body. Once approved, the program initiation phase begins.

Although the business case is prepared to initiate the program, it should be revisited and updated as required on a regular basis to ensure that the program continues to meet its objectives and is delivering its expected benefits.

Program strategic objectives: This section describes the expected results from the program. It shows how these expected results complement the organization's strategic objectives. It states the vision or end state of the program, the mission or why the program is important, and the values to be used in making decisions concerning program activities. The program's objectives must be aligned with the organization's strategic plan and goals.

Program benefits: A benefit is an improvement to the running of an organization that provides utility to the organization. Benefits may be financial or nonfinancial, tangible or intangible. This section describes the expected benefits to be delivered through the program, such as to enhance existing capabilities or develop new capabilities. It explains why it is more appropriate to manage this initiative as a program rather than as separate projects, and describes the types of projects that probably will be part of the program and the collective benefits to be realized through a program management structure.

Required resources: This section provides a high-level estimate of the resources required for the program. It includes all resources, not just human resources, and shows why they are needed and when they will need to be available. It highlights the value of the program against the resources that are required for its successful implementation.

Financial analysis: This section contains the financial analysis of the program in terms of financial indices, such as the return on investment, net present value, and the payback period. It shows the costs to execute the program compared to the benefits to be realized by the program. These indicators should be tracked throughout the program. This section describes sources of program funding, trends in labor and material costs, and contract costs as appropriate.

Internal and external influences: Programs may be initiated for a number of reasons, and there are a wide range of internal and external influences that can affect the program or show the reason it should be undertaken. This section describes these influences. If it is an external program, this section states the market demand for the program and any barriers to entry. Time-to-market data are included in this section. In addition, these influences may affect the execution of the program. This section describes these influences and why they are significant to the program, as they often become program constraints.

Alternative analysis: Because of resource limitations and other constraints, it is necessary to recognize that competing initiatives exist in the organization as all possible projects and programs cannot be approved. This section describes the results of alternative analyses, or "what if" analyses, to show different approaches that could be considered in order to meet the program's intended objectives. Feasibility studies may be included as well in this section. It is used to show that initiating this program is the most effective way to meet these objectives and deliver the expected benefits.

Program complexity: Programs are initiated because of the need for some type of change to implement new capabilities to be used within the organization or by customers or to enhance existing capabilities. This section describes the complexity of this change initiative to best determine whether or not it should be managed as a program and undertaken by the organization.

Approvals: This section contains the written approval of the program business case by the members of the portfolio review board or similar group and any other key stakeholders as appropriate.

Program Business Case Template

<Insert Program Name>
Program Business Case

Program name:	
Program sponsor:	
Proposed start date:	
Proposed end date:	
Date prepared:	
Revision history:	
Business unit:	

A. PURPOSE

A brief introductory statement defining the purpose of the business case, such as:

> The program business case describes the need, feasibility, and justification for the program.

_____
_____
_____

B. PROGRAM STRATEGIC OBJECTIVES

This section describes the expected results from the program and how they complement the organization's strategic objectives.

_____
_____
_____

C. PROGRAM BENEFITS

This section describes the expected benefits to be delivered by the program. It describes why it is more appropriate to manage this initiative as a program rather than as separate projects.

_____
_____
_____

D. REQUIRED RESOURCES

This section provides a high-level estimate of the resources required for the program. It highlights the value of the program against the resources that are required for its successful implementation.

_____
_____
_____

E. FINANCIAL ANALYSIS

This section describes the results of the financial analyses that were conducted and describes sources of program funding, trends in labor and material costs, and contract costs as appropriate.

_____
_____
_____

F. INTERNAL AND EXTERNAL INFLUENCES

This section describes the internal and external influences that show why the program should be undertaken and also that may affect the program if it is approved.

_____
_____
_____

G. ALTERNATIVE ANALYSIS

This section describes the results of any alternative analyses that have been undertaken to show different approaches that could be used in order to meet the program's intended objectives. Any feasibility studies that were undertaken can be attached to this section.

_____
_____
_____

H. PROGRAM COMPLEXITY

This section describes the complexity of the initiative to determine whether or not it should be managed as a program and undertaken by the organization.

_____

_____

_____

I. APPROVALS

This section contains the approval of the program business case by the members of the portfolio review board and other key stakeholders as required.

SIGNATURES AND DATE APPROVAL OBTAINED

Portfolio review chairperson　　　　　　　_____

Portfolio review board member 1　　　　 _____

Portfolio review board member 2　　　　 _____

Portfolio review board member N　　　　_____

Stakeholder 1　　　　　　　　　　　　　 _____

Stakeholder 2　　　　　　　　　　　　　 _____

Stakeholder N　　　　　　　　　　　　　 _____

Program Brief

The program brief typically is the single document that will be used to gain approval to proceed to program initiation. The program charter will then be the desired output of the (hopefully) subsequent program initiation phase. The *Standard for Program Management*—Second Edition (2008) also uses the term *program mandate*.

Program Brief Instructions

The program brief includes the following:

> **Purpose:** A brief introductory statement defining the purpose of the program brief, such as:
>
>> The program brief describes the importance for this program to be part of the organization's portfolio.

The program brief is often the first program document that is prepared before the program is initiated. The program sponsor typically prepares the program brief, since he or she is the person who will provide funding for the program, with input from other key stakeholders. A client may suggest that the program be undertaken and may provide supporting details concerning its importance. It serves as the document that is provided to members of the organization's portfolio review board or comparable group to approve the program and to put it in the portfolio. It is followed by the program business case, which then leads to the formal initiation process.

This template provides guidance for the generic factors that should be included as part of the program brief, recognizing that it will be tailored, since each organization will have different criteria that it uses to select and prioritize programs, projects, and ongoing operations. The program brief should address these specific criteria used by the organization.

Program importance: This section sets the stage for the remainder of the document, as it shows the importance of the program to the organization. It provides a description of what the program is intended to achieve and why this initiative should be managed as a program rather than as a project.

Program vision: This section contains the vision for the program or its end state to provide more details as to what the program will achieve.

Program strategic objectives: This section states the strategic objectives of the program and shows how each objective relates to the organization's strategic objectives and strategic plan. It shows how these objectives then will achieve the program's vision. This section also shows how this program will interface with other programs and projects in the organization that are under way and are part of the overall strategic initiatives.

Program benefits: A benefit is an outcome of the program, such as an improvement to the overall operations of the organization or a desired product or service for clients. This section describes the benefits of the program to the organization and how they will be realized through the various components of the program—projects and nonproject work.

Program scope and components: This section states the scope of the program in terms of the products, services, and results that will be delivered in order to realize the benefits. It describes identified components, which will comprise the program and how they will relate to one another; often these components already are under way as individual projects. If this is the case, this section shows how these components, if managed as a program, will achieve more benefits than if they were continued as individual projects. This section also describes what is considered to be outside of the scope of the program.

Assumptions and constraints: This section states the assumptions and constraints that are expected to affect the proposed program. Assumptions are those items that are considered to be true, real, or certain without any backup documentation, while constraints represent any milestones to be imposed on the program or limits in terms of schedule, costs, and resources.

Program schedule: This section presents a high-level schedule of the program's deliverables and key milestones.

Resource requirements: This section states the resource requirements for the program and includes all resources, not just people. It also notes when specific resources will be required according to the high-level schedule.

Risks and issues: Various risks and issues will affect the program. This section presents those risks and issues that may affect the program, positively or negatively, and that have been identified at the time the program is proposed in order that the organization can determine whether the level of risk is acceptable before proceeding further.

Stakeholder considerations: Stakeholders play a key role in any program. This section presents a list of those stakeholders that are expected to influence the program, positively or negatively, and others who will have an interest in the program at certain phases in the life cycle.

Governance requirements: This section states the governance requirements for the program as it specifies the use of a governance board or similar group and suggests key members for this board. It states whether it is necessary to modify existing governance procedures used in the organization for the program and shows how the board will meet to oversee the program according to the schedule. This section also states the governance processes at the program level that are proposed to oversee the various components. It describes reporting requirements to the governance board from the program manager, and to the program manager from component managers.

Approvals: This section contains the written approval of the program brief by the members of the portfolio review board or similar group and any other key stakeholders as appropriate.

Program Brief Template

<Insert Program Name>
Program Brief

Program name:	
Program sponsor:	
Proposed start date:	
Proposed end date:	
Date prepared:	
Revision history:	
Business unit:	

A. PURPOSE

A brief introductory statement defining the purpose of the program brief, such as:

> The program brief describes the importance for this program to be part of the organization's portfolio.

_____
_____
_____

B. PROGRAM IMPORTANCE

This section provides a description of the program and why it is important to the organization. It also states why the initiative should be managed as a program rather than as individual projects.

_____
_____
_____

C. PROGRAM VISION

This section contains the vision for the program or its end state.

_____
_____
_____

D. PROGRAM STRATEGIC OBJECTIVES

This section states the strategic objectives of the program and shows how each objective relates to the organization's strategic objectives and strategic plan. It shows how these objectives will achieve the program's vision and describes how this proposed program relates to other programs and projects under way in the organization.

_____
_____
_____

E. PROGRAM BENEFITS

This section describes the benefits of the program to the organization and how they will be realized through the various program components.

_____
_____
_____

F. PROGRAM SCOPE AND COMPONENTS

This section states the scope of the program in terms of the products, services, and results to be delivered to realize benefits. It also describes what is considered to be outside of the scope of the program.

_____
_____
_____

G. ASSUMPTIONS AND CONSTRAINTS

This section describes the assumptions and constraints that are expected to affect the proposed program.

_____
_____
_____

H. PROGRAM SCHEDULE

This section presents a high-level schedule of the program's deliverables and key milestones.

_____
_____
_____

I. RESOURCE REQUIREMENTS

This section states the resource requirements for the program and notes when they will be required according to the high-level schedule.

_____
_____
_____

J. RISKS AND ISSUES

This section presents the possible risks and issues that could affect the program, positively or negatively, that have been identified at the time the program brief is prepared.

_____
_____
_____

K. STAKEHOLDER CONSIDERATIONS

This section presents a list of those stakeholders that are expected to influence the program, positively or negatively, or have an interest in its outcome.

_____
_____
_____

L. GOVERNANCE REQUIREMENTS

This section states the governance requirements for the program at the program level and also at the component level.

_____
_____
_____

M. APPROVALS

This section contains the approval of the program brief by the members of the portfolio review board and other key stakeholders as required.

SIGNATURES AND DATE APPROVAL OBTAINED

Portfolio review chairperson	_____
Portfolio review board member 1	_____
Portfolio review board member 2	_____
Portfolio review board member 3	_____
Stakeholder 1	_____
Stakeholder 2	_____
Stakeholder N	_____

Chapter 4

The Program Initiation Phase

> Without a roadmap, program execution is like flying with visual flight ranging in a cloud. Almost certainly in the hear of the moment you'll veer seriously toward somewhere you had no intention of going.
>
> **—Anonymous**

In his children's book, *Oh, the Places You'll Go!*,[4] Dr. Seuss coined program management wisdom for the ages, warning eloquently of the scary proposition of making quick decisions "where the streets are not marked" and winding up in "weirdish wild space" and "useless places."

Having no use for useless places or weirdish wild space, in the program initiation phase we produce a high-level road map for the program—guideposts along the path to success. We also have our program charter, which then links the program to the organization and its strategic goals and objectives. During this phase, we also may need to update the business case from the pre-program preparations phase as the program's financial framework is established and as the program charter and program road map are prepared.

Program Charter

Without a charter, the program manager has no authority to use resources and execute the program, and in fact, the program has no right to exist. The program charter is an output of the initiate program process in the *Standard for Program Management*—Second Edition (2008).

Program Charter Instructions

The program charter is a key program document. At the time the program is approved, it states the program vision, key objectives, expected benefits, constraints, and assumptions. It serves to link the program to the ongoing work of the organization. It also states the authority level of the program manager. When the program charter is approved, the program is officially authorized. A suggested format is:

Purpose: A brief introductory statement defining the purpose of the charter, such as:

The program charter states the vision statement that defines the organization's end state for the program—a vital concept for successful program completion. It also states the program manager's authority and responsibility and formally authorizes the program.

Program vision: The program vision is the desired end state for the program. It describes why that state will benefit the organization. It also describes the outcomes required to achieve the vision.

Justification: Each program has a key set of objectives to be accomplished. Objectives may involve the organization's business need for the program, a customer request, market demand, a regulation, etc. The program's objectives support the organization's business plan and strategic goals. The objectives should be measureable and state success criteria.

Benefits: Programs are established in order to deliver benefits that may not be realized if projects within the program were managed on an individual basis. Benefits enhance current capabilities or enable development of new capabilities. A benefit is an outcome of actions or behaviors to provide utility to the program's stakeholders. It is an improvement to the running of the organization, such as increased sales, reduced costs, or decreased waste. Benefits may be tangible (such as financial objectives) or intangible (such as customer satisfaction or improved employee morale). Benefits should be specific, measureable, actual, realistic, and time based. This section describes the benefits and how they are to be realized.

Program constraints: Constraints are factors that limit the options of the program team. For example, a constraint may involve a regulatory requirement that must be met by a certain date. Constraints typically fall into categories such as time, cost, resources, or deliverables. Constraints are expected to change throughout the life of the program.

Program assumptions: This section describes the assumptions or any factors that are considered to be true, real, or certain in planning the program.

Assumptions generally involve some degree of risk. They are expected to change throughout the life of the program.

Scope: This section describes what is within the scope of the program and what is excluded from it. It serves as the basis to avoid possible scope creep from the beginning of the program. It also states the various components to be part of the program to show how they will interface and interrelate throughout the program's life cycle in terms of a high-level plan for these components.

Known risks and issues: This section lists any risks and issues known at this time.

Schedule: This section describes the planned length of the program and any milestones that are known at this time.

Resource requirements: This section lists required resources, human and other resources, for the program and the cost of each resource for later in-depth planning.

Stakeholder issues: This section builds on the initial stakeholder identification in the pre-program preparations phase to list any key concerns of the stakeholders and the attitudes of the stakeholders who are expected to influence the program and be active in it at various phases of the program life cycle. It also includes a draft program communications management plan for these stakeholders since active communications are required at the time of program initiation.

Governance: This section describes the program's governance structure as well as the governance structure for the various projects and nonproject work that are part of the program.

High-level road map: This section presents a high-level plan to move forward with the program and to show the order in which various other artifacts will be prepared.

Program manager authority: The charter lists the program manager and describes his or her authority and responsibilities, especially in terms of being able to apply resources to the program.

Approvals: This section contains the approval of the program charter by the members of the portfolio review board and other key stakeholders as required.

Program Charter Template

<Insert Program Name>
Program Charter

Program name:	
Progam manager:	PM's email address here as a hyperlink
Program sponsor:	
Actual start date:	

Approved end date:	
Program no.:	
Revision history:	
Business unit:	

A. PURPOSE

A brief introductory statement defining the purpose of the program charter, such as:

> The program charter states the vision statement that defines the organization's end state for the program to follow to successfully complete the program. It also states the program manager's authority and formally authorizes the program.

_____

_____

_____

B. PROGRAM VISION

This is a statement that describes the end state of the program and how it will benefit the organization. It also describes the outcomes required to achieve the vision.

_____

_____

_____

C. JUSTIFICATION

This section states the key objectives of the program as they support the business plan and strategic goals. Describe the objectives in measurable terms with specific success criteria.

_____

_____

_____

D. BENEFITS

This section states the expected benefits of the program to the organization and how they are planned to be realized.

_____

_____

_____

E. CONSTRAINTS

This section states the key constraints of the program. Constraints are factors that limit the program team's options. They are expected to change during the life of the program.

_____
_____
_____

F. ASSUMPTIONS

This section describes the assumptions that may affect the program. They are expected to change during the life of the program.

_____
_____
_____

G. SCOPE

This section describes what is within the scope of the program and what is excluded from it. It also states the various components to be part of the program in terms of a high-level plan for them.

_____
_____
_____

H. KNOWN RISKS AND ISSUES

This section lists any risks and issues known at this time.

_____
_____
_____

I. SCHEDULE

This section describes the planned length of the program and any milestones that are known at this time.

_____
_____
_____

J. RESOURCE REQUIREMENTS

This section lists required resources and the cost of each resource.

_____

_____

_____

K. STAKEHOLDER ISSUES

This section lists any concerns of the key stakeholders who are expected to influence the program and be actively involved in it at various phases of the life cycle. It also includes a draft program communications management plan.

_____

_____

_____

L. GOVERNANCE

This section describes the program's governance structure and the governance structure planned for the program's components.

_____

_____

_____

M. HIGH-LEVEL ROAD MAP

This section presents a high-level plan to move forward with the program and to show the order in which the various artifacts will be prepared.

_____

_____

_____

N. PROGRAM MANAGER'S AUTHORITY

This section lists the program manager and describes his or her authority and responsibilities.

_____

_____

_____

O. APPROVALS

This section contains the approval of the program charter by the members of the portfolio review board and any other key stakeholders as required.

SIGNATURES AND DATE APPROVAL OBTAINED

Portfolio review chairperson   _____

Portfolio review board member 1   _____

Portfolio review board member 2   _____

Portfolio review board member 3   _____

Stakeholder 1   _____

Stakeholder 2   _____

Stakeholder N   _____

Program Road Map

Timing of major milestones is important in the selling and execution of a program. The program road map (Figure 4.1) provides a guide or "map" through time of the program's scope and execution. There is considerable similarity of the program road map to the concept of the integrated master plan in the United States Department of Defense.[2] During the initiate program process, in the *Standard for Program*

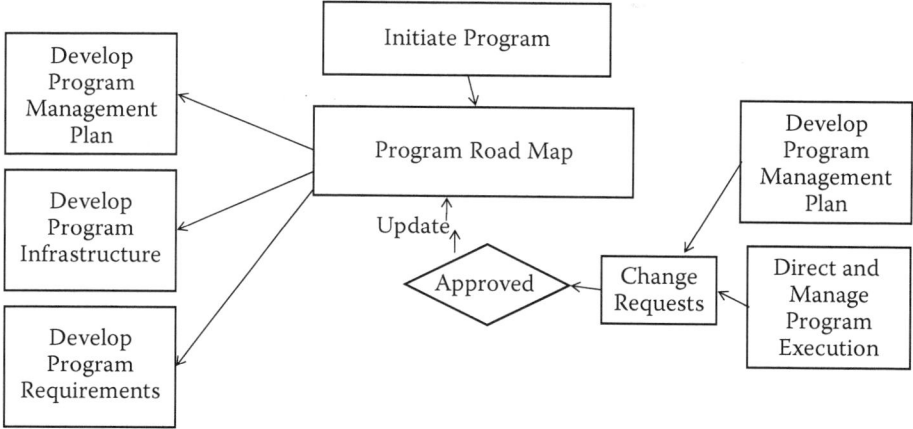

Program Management Life Cycle: Program Initiation

Figure 4.1   Program road map.

Management—Second Edition (2008), this road map is high level in nature. It is greatly refined later in the program, as part of the develop program management plan process.

Program Road Map Instructions

The program road map includes the following:

Purpose: A brief introductory statement defining the purpose of the program road map, such as:

The program road map shows, in a chronological way, the program's intended direction as it describes major milestones, key dependencies, the link between the planned and prioritized work, and key decision points.

The program road map helps in program execution and management, as it is used to assess progress in delivering benefits. It shows the program's high-level, overall scope and execution. It is prepared based on the program's business case and the organization's strategic objectives.

Although the program road map is prepared as the program is initiated, it is an iterative document, developed in a rolling-wave format, and should be reviewed periodically by the program management team, other key stakeholders, and the members of the governance board, as the work of the program continues throughout the various phases in its life cycle, especially when there are schedule, financial, and other program changes.

The program road map is a subsidiary document to the program management plan and evolves with it.

Endpoint objectives: This section describes the overall objectives of the program, especially in terms of benefits realization and ultimate benefits sustainment. It describes the link between the business strategy and the planned and prioritized work to be done in the program. It may include any needed resources or competencies required for program success.

Key challenges and risks: This section describes the key challenges associated with the program and the identified risks to the program. By noting these challenges and risks as part of the road map, deviations from them then may indicate other threats to the program or potential opportunities.

Key milestones and decision points: This section describes the key milestones and decision points in the program. As part of the road map, the high-level, overall scope and execution of the program are shown. These milestones and key decision points will increase as the program ensues and as components are completed, and others are initiated as part of the program. As decisions are made, and as change requests from other areas cause milestones to change, the road map may require updates.

Program organization: This section describes the dependencies between the program components, such as releases in a software program or stages in a construction program. It describes when components are to be implemented and how requests to initiate components are processed.

Supporting infrastructure: This section describes the support structure and needed capabilities for the program, such as use of a program management office; guidelines, procedures, and templates; facilities; and tools and techniques.

Approvals: This section contains the written approval of the program road map by the program sponsor, program manager, program management office, members of the governance board, and any other key stakeholders as appropriate.

Program Road Map Template

<Insert Program Name>
Program Road Map

Program name:	
Program manager:	PM's email address here as a hyperlink
Program sponsor:	
Actual start date:	
Approved end date:	
Program no.:	
Revision history:	
Business unit:	

A. PURPOSE

A brief introductory statement defining the purpose of the program road map, such as:

> The program road map shows, in a chronological way, the program's intended direction as it describes major milestones, key dependencies, the link between the planned and prioritized work, and key decision points.

_____
_____
_____

B. ENDPOINT OBJECTIVES

This section describes the program's overall objectives, especially in terms of benefits realization and ultimately benefits sustainment. It describes the link between business strategy and the planned and prioritized program work.

_____

_____

_____

C. KEY CHALLENGES AND RISKS

This section describes the key challenges associated with the program and identified program risks.

_____

_____

_____

D. KEY MILESTONES AND DECISION POINTS

This section describes the program's key milestones and decision points. It also presents the overall scope and execution of the program.

_____

_____

_____

E. PROGRAM ORGANIZATION

This section describes the dependencies between the program components, when they will be implemented, and how requests to initiate components are processed.

_____

_____

_____

F. SUPPORTING INFRASTRUCTURE

This section describes the support structure and needed capabilities for the program, such as use of a program management office; guidelines, procedures, and templates; facilities; and tools and techniques.

_____

_____

_____

G. APPROVALS

This section contains the approval of the program road map by the program sponsor, program manager, program management office, members of the program board or governance board, and other key stakeholders as required.

Signatures and Date Approval Obtained

Governance board chairperson	_____
Governance board member 1	_____
Governance board member 2	_____
Governance board member 3	_____
Program sponsor	_____
Program manager	_____
Program management office director	_____
Stakeholder 1	_____
Stakeholder 2	_____
Stakeholder N	_____

Chapter 5

The Program Setup Phase

> When you don't invest in infrastructure, you are going to pay sooner or later.
>
> —Mike Parker

In the program setup phase, the program infrastructure, including selection of projects to be part of the program, occurs. The high-level program road map from the program initiation phase is morphed into a detailed program road map. Here, the program charter is progressively elaborated to include much more detailed information, such as budget, schedule, and indeed a complete program management plan that describes the program's management infrastructure as prepared. That plan, by design, includes the tools and techniques that will eventually allow these "living documents" to evolve with developing realities.

Benefits Realization Plan

The benefits realization plan (Figure 5.1) is the "one-stop shop" for benefits identification, monitoring and implementation of benefits achievement, and defining them in terms of measurable program outcomes. It is prepared in the define program goals and objectives process in the *Standard for Program Management*—Second Edition (2008).

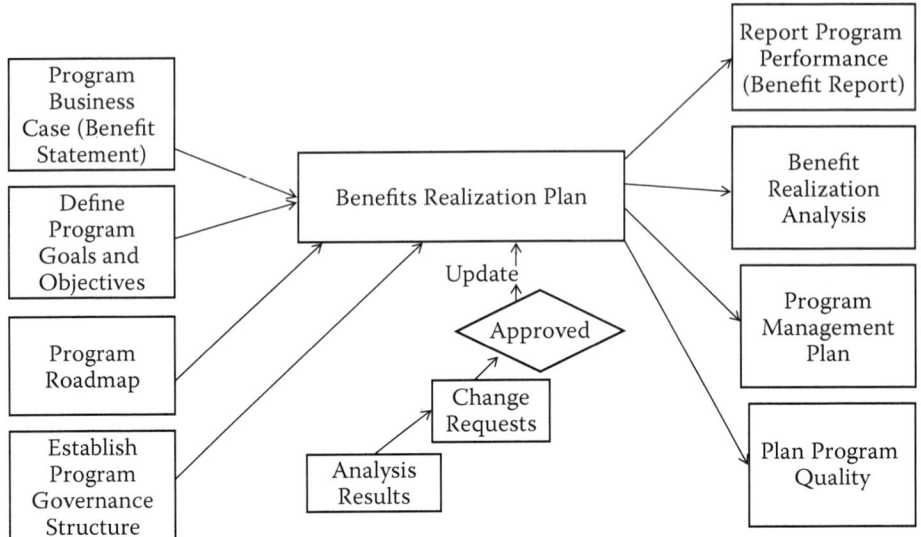

Figure 5.1 Benefits realization plan.

Benefits Realization Plan Instructions

The benefits realization plan includes the following:

Purpose: A brief introductory statement defining the purpose of the benefits realization plan, such as:

The benefits realization plan assesses the value and organizational impact of the program. It identifies the benefits to be realized from the projects and other work of the program and ensures the benefits are specific, measurable, attainable, realistic, and time based.

It also analyzes the impact of changes on the overall outcome of the program and assigns roles and responsibilities to ensure the identified benefits are attained. Although the plan is drafted early in the program, it is an iterative document that should be further refined as the program progresses through the life cycle. This plan is included in the program management plan as it helps to determine how benefits will be realized and provides a baseline for tracking progress and reporting variances.

In the Project Management Institute's *Standard for Program Management—Second Edition* (2008), the benefits realization plan is noted in the benefits management life cycle under phase two, benefits analysis and planning. During the pre-program preparations phase in the program management life cycle, the importance of benefits is noted along with a plan to show how program benefits will be realized. Benefits are described in the program's business case as well as in the business case for each of the projects in the program. During the program initiation process, the benefits the program is to deliver are clarified, and the program road map, as an output of this process, shows the linkage between program activities and expected benefits. The benefits realization plan is an output of the define program goals and objectives process and the plan and establish program governance structure process. The management program benefits process uses benefits realization analysis as a tool and technique. This plan also is an input to report performance process and the plan program quality process.

Definition of each program benefit: This section defines each benefit in the program—both tangible and intangible. It also shows how the benefit is to be realized. The benefits described in this section should be in line with those in the program's business case and the organization's overall strategy. Benefits are identified through interviews, brainstorming sessions, and review sessions.

Each benefit's impact to the program's outcomes: This section shows how each benefit relates to the outcomes of the program. It further shows the value of the program in terms of the benefits to be realized, and it describes the interdependencies between the program's benefits.

Metrics and procedures to measure benefits: In order to ensure that the program is realizing its intended benefits, this section describes the key metrics that will be collected, and the processes that will be used, to measure the program benefits. Suggested metrics include scheduled time for benefits realization versus actual time, extent of the benefits realized versus those planned in the business case, impact of the realized benefit on other components of the program, the need to change the benefits as the program progresses versus those in the plan, the value of the benefits that were realized, the extent of the sustainment of benefits after the program ends, and other benefits realized that were not planned. The metrics can be used if the benefits are not realized as planned in order that corrective actions can be implemented.

Roles and responsibilities for benefits realization and management: Benefits realization and management is a team effort. This section describes specific roles and responsibilities of the program team members to deliver final and intermediate benefits in the program. These roles and responsibilities can be displayed in a responsibility assignment matrix (RAM) or in a Responsible, Accountable, Consult, Inform (RACI) chart to show whether the team member is responsible for the benefit, should be involved in its realization in terms of monitoring and control, should be performing an ongoing analysis of the program for incremental benefits to make adjustments to the benefits delivery schedule, should be consulted as the benefit is realized, or should sign off once the benefit has been realized.

Benefits management communications plan: Program stakeholders require information concerning how the proposed program benefits are being realized. This section describes the communications methods to be used to ensure each stakeholder has the information he or she requires regarding benefits management. It also describes how benefits will be reviewed with stakeholders. It discusses the preparation on a regular basis of the benefits realization report, since this report is an output of the report performance process, and describes the benefits realization plan versus the actual benefits delivered and serves to monitor overall benefits delivery. The benefits management communications plan can be an appendix or section in the program's communications management plan.

Benefits delivery schedule: All program benefits will not be realized at the same time. Also, some projects in the program will need to integrate the benefits from their projects with other projects or ongoing work of the program. This section presents a schedule, typically in a Gantt or network chart format, to show the planned and actual dates for each of the identified benefits in the program. The schedule should show the interdependencies between benefits from the various projects in the program and the other work that is part of the program. This schedule should be part of the program's master schedule.

Benefits-related risks: Each benefit will have some type of risks associated with its realization. This section describes the risks and stresses the risks that may occur based on the component risks on benefits delivery so they can be evaluated.

Required changes to processes and systems: This section discusses new processes and systems and those already in existence, which must be changed in order to track and monitor benefits as they are being realized in the program.

Transition of the program into ongoing operations and benefits sustainment: When the program is officially closed, the program is transitioned into ongoing operations. This section describes how the program will transition and how the program's benefits will be sustained. It is important to ensure that the transition activities provide for continued management of the benefits within the framework of the customer organization as appropriate. Recognize that benefits management transcends the program's life cycle and continues into transfer and sustainment of the benefits of the program.

Approvals: This section contains the written approval of the benefits realization plan by the program sponsor, program manager, program management office, members of the program board or governance board, and other stakeholders.

Benefits Realization Plan Template

<Insert Program Name>
Benefits Realization Plan

Program name:	
Program manager:	PM's email address here as a hyperlink
Program sponsor:	
Actual start date:	
Approved end date:	
Program no.:	
Revision history:	
Business unit:	

A. PURPOSE

A brief introductory statement defining the purpose of the benefits realization plan, such as:

> The benefits realization plan assesses the value and organizational impact of the program. It identifies the benefits to be realized from the projects and other work of the program and ensures the benefits are specific, measurable, attainable, realistic, and time based.

_____
_____
_____

B. DEFINITION OF EACH PROGRAM BENEFIT

This section defines each benefit in the program—both tangible and intangible. It also shows how the benefit is to be realized.

_____
_____
_____

C. EACH BENEFIT'S IMPACT TO THE PROGRAM'S OUTCOMES

This section shows how each benefit relates to the outcomes of the program. It further shows the value of the program in terms of the benefits to be realized.

D. METRICS AND PROCEDURES TO MEASURE BENEFITS

This section describes the key metrics that will be collected, and the processes that will be used to measure the program benefits.

E. ROLES AND RESPONSIBILITIES FOR BENEFITS REALIZATION AND MANAGEMENT

This section describes specific roles and responsibilities of the program team members to deliver the final and intermediate benefits in the program. Attach a Responsibility Assignment Matrix (RAM) or a Responsible, Accountable, Consult, Inform (RACI) chart as appropriate.

F. BENEFITS MANAGEMENT COMMUNICATIONS MANAGEMENT PLAN

This section describes the communications methods to be used to ensure each stakeholder has the information he or she requires regarding benefits management. It also describes how benefits will be reviewed with stakeholders and describes the content of the benefits realization report.

G. BENEFITS DELIVERY SCHEDULE

This section presents a schedule, typically in a Gantt or network chart format, to show the planned and actual dates for each of the identified benefits. The schedule should show the interdependencies between benefits from the various projects in the program and other work that is part of the program.

H. BENEFITS-RELATED RISKS

This section describes the risks associated with benefits realization.

_____
_____
_____

I. REQUIRED CHANGES TO PROCESSES AND SYSTEMS

This section discusses new processes and systems and those already in existence that must be changed to handle benefits realization and management.

_____
_____
_____

J. TRANSITION OF THE PROGRAM INTO ONGOING OPERATIONS AND BENEFITS SUSTAINMENT

This section describes how the program will transition into ongoing operations with an emphasis on how the program's benefits will be sustained.

_____
_____
_____

K. APPROVALS

This section contains the approval of the benefits realization plan by the program sponsor, program manager, program management office, members of the program board or governance board, and other key stakeholders.

SIGNATURES AND DATE APPROVAL OBTAINED

Program sponsor	_____
Program manager	_____
Program management office director	_____
Governance board chairperson	_____
Governance board member 1	_____
Governance board member N	_____
Stakeholder 1	_____
Stakeholder 2	_____
Stakeholder N	_____

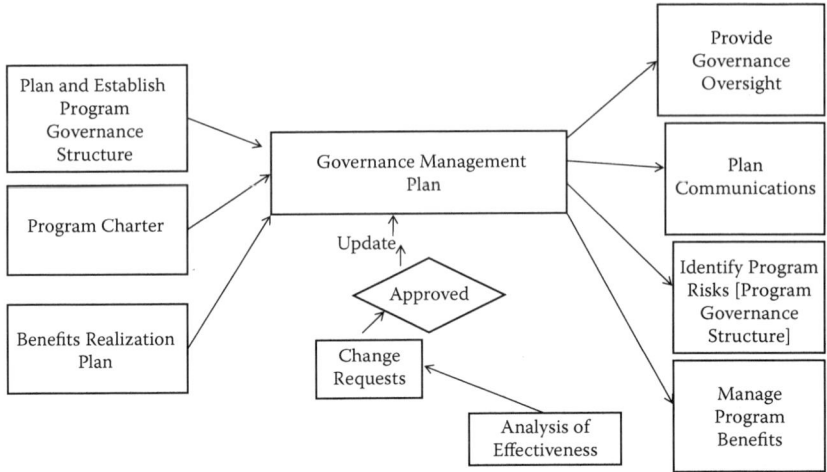

Program Management Life Cycle: Program Initiation and Program Setup

Figure 5.2 Program governance plan.

Program Governance Plan

This seemingly mundane topic is one of the most prominent areas of current interest due in part to legal matters surrounding accurate project reporting. Entire books are being devoted to various aspects of governance.

When some aspect of the program threatens to get out of control, action is required. Resulting interorganizational and intraorganizational struggles can be divisive and counterproductive. Who has the authority to make such decisions and how will they keep tabs on things? Of course, at times, the program manager may be too close to the situation to know what should be done. The governance process is the answer. Thus, the importance of preparing a governance plan (Figure 5.2) during the plan and establish program governance structure process in the *Standard for Program Management*—Second Edition (2008) is clear.

Program Governance Plan Instructions

The program governance plan includes the following:

Purpose: A brief introductory statement defining the purpose of the program governance plan, such as:

> The governance plan describes the process that will be followed to execute the program's governance activities. Its focus is on goals, structure, roles and responsibilities, and overall logistics for the governance board.

The program governance plan is a subsidiary plan to the program management plan. Effective program governance is key to successful program management. The program governance board is the major stakeholder in every program, to focus on benefits realization, stage gate reviews, and effective decision making. The governance board, also known as a program board or a steering committee in many organizations, emphasizes proactive actions rather than the need for corrective actions. The governance board, as noted through this plan, serves to identify, analyze, and respond to internal and external events in the program and to change, initiate, terminate, or transition components as required. The governance plan states the process to ensure that decisions are made in a timely manner to not impede program progress.

This plan is an iterative document and should be reviewed periodically by the program management team and the members of the governance board, as the work of the program continues throughout the various phases in its life cycle.

In the Project Management Institute's *Standard for Program Management—Second Edition (2008)*, the program governance management is an output from the following:

- Planning and establishing governance structure process
- Program charter
- Benefits realization plan

It is an input to the following processes:

- Provide governance oversight
- Plan communications
- Identify program risks (program governance structure)
- Manage program benefits

Goals: This section describes the goals for program governance, such as the importance of ensuring that the program remains in alignment with the organization's strategic goals and objectives. Additionally, it ensures that interfaces between the program with other programs, projects, and ongoing operations within the organization are managed effectively to minimize conflicts and maximize opportunities. Furthermore, this section discusses the role of risk management in governance activities. Recognizing that often programs involve alliances with other organizations, this section describes the adherence to key policies, procedures, and standards as applicable.

Organizational structure: This section describes the structure of the governance board. Existing organizational charts are used since they show accountabilities and authority levels within the organization. Also, different programs in the organization will use different structures, meaning that the emphasis in this section is to determine a structure that will facilitate effective program governance.

Roles and responsibilities: This section lists the members of the governance board and the board's specific responsibilities. It should be noted that while consensus is desired among the board members, it is not a prerequisite. An executive director or a program director typically chairs the board and is the ultimate decision maker. This individual generally is a senior manager and provides organizational resources to the program. He or she has overall responsibility for program success. If partner organizations are part of the program, they should be represented on the governance board. On certain programs, the customer may be represented. This section states the involvement of the portfolio manager, business change manager, functional managers, program sponsor, program manager, director of the program management office, project managers, and program team members as appropriate in terms of serving as board members or in interactions with the board. This section also describes specific accountabilities for benefits realization, communication with stakeholders, and oversight of the program and its components.

Governance decisions: This section describes the decision-making approach the board will follow. It states how decisions will be documented and communicated to program stakeholders, perhaps through the use of a governance decision register. It also describes an escalation process to follow if the board does not feel it is empowered to make certain types of decisions. Since decisions of the board impact the overall benefits delivery of the program and strategic alignment, each member of the board should be aware of the organization's strategic plan, vision, mission, and values.

Meeting schedule: This section presents an overview of the frequency of the governance board's meetings. Regularly scheduled meetings should be shown on the program's schedule. It also notes that meetings may be called as needed. It describes the process to be used to conduct each meeting, including responsibilities for handling logistics, preparing and distributing the agenda, taking and distributing meetings, escalating issues as required, and documenting decisions that are made. It describes others who can attend various meetings.

Gate review requirements: Since programs typically span a longer duration than projects and are more complex, stage gate reviews are a recommended best practice, especially when programs have completed a phase in the life cycle. This section states the requirements for these reviews. They serve as go/no-go decisions. These gate reviews assist in overall program monitoring and control to ensure that not only is the program being managed effectively but also program components are being managed as planned. These reviews also provide a way to assess the strategic and quality criteria, such as ensuring that the program remains aligned with the organization's overall strategic direction; that program benefits are being realized as planned; that the level of risk to the program is one that fits the organization's overall tolerance for risks; that variances in scope, schedule, and cost are consistent with the organization's practices; and that best practices in program management continue to be followed. This section discusses what will occur at these reviews, when they will be scheduled, the items to be covered, roles and responsibilities, and measurement criteria.

Program performance review requirements: In addition to gate reviews, the governance board typically reviews the program at various times. These reviews concentrate on overall program performance and management. They evaluate existing plans to see if they are effective or require changes; the program tools and techniques that are being used, such as the program management information system; overall performance against desired outcomes and benefits realization; alternatives to contribute to overall program success; and whether the existing processes and procedures remain helpful or need change.

Process to initiate, terminate, and transition components: The governance board approves the initiation of new components to be part of the program and determines whether a component should be terminated because it has completed its deliverables and delivered its expected benefits or should be terminated because it no longer is supportive of the program's goals and objectives. It also approves when a component should be transitioned to ongoing operations, such as to a product or customer support group, or to the customer when it has completed its goals and objectives and its benefits have been realized. This section describes the process the board follows for initiation, termination, and transition.

Assessment of effectiveness: On a periodic basis, it is incumbent to ensure that the program governance plan is effective and to determine whether any changes are required to it. It also is necessary to see whether or not the principles set forth in this plan are being followed. This section describes how effectiveness is determined and who is responsible for this evaluation.

Approvals: This section contains the written approval of the governance management plan by its members and any other key stakeholders as appropriate.

Program Governance Plan Template

<Insert Program Name>
Governance Management Plan

Program name:	
Program manager:	PM's email address here as a hyperlink
Program sponsor:	
Actual start date:	
Approved end date:	

Program no.:	
Revision history:	
Business unit:	

A. PURPOSE

A brief introductory statement defining the purpose of the program governance plan, such as:

> The program governance plan describes the process that will be followed to execute the program's governance activities. Its focus is on goals, structure, roles and responsibilities, and overall logistics of the governance board.

B. GOALS

This section describes goals of program governance in the program such as to ensure that the program remains aligned with the organization's strategic goals and objectives and that interfaces are managed effectively. It also discusses the role of risk management in governance activities and states the importance of adherence to key policies, procedures, and standards as applicable.

C. ORGANIZATIONAL STRUCTURE

This section describes the structure of the governance board.

D. ROLES AND RESPONSIBILITIES

This section lists the members of the governance board and specific responsibilities. It describes specific accountabilities for benefits realization, stakeholder communications, and oversight of the program and its components.

E. GOVERNANCE DECISIONS

This section describes the decision-making approach the board will follow. It states how decisions will be documented and communicated to stakeholders and describes an escalation process to follow if the board does not feel it is empowered to make certain types of decisions.

_____
_____
_____

F. MEETING SCHEDULE

This section presents an overview of the frequency of board meetings and notes that meetings may be called as needed. It describes the process to follow for meeting logistics and who can attend various meetings.

_____
_____
_____

G. GATE REVIEW REQUIREMENTS

This section states the requirements for program gate reviews. It describes the purpose of these reviews and the items that are covered during each review.

_____
_____
_____

H. PROGRAM PERFORMANCE REVIEW REQUIREMENTS

This section describes the process to follow for the board to review overall program performance at various times. It discusses the objectives of these reviews.

_____
_____
_____

I. PROCESS TO INITIATE, TERMINATE, AND TRANSITION COMPONENTS

This section describes the process the board follows to initiate new components to be part of the program, to terminate existing components, and to transition components when the work is complete and benefits have been realized.

_____
_____
_____

J. ASSESSMENT OF EFFECTIVENESS

This section describes how program governance is assessed for its effectiveness in terms of overall delivery of program benefits and describes who is responsible for this evaluation.

_____

_____

_____

K. APPROVALS

This section contains the approval of the program governance plan by the members of the program board or governance board, and other key stakeholders as required.

Signatures and Date Approval Obtained

Governance board chairperson	_____
Governance board member 1	_____
Governance board member 2	_____
Governance board member 3	_____
Stakeholder 1	_____
Stakeholder 2	_____
Stakeholder N	_____

Phase Gate Review Agenda

One of the reasons programs continue beyond their usefulness is the lack of a systematic decision process. Phase gates occur at the end of each of the five phases described in the *Standard for Program Management*—Second Edition (2008), with a resulting go or no-go decision in the plan and establish program governance structure process. As with any meeting, it is important to have an agenda that ensures an orderly and thorough meeting.

Phase Gate Review Agenda Instructions

At different points in the program life cycle, phase gate reviews will be held as described in the program's governance management plan. They may result from a formal submission of a gate review decision request, an input to the provide governance oversight process in the Project Management Institute's *Standard for Program*

Management—Second Edition (2008). These meetings are used for decisions to move from one gate in the program management life cycle to another and to assess progress against specific criteria. They serve as go/no-go decisions to move to the next phase in the life cycle and to confirm that generally accepted best practices have been followed.

An agenda for these reviews is as follows:

PARTICIPANTS (NAMES/ORGANIZATION)

Date: _____

Time: _____

Place: _____

- **Program overview:** The program manager presents a brief overview of the program as to why the program was undertaken and where it stands in the program management life cycle. The purpose is to enable participants to ask questions to see that objectives of the program and its components are still in alignment with the organization's strategic objectives.
- **Deliverables completed:** The program manager describes the status of any completed deliverables. This section describes the program management processes that are being followed so participants can ask questions to ensure that best practices are being used.
- **Benefits realized:** The program manager describes the status of the program benefits that have been realized to date. The purpose is to enable participants to determine if the benefits are being realized as stated in the benefits realization plan and are ones that support the program's business case.
- **Exit criteria satisfaction:** The program manager describes the exit criteria for the previous phase and how it has been satisfied.
- **Risks:** The program manager presents an overview of the risks that have affected the program since the last meeting or are expected to affect the program during the next phase in the life cycle. The purpose is to enable participants to ask questions to determine if the level of tolerance for risks is acceptable to the members of the governance board and the organization.
- **Expected date of the next meeting:** The program manager states when he or she expects the next meeting will be held for planning purposes.
- **Decisions:** This section documents the decisions made during this review.

SIGNATURES OF PARTICIPANTS

Governance board chairperson _____

Board member 1 _____

Board member 2 _____

Board member N _____

Program Review Agenda

In addition to the phase gate reviews, it is also useful to hold program reviews. The *Standard for Program Management*—Second Edition (2008) refers to these meetings as "periodic health checks," and they are also in the plan and establish program governance structure process. Clearly, these review meetings need to be conducted during longer phases on longer programs but are less formal. These reviews also need an agenda for an orderly and thorough meeting.

Program Review Agenda Instructions

At different points in the program life cycle, program reviews will be held as described in the program's governance management plan. These meetings are used in addition to phase gate reviews to assess overall program performance against outcomes and expected benefits and to determine if any preventive or corrective actions are needed. Also, since the phases in the life cycle may be long for many programs, these reviews provide a way to assess progress on a more frequent basis and keep the members of the governance board involved in the program to evaluate performance and to see if best practices are being followed. The program manager uses these reviews to focus on areas in the program rather than specifics and to describe overall status, concerns, and issues. The program manager also can use these reviews to discuss any alternatives with the governance board to improve opportunities for overall program success. Since these reviews are not go/no-go decisions, they generally are viewed in a more positive way and are conducted in a more informal manner.

An agenda for these reviews is as follows:

PARTICIPANTS (NAMES/ORGANIZATION)

Date: _____

Time: _____

Place: _____

- **Program overview:** The program manager presents a brief high-level overview as to why the program was undertaken and where it stands in the program management life cycle. He or she should remind participants when the last phase gate review and program review were held. Participants can ask questions to see that objectives of the program and its components are still in alignment with the organization's strategic objectives and to see whether the business case requires revision.
- **Status of milestones and deliverables:** The program manager describes the status of completed deliverables and those that are expected to be completed in the near future as well as the status of key milestones. Participants can ask questions about the status of upcoming milestones and deliverables to see whether the schedule management plan is being followed and whether the schedule

requires updating. They also can address customer satisfaction concerns, if any, and can see if the scope management plan is being followed.

Benefits status: The program manager describes the status of the program benefits that have been realized to date and are coming in the near future. Participants can ask questions to determine if the benefits are being realized as stated in the benefits realization plan and are ones that support the program's business case. They also can assess whether the benefits are ones that can be sustained.

Resource status: The program manager describes resource use in the program and whether additional resources are required or if any dedicated resources can be released. The program manager describes whether there are any problems in obtaining resources as agreed upon to support the program. Participants can ask questions to see that the program resource plan is being followed and to determine whether changes are required to the program manager's charter.

Component status: The program manager states whether any components have been transitioned to the customer or to ongoing operations and whether any new components are being added to the program. Participants can ask questions to see that closeout has occurred according to plans and that benefits are being sustained or, if components are being added, whether the program documentation is being updated. They can see if the program road map remains valid and if the architecture plan is being followed.

Budget status: The program manager provides an overview of the budget and discusses key earned value performance metrics, if earned value management is being used. Participants can ask questions to see that the financial plan is being followed.

Change request status: The program manager states the number of change requests that have been received and analyzed and explains whether those that have been approved have been implemented. The purpose is not only to describe the number of change requests to date but to enable participants to see that the change request process is being followed and to identify any items of concern that may affect future program performance.

Issue status: The program manager provides an overview of the status of issues on the program issues register. Participants then can ensure that the program issues register is being used and can ask questions about outstanding issues affecting the program.

Stakeholder communications: The program manager uses the communications log and discusses communications with stakeholders to show the frequency of communication and to discuss any issues. He or she also describes other requests for information from stakeholders and whether these requests have led to the need to issue any other formal reports. Participants can ask questions to see that the program communications management plan and the program stakeholder management plan are being followed and can address any outstanding issues regarding program stakeholder management.

Risks: The program manager presents an overview of the risks that have affected the program since the last meeting or are expected to affect the program in the near future using the risk register. Participants can ask questions to determine if the level of tolerance for risks is acceptable and to see that the risk management plan and the risk response plan are being followed. They can check on possible opportunities that have been identified and how they are being maximized.

Contract status: The program manager provides an overview of the contractor/ supplier status. He or she describes completed deliverables, any issues, whether agreements and contract terms and conditions are being followed, and the need for additional contracts in other areas. Participants can ask questions to see that the procurement management plan and contracts management plan are being followed.

Lessons learned: The program manager discusses lessons learned in the program to date using the lessons learned log. Participants can ask questions to see if program management processes and procedures require change, are being used as intended, and are adding value to the program. They also may see opportunities to leverage these lessons learned to other programs and projects under way in the organization or to transfer knowledge assets from other areas to this program. The emphasis during this part of the review is to review these lessons learned to improve overall program success.

Additional comments: The program manager provides additional comments about the program, and participants ask questions in other areas as appropriate.

Expected date of the next meeting: The program manager states when he or she expects the next meeting will be held for planning purposes.

Decisions: This section documents any decisions made during this review.

SIGNATURES OF PARTICIPANTS

Governance board chairperson   _____

Governance board member 1   _____

Governance board member 2   _____

Governance board member 3   _____

Stakeholder 1   _____

Stakeholder 2   _____

Stakeholder 3   _____

Issue Escalation Process

Questions surrounding unplanned occurrences must be referred to the program from its components (projects and other work), and from the program to organizational executive management. Seasoned program managers know when it is and when it is not important to make those referrals and how to do them properly. This is the purview of the issue escalation process noted in the plan and establish program governance structure process in the *Standard for Program Management*—Second Edition (2008). The issue escalation process is established as a planning process and then is used as the program is executed and monitored and controlled.

Issue Escalation Process Instructions

Purpose: Each program will have issues, or unplanned events, actions, or disputes that may impact program areas and that will need resolution, following the program's governance plan and using the program issues register or log. One of the program manager's responsibilities is to resolve these issues that are escalated from program components through a synergistic approach to enable the program's benefits to be realized. It is also a key part of the program charter and program management plan to describe the identified risks and issues at the beginning of the program so they do not turn into problems later during execution. Additionally, identifying and managing issues is a major part of program integration management, as defined in the *Standard for Program Management*—Second Edition (2008), to anticipate issues and manage them effectively.

An issue resolution process can facilitate the steps to follow when there are issues that cannot be resolved by a component manager, a team member, or the program manager. It is important to recognize that issues may affect any aspect of the program.

In the *Standard for Program Management*—Second Edition (2008), this issue escalation process is an output of the plan and establish program governance structure process.

This document describes an issue escalation process to follow:

1. Set up the program issues register at the beginning of the program, even though it is an output of the direct and manage program execution process in the *Standard for Program Management*—Second Edition (2008). Use the program issues register to identify the issue and to track it throughout the process. Assign a number to the issue and link it to the program work breakdown structure (PWBS) number. Those issues noted in the program brief and in the program charter should be added to the program issues register once the program is officially initiated.
2. Determine if a change request is required for the issue, and if so, have someone on the program management team prepare it. Ideally, the change request should be prepared by the person who first identified the issue.
3. Determine the issue's priority and identify someone on the program management team who will be responsible for tracking the progress of the issue through its resolution and subsequent implementation. Often, the program management office handles the issue log for the program.
4. Determine whether a feasibility study may be required to help analyze the issue and determine the most appropriate way to resolve it, and if so, identify a program management team member to conduct this study and prepare a plan for it so it can be completed in a timely manner. Use this feasibility study as part of the overall issue analysis process to determine if additional funding is required for the issue resolution process or to implement corrective action.
5. Inform the governance board that an issue has been identified through a regularly scheduled status report or by other means if it is an issue that has been identified to have a major impact on the program or

the organization, in case it cannot be resolved by the program manager. The governance board should be informed as soon as possible following the information distribution process in case a special meeting may need to be held to resolve the issue.

6. Review the program manager's charter to see if he or she has the authority to resolve the issue. Typical resolution methods are to accept the issue and not require other change or to change the program management plan and other associated documents because of the issue. The issue escalation process and the people to be involved typically are covered in the program communications management plan.
7. Determine the stakeholders that will be affected by the issue and engage them as appropriate in the issue resolution process. Identify possible stakeholders who may be affected by reviewing the type of issue as noted in the program issues register. Update the stakeholder register accordingly to ensure all stakeholder concerns have been addressed.
8. If the program manager cannot resolve the issue effectively, escalate it to the governance board for resolution. Even if the program manager has the authority to resolve the issue, it may be one that affects other programs or projects or the entire organization, so the program manager may decide to involve the governance board because of the issue's scope and impact.
9. If the issue is escalated to the governance board, the program manager should describe the importance of the issue. It may be appropriate to have a member of the program management team, or someone from the program management office, to facilitate the meeting so a decision concerning the issue can be made quickly and to see that the governance board member's questions are answered during the meeting. The program manager then should communicate the resolution of the issue after the meeting to affected stakeholders, and the team member responsible for the program issues register should note the decision in the issue register.
10. Ensure that once a resolution for the issue has been determined that corrective actions are taken. Also determine whether preventive actions are required so the issue does not surface in the future.
11. Document the issue and its resolution as part of the lessons learned register.
12. In the next meeting with the governance board, state that the issue has been resolved and the corrective actions that have been taken. Note that it is part of the lessons learned register in case there are other projects or programs under way that could benefit from learning about this issue and its resolution.
13. In a status report that is distributed to stakeholders and members of the governance board, state that the issue was resolved and describe its resolution.
14. Ensure that as part of the transition plan after the program is officially closed, there is customer support in case a comparable issue arises later after the program deliverables are completed.

Audit Plan

Audits can be conducted by elements internal to the program or external to it. In contrast to meetings where progress and status are reported, audits focus more on the supporting data and record keeping. The objectives and timing of audits are laid out in the audit plan (Figure 5.3), described in the plan and establish program governance structure process in the *Standard for Program Management*—Second Edition (2008).

Audit Plan Instructions

The audit plan includes the following:

Purpose: A brief introductory statement defining the purpose of the audit plan, such as:

The audit plan describes the process that will be followed to periodically review the overall performance of the program at all levels to enhance effectiveness and ensure that the program benefits are being delivered as set forth in the benefits realization plan and that the program is being executed as stated in the program management plan.

Audits are common in programs. They are necessary for a number of reasons and should be viewed in a positive manner rather than as necessary for compliance or for pinpointing specific problems and associating them to specific individuals.

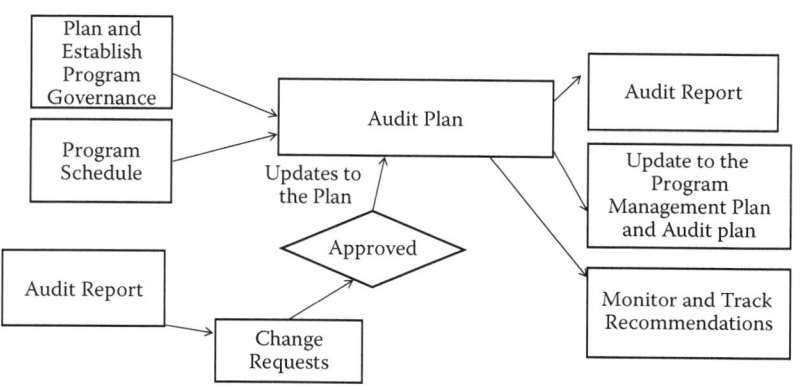

Figure 5.3   Audit plan.

Audits may be internal or external. Ideally, the program manager should request internal audits at various times in the program and should establish a process so that everyone on the team views the auditors in a positive way, with the audit results then used to improve the program's overall effectiveness.

This plan is an iterative document and should be reviewed periodically by the program management team and other key stakeholders, especially the members of the governance board, as the work of the program continues throughout the various phases in its life cycle. It also should be reviewed after each audit is conducted.

In the Project Management Institute's *Standard for Program Management—Second Edition* (2008), the audit plan is an output of the plan and establish program governance structure process and is an input to the plan for audits process. The audit plan is a subsidiary plan to the overall program management plan.

Goals: This section states the goals for program audits. Examples are to examine the financial status of the program; to review the effectiveness of the program management processes, procedures, and guidelines that are being used; to determine whether or not there is compliance with specific standards and regulations; and to assess whether there may be evidence of fraud or mismanagement. The specifics of each program dictate the various types of audits that may be required; however, each program on a periodic basis should conduct audits to assess overall program management effectiveness and to determine whether changes in procedures, processes, and guidelines are needed to help ensure overall program success.

Roles and responsibilities: This section describes the roles and responsibilities of the program management team and other key stakeholders in preparing for an audit and during an audit. While the auditors, whether internal or external, will prepare a plan for the audit, the program manager and other members of the program management team will also need to plan for the audit and participate in the audit. A number of people on the team and other stakeholders may need to be interviewed, and the program manager will need to ensure that the auditors have access to program documentation. The program manager should set the stage for the audit with the team to promote an atmosphere of cooperation. Everyone on the team should view the results of the audit as ones that can improve overall program effectiveness. The program manager must serve as the facilitator for the auditors.

Schedule: This section presents the schedule for program audits. Although some audits will occur on a random basis and cannot be scheduled, others can be part of the program master schedule. The program manager ideally should request audits at certain times for a self-assessment during the program's life cycle, such as at key milestones in the program, at the end of a phase gate review, or before a scheduled program review to help prepare for such reviews and to have other suggestions to note to the board during these review meetings.

Audit results: The auditors, whether internal or external, will present a report that documents the results and gives recommendations. This section describes how these audit results will be documented and made available to key stakeholders. Ideally, a practice of "no secrets" will be followed. This means that the results should be available in an easily accessible format so every stakeholder, especially those on the program management team, can review the suggested recommendations. This section also describes how the program management team will implement the suggested recommendations. Some recommendations may be mandatory, especially if the audit is conducted to determine compliance with regulations or standards. If the program management team believes it cannot implement a mandatory recommendation, this section describes the process to request a waiver. It also states the process to follow if the program management team wants to implement a recommendation at a different time than specified in the audit report. The program manager may need to escalate these requests to the governance board for approval. Additionally, this section describes the process to update other plans and documents as needed based on the findings and recommendations in the audit report. Each recommendation will require a change request and should be handled through the program's change control system.

Monitoring and tracking: This section describes the approach the program management team will use to monitor and track the implementation of the recommendations from each audit. It describes the use of a log or register to assist in this process. In subsequent audits, this log then can be provided to the auditors.

Approvals: This section contains the written approval of the audit plan by the program sponsor, program manager, program management office, members of the program board or governance board, and any other key stakeholders as appropriate.

Audit Plan Template

<Insert Program Name>
Audit Plan

Program name:	
Program manager:	PM's email address here as a hyperlink
Program sponsor:	
Actual start date:	
Approved end date:	

Program no.:	
Revision history:	
Business unit:	

A. PURPOSE

A brief introductory statement defining the purpose of the audit plan, such as:

> The audit plan describes the process that will be followed to periodically review the overall performance of the program at all levels to enhance effectiveness and ensure that the program benefits are being delivered as set forth in the benefits realization plan and that the program is being executed as stated in the program management plan.

_____
_____
_____

B. GOALS

This section states the goals for the audits.

_____
_____
_____

C. ROLES AND RESPONSIBILITIES

This section describes the roles and responsibilities of the program management team and other key stakeholders in preparing for an audit and during an audit.

_____
_____
_____

D. SCHEDULE

This section presents a schedule for program audits, even though some will occur on a random basis.

_____
_____
_____

E. AUDIT RESULTS

This section describes how the audit results will be documented and made available to program stakeholders. It describes a process that the program management team will follow if the team believes a mandatory recommendation from an audit cannot be implemented or can be implemented but at a later time than that recommended. It describes the process to update plans and other documents as needed based on the audit findings and recommendations.

F. MONITORING AND TRACKING

This section describes the approach the program management team will use to monitor and track the implementation of the recommendations from each audit.

G. APPROVALS

This section contains the approval of the audit plan by the program sponsor, program manager, program management office, members of the program board or governance board, and other key stakeholders as required.

SIGNATURES AND DATE APPROVAL OBTAINED

Program manager

Program sponsor

Program management office director

Governance board chairperson

Governance board member 1

Governance board member 2

Governance board member N

Stakeholder 1

Stakeholder 2

Stakeholder N

Change Management Plan

According to the *Standard for Program Management*—Second Edition (2008), program managers accept and embrace change—more so than project managers. Change is inevitable. Success requires control of change and, where that is not possible or desirable, adaptation to it. A change management plan is a guidebook to make this happen.

Change Management Plan Instructions

The change management plan will include the following:

> **Purpose:** A brief introductory statement defining the purpose of the change management plan, such as:
>
> The change management plan describes the processes and procedures to influence and manage program changes. It outlines the approaches to follow when there is a program change and assesses its impact on the overall program.
>
> It also analyzes the impact of changes on the overall outcome of the program and assigns roles and responsibilities to ensure the impact of the change is assessed accordingly, especially since each program involves changes. It focuses on factors that may influence program change to maximize them for the benefits of the program. It helps to coordinate changes across the program.
>
> Although the plan is drafted early in the program, it is an iterative document that should be further refined as the work of the program continues throughout the various phases in its life cycle. It involves redirecting or modifying the program as required based on changes that do in fact occur. It identifies standard change process information used within the organization as well as program-specific information. It should be provided to all program stakeholders.
>
> **Definition of the change process:** This section describes the change process to be followed in the program. It differentiates between program changes and product/services changes accordingly but integrates the product/services changes into the overall plan. It notes that changes may be either internal to the program or external to it. It identifies the key stakeholders who may be involved and the communication process to follow. It describes how the program manager must communicate the importance of changes to affected stakeholders. The program manager must plan for change, provide resources and support for changes, monitor and track changes, provide feedback on changes to stakeholders, and manage any issues stakeholders may have with each change. It states that changes may be approved, deferred, or rejected; the priority of the change; and its severity in terms of the program. It describes the specific roles and responsibilities of the program stakeholders regarding change management.
>
> **Change type:** This section shows the types of changes that may occur in the program. Some changes may be mandatory, while others are ones that may benefit the program or may clarify an existing requirement. Regardless, different types of changes will then require different levels of detail to be provided concerning the change, and will require different approval conditions. Some changes will involve more risks than others. The type of change also

may impact other program documents that may require modification if the change is approved and implemented.

Identification of controlled/configuration items: This section describes the controlled items in the program, sometimes referred to as configuration items. The emphasis of the identification of these items to be controlled should focus on physical items, documents, forms, and records. They are items that may be legal and regulatory requirements, health and safety guidelines, ones that are sent to contractors, ones that have an impact on the process or deliverables that are outside of the current program, and ones that involve the program's deliverables. For example, certain program artifacts, such as the program charter, program work breakdown structure, program management plan, approved schedule, approved budget, risk register, metrics, and contracts, are examples of possible controlled items or configuration items that require control. Each configuration item should be uniquely identified for control, processing, and tracking. Ideally, the configuration item should be linked to the program work breakdown structure program package identification number.

Change evaluation and approval processes and procedures: This section describes how a change request is to be used, how the change request will be analyzed, how decisions will be made based on the change impact analysis, and metrics to be reported as to the impact of the change. It notes the importance of documenting all change requests. It also describes how notifications to stakeholders regarding the disposition of the change will be made, states the process to implement the approved changes, and verifies that the implementation has occurred.

Change control: This section describes the process to be followed for change control. It explains how the change management process is integrated with the program management information system. It notes the importance of a full audit trail and reporting of the status of change requests. It describes how specific change control systems, such as those for contracts or cost, are part of an integrated change control system across the program.

Change status accounting and metrics: This section describes how information about the changes is communicated and actions are validated. It serves as a feedback mechanism for the overall program change management process. It describes the process to follow to acquire and enter information about the change into the appropriate repository. It also provides the data through established metrics to validate if the approved changes have been consistent with the program's objectives and can be tracked to its scope and evolution. The status of approved changes is tracked to inform the program manager and other stakeholders about the results of an approved change. Metrics are part of the change management plan and include items such as what was changed, when it was changed, what impact it has on the previously captured data and potential effects of new data, and the impact on other related programs and projects. The purpose is to assist the program manager in identifying trends in the productivity of implementing various changes, determine if estimating techniques are still valid, track customer satisfaction, and track rework. The metrics should be ones that are analyzed and used to facilitate communication across the program. Ad hoc and periodic reports to be prepared for stakeholders are included in this section.

Change verification and audits: This verification process of this section ensures the program change management goals are achieved through a systematic comparison of requirements with the initial, interim, and final results. The audit process of this section ensures the program configuration items have been handled according to their defined documentation. The actual process used is compared to the documented process to uncover any deficiencies or areas for improvement. This section also describes how results from the audits will be communicated to program stakeholders.

Approvals: This section contains the written approval of the change management plan by the program sponsor, program manager, program management office, members of the program board or governance board, and other stakeholders.

Change Management Plan Template

<Insert Program Name>
Change Management Plan

Program name:	
Program manager:	PM's email address here as a hyperlink
Program sponsor:	
Actual start date:	
Approved end date:	
Program no.:	
Revision history:	
Business unit:	

A. PURPOSE

A brief introductory statement defining the purpose of the change management plan, such as:

> The change management plan describes the processes and procedures to influence and manage program changes. It outlines the approaches to follow when there is a program change and assesses its impact on the overall program.

B. DEFINITION OF THE CHANGE PROCESS

This section defines the change process to be followed in the program. It notes the different changes that may affect the program, the key stakeholders and communications processes to follow, the disposition of changes, the priority of changes, and the roles and responsibilities of the stakeholders.

C. CHANGE TYPE

This section shows the types of changes that may occur in the program. It explains that based on the types of changes, different levels of detail to be provided concerning the change will be required as well as different approval requirements. The section also states the effect of the type of change on the impact of other program documents if the change is approved and implemented.

D. IDENTIFICATION OF CONTROLLED/CONFIGURATION ITEMS

This section describes the controlled items in the program or configuration items. Each one should be uniquely identified for control, processing, and tracking.

E. CHANGE EVALUATION AND APPROVAL PROCESSES AND PROCEDURES

This section describes how a change request is to be used, how it will be analyzed, how decisions will be made based on the analysis, and how metrics will be reported. It also includes how notifications to stakeholders concerning the disposition of the change request will be made, the process to implement approved changes, and the process to verify that implementation has occurred.

F. CHANGE CONTROL

This section describes the process to be followed for change control and explains how the change management process is integrated with the program management information system. It notes the importance of a full audit trail and reporting on the status of change requests.

_____

_____

_____

G. CHANGE STATUS ACCOUNTING AND METRICS

This section describes how information about changes is communicated and actions are validated. It describes the process to follow to acquire and enter information about the change into the appropriate repository and provides data through established metrics to validate if the approved changes are consistent with the program's objectives and can be tracked to its scope and evolution. The metrics to be collected are described in this section as well as various ad hoc and periodic reports to be prepared.

_____

_____

_____

H. CHANGE VERIFICATION AND AUDITS

This verification part of this section states how the program change management goals have been achieved through a systematic comparison of requirements with the initial, interim, and final results. The audit part of this section states that the program configuration items have been handled as planned and compares the actual process used to the documented process. It also describes how results from the audits will be communicated to stakeholders.

_____

_____

_____

I. APPROVALS

This section contains the approval of the change management plan by the program sponsor, program manager, program management office, members of the program board or governance board, and other key stakeholders.

SIGNATURES AND DATE APPROVAL OBTAINED

Program manager   _____

Program sponsor   _____

Program management office director   _____

Governance board chairperson	_____
Governance board member 1	_____
Governance board member 2	_____
Governance board member N	_____
Stakeholder 1	_____
Stakeholder 2	_____
Stakeholder N	_____

Program Scope Management Plan

Just as the program scope statement defines the extents and boundaries within which to manage the program, the program scope management plan defines how to prepare and manage the program scope statement. It also is developed in the plan program scope process in the *Standard for Program Management*—Second Edition (2008).

Program Scope Management Plan Instructions

The scope management plan will include the following:

Purpose: A brief introductory statement defining the purpose of the scope management plan, such as:

The scope management plan describes the process of managing scope throughout the program.

This plan describes the process to follow to develop a detailed program scope statement, the program work breakdown structure (PWBS), and the approach to follow for effective scope change control. It also sets forth the relationship between product scope and program scope as it serves to identify the process and activities to produce deliverables and benefits to achieve program goals. This plan then is used to define the program's goals and objectives.

In the Project Management Institute's *Standard for Program Management—Second Edition* (2008), the scope management plan is an output of plan program scope process. It is an input to the define program goals and objectives process.

Product scope and program scope: This section states the difference between product scope and program scope. It recognizes that product scope involves the features and functions that characterize the products, services, and results of the program, while program scope describes the work required to deliver a major product, service, or benefit. Separate processes may be needed for product scope and program scope, which would be stated in this section. This section notes that completion of product scope is measured against program requirements, while completion of program scope is measured according to the program management plan and the benefits realization plan.

Expected stability of the scope of the program: This section describes the expected stability of the scope of the program based on information from program stakeholders. The stakeholder register, and its accompanying analysis, is reviewed and analyzed, and stakeholders are contacted to define and prioritize their requirements and to obtain inputs concerning program scope acceptance. Program deliverable acceptance criteria are defined in this section for use in determining the overall stability of the scope of the program.

Scope statement development process: This section describes the process to follow to develop the scope statement for the program. A detailed program scope statement is critical to program success. The scope statement addresses the vision, range, capacity, and extent of the program endeavor. It serves to provide a common understanding of the program's scope by the stakeholders, as it establishes the direction to be taken and the essential aspects of the program to be accomplished. The process notes appropriate policies, procedures, and templates, which may be helpful in the development of the scope statement. It also describes tools and techniques to be used in the development of the scope statement, such as expert judgment, interviews, focus groups, and customer acceptance reviews.

Program work breakdown structure development process: This section describes the process to follow to develop the PWBS. The PWBS provides the framework for organizing and managing the work in the program. The objective is to structure the work in order that future activities and scope are easily managed. This section notes specific PWBS templates that may be considered, the use of expert judgment, lessons learned from previous programs, the various options to consider in program management in order that there is a balance between program deliverables and business objectives, the roles and level of involvement of specific individuals in the ownership of key activities, and methods to verify that the level of decomposition desired is necessary and sufficient.

Program scope change control process: This section describes the methods to use to identify program scope changes. The classification of these changes also is included in this section to determine the types of changes that the program manager can approve and others that need escalation to the program governance board. It also describes the process to follow to manage scope so scope creep does not occur, and states how program scope changes will be integrated into the overall program. Specific configuration management tools to be used are stated in this section to be able to monitor change control while enhancing organizational control so there is consistent documentation and product versions throughout the program.

Approvals: This section contains the written approval of the scope management plan by the program sponsor, program manager, program management office, members of the program board or governance board, and other stakeholders.

Scope Management Plan Template

<Insert Program Name>
Scope Management Plan

Program name:	
Program manager:	PM's email address here as a hyperlink
Program sponsor:	
Actual start date:	
Approved end date:	
Program no.:	
Revision history:	
Business unit:	

A. PURPOSE

A brief introductory statement defining the purpose of the scope management plan, such as:

> The scope management plan describes the process of managing scope throughout the program.

___
___
___

B. PRODUCT SCOPE AND PROGRAM SCOPE

This section states the difference between product scope and program scope. It describes how product scope and program scope are measured and states whether there is a need for separate processes to be used for product scope and program scope.

___
___
___

C. EXPECTED STABILITY OF THE SCOPE OF THE PROGRAM

This section describes the expected stability of the scope of the program based on information from program stakeholders. It defines program deliverable acceptance criteria as part of this process.

D. SCOPE STATEMENT DEVELOPMENT PROCESS

This section describes the process to follow to develop the scope statement for the program. It notes appropriate policies, procedures, and templates that may be helpful in the development of the scope statement and describes specific tools and techniques that will be used.

E. PROGRAM WORK BREAKDOWN STRUCTURE DEVELOPMENT PROCESS

This section describes the process to follow to develop the PWBS. It notes the tools and techniques to be used, and the methods to verify that the level of decomposition desired is necessary and sufficient.

F. PROGRAM SCOPE CHANGE CONTROL PROCESS

This section describes the methods to use to identify program scope changes. It includes how changes are classified and the process to follow to manage scope so scope creep does not occur. It states how program scope changes will be integrated into the overall program. It also describes specific configuration management tools to be used.

G. APPROVALS

This section contains the approval of the scope management plan by the program sponsor, program manager, program management office, members of the governance board, and other key stakeholders.

SIGNATURES AND DATE APPROVAL OBTAINED

Program manager   _____

Program sponsor   _____

Program management office director   _____

Governance board chairperson   _____

Governance board member 1   _____

Governance board member N   _____

Stakeholder 1   _____

Stakeholder 2   _____

Stakeholder N   _____

Program Scope Statement

Programs often fail because they do too many things in the heat of the battle that are being done by another team or organization, were not even part of the contract, or were not really needed for success. Ignoring this step can result in unnecessary requirements and serious cost overruns. The program scope statement (Figure 5.4) is a living document for avoiding this type of failure and is used throughout the

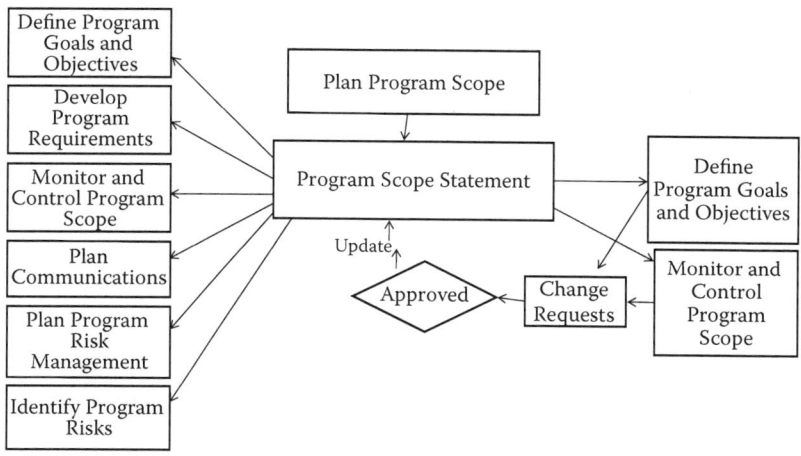

Program Management Life Cycle: Program Setup

Figure 5.4 Program scope statement.

program life cycle. It is prepared in the plan program scope process in the *Standard for Program Management*—Second Edition (2008).

Program Scope Statement Instructions

The program scope statement includes the following:

Purpose: A brief introductory statement defining the purpose of the scope statement, such as:

> The program scope statement defines the benefits, intent, and reason for pursuing a program by documenting what will be accomplished by the program.

It serves as the basis for future program decisions and describes the scope boundaries of the program. It identifies how scope will be managed throughout the program. It is an iterative document that can be further refined as the program progresses through the life cycle.

In the Project Management Institute's *Standard for Program Management*—Second Edition (2008), the program scope statement is an output of the plan program scope process. It is an input to the following processes:

- Define program goals and objectives
- Develop program requirements
- Monitor and control program scope
- Plan communications
- Plan program risk management
- Identify program risks

Updates to the scope statement result from the following processes:

- Define program goals and objectives
- Monitor and control program scope

Objectives and success criteria: This section includes the measurable success criteria of the program, including cost, schedule, technical, and quality objectives. Cost, schedule, and quality targets can be included. Benefits to be realized by the program should be mentioned with a reference to the benefits realization plan.

Program scope (inclusions and exclusions): This statement describes the characteristics of the product, service, or result that the program is undertaken to create. It is expected that these characteristics will be progressively elaborated as the project ensues.

Assumptions: This section lists and describes the specific program assumptions associated with the program scope, and the potential impact of the assumptions should they prove to be false.

Constraints: This section lists and describes the specific program constraints associated with the program scope that limit the team's options.

Resources: This section identifies the members of the program team, key stakeholders, and the program organization.

Deliverables and milestones: This section lists the deliverables, including both the outputs that comprise the product, service, or result, and the ancillary results, such as the program management reports and documentation. The milestones, proposed dates for those activities, and the deliverables are identified here, or a reference to the master program schedule may be used.

Acceptance criteria: This section identifies approval requirements that can be applied to items such as program objectives, deliverables (such as the manuals), documents (such as the component project plans and the performance tracking reports), and work products.

Risks: This section identifies the known risks to the program. It will be progressively elaborated during the course of the program.

Definitive cost estimate: This section shows the program's cost estimate. It is usually preceded by a modifier that provides some indication of accuracy.

Approvals: This section contains the written approval of the program scope statement by the program sponsor, program manager, program management office, members of the governance board, and other stakeholders.

Program Scope Statement Template

<Insert Program Name>
Program Scope Statement

Program name:	
Program manager:	PM's email address here as a hyperlink
Program sponsor:	
Actual start date:	
Approved end date:	
Program no.:	
Revision history:	
Business unit:	

A. PURPOSE

A brief introductory statement defining the purpose of the scope statement, such as:

> The program scope statement defines the benefits, intent, and reason for pursuing a program by documenting what will be accomplished by the program.

_____

_____

_____

B. OBJECTIVES AND SUCCESS CRITERIA

This section includes the measurable success criteria of the program, including cost, schedule, technical, and quality objectives and achievement of program benefits.

_____

_____

_____

C. PROGRAM SCOPE (INCLUSIONS AND EXCLUSIONS)

This statement describes the characteristics of the product, service, or result that the program is undertaken to create.

_____

_____

_____

D. ASSUMPTIONS

This section lists and describes the specific assumptions associated with the program scope, and the potential impact of the assumptions should they prove to be false.

_____

_____

_____

E. CONSTRAINTS

This section lists and describes the specific constraints associated with the program scope that limit the team's options.

_____

_____

_____

F. RESOURCES

This section identifies the members of the program team, the program governance board, key stakeholders, and the program organization.

G. DELIVERABLES AND MILESTONES

This section is a statement of the deliverables, including both the outputs that comprise the product, service, or result, and the ancillary results, such as the program management reports and documentation.

H. ACCEPTANCE CRITERIA

This section identifies approval requirements for items such as objectives, benefits realization plan, deliverables, documents, and work products.

I. RISKS

This section identifies the known risks to the program.

J. DEFINITIVE COST EXAMPLE

This section shows the program's cost estimate. It is usually preceded by a modifier that provides some indication of accuracy.

K. APPROVALS

This section contains the written approval of the program scope statement by the program sponsor, program manager, program management office, members of the governance board, and other stakeholders.

SIGNATURES AND DATE APPROVAL OBTAINED

Program manager　　　　　　　　＿＿＿＿＿＿＿＿＿＿＿＿＿＿＿＿
Program sponsor　　　　　　　　＿＿＿＿＿＿＿＿＿＿＿＿＿＿＿＿
Program management office director　＿＿＿＿＿＿＿＿＿＿＿＿＿＿＿＿
Governance board chairperson　＿＿＿＿＿＿＿＿＿＿＿＿＿＿＿＿
Governance board member 1　　＿＿＿＿＿＿＿＿＿＿＿＿＿＿＿＿
Governance board member 2　　＿＿＿＿＿＿＿＿＿＿＿＿＿＿＿＿
Governance board member N　　＿＿＿＿＿＿＿＿＿＿＿＿＿＿＿＿
Stakeholder 1　　　　　　　　　＿＿＿＿＿＿＿＿＿＿＿＿＿＿＿＿
Stakeholder 2　　　　　　　　　＿＿＿＿＿＿＿＿＿＿＿＿＿＿＿＿
Stakeholder N　　　　　　　　　＿＿＿＿＿＿＿＿＿＿＿＿＿＿＿＿

Program Stakeholder Management Plan

Having identified a preliminary list of stakeholders (organizations and people that hurt, help, or kill your program) in the pre-program preparations phase, it is now time to devote some thought to how you are going to deal with them. Do not forget that some stakeholders could be less than friendly just because you ignored or did not involve them. A plan to manage these diverse stakeholders is essential and is done in the program stakeholder management plan (Figure 5.5) process in the *Standard for Program Management*—Second Edition (2008).

Program Stakeholder Management Plan Instructions

The program stakeholder management plan includes the following:

Purpose: A brief introductory statement defining the purpose of the plan, such as:

> The program stakeholder management plan defines the program's key stakeholders and identifies their expectations and concerns for the program. Also, it ensures their commitment and support of the program. It is essential to understand and address the stakeholders' expectations and concerns to leverage them to support the program's business case and its continuation throughout its life cycle.
>
> The program stakeholder management plan does not need to be an extensive document. It needs to address key stakeholders, their information needs, concerns, expectations, and commitment to the program. Examples of possible program stakeholders follow the template. During the initial phases of the program, it serves to win support for the business case so the program may be initiated. Later, it serves to ensure that stakeholder commitment to the program remains strong.

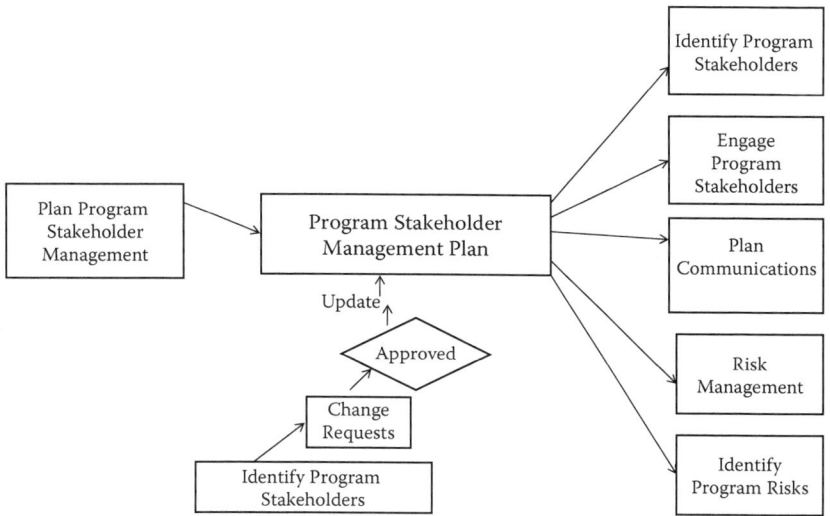

Figure 5.5 Program stakeholder management plan.

This plan should identify how the program will impact the stakeholders, the program's effect on the organization's culture and current major issues, and its likelihood to meet resistance and barriers to change. The plan provides a communications strategy for engaging the stakeholders, managing their expectations, and improving their acceptance and support of program objectives. Steps to consider in preparing the plan follow the template.

The plan also should relate to the program communications management plan so collectively these plans facilitate a clear understanding of issues, explain program goals and objectives, and target the delivery of key messages and the engagement of key stakeholders when required.

In the Project Management Institute's *Standard for Program Management—Second Edition* (2008), the program stakeholder management plan is an output of the plan program stakeholder management process. It is an input to the following processes:

- Identify program stakeholders
- Engage program stakeholders
- Plan communications
- Plan program risk management
- Identify program risks

Updates to the plan may occur from the identify program stakeholders process.

Stakeholder analysis chart: This chart is usually implemented as a spreadsheet, which requires the name, contact information, area of concern, level of involvement, primary concerns, requirements, and expectations of the responsible team member for every key program stakeholder. Its purpose is to assess each stakeholder's power, interests, expectations, and concerns. Recognize, as this chart is prepared, that stakeholders may have different areas of interest in the program, and these interests may change over the life cycle of the program.

Stakeholder communications approach: This section describes the methods to be used to communicate with stakeholders. An expanded version is included in the program communications plan. Here, the emphasis is on ensuring that the stakeholders are supportive of the program's mission, vision, goals, and objectives. It also should provide a strategy to engage each affected stakeholder, manage his or her expectations, and improve his or her acceptance of program objectives.

Stakeholder commitment: This section describes the approach the team will use to ensure stakeholder commitment to the program.

Approvals: This section contains the written approval of the program stakeholder management plan by the program sponsor, program manager, program management office, members of the governance board, and other stakeholders.

Program Stakeholder Management Plan Template

<Insert Program Name>
Program Stakeholder Management Plan

Program name:	
Program manager:	PM's email address here as a hyperlink
Program sponsor:	
Actual start date:	
Approved end date:	
Program no.:	
Revision history:	
Business unit:	

A. PURPOSE

A brief introductory statement defining the purpose of the program stakeholder management plan, such as:

> The program stakeholder management plan defines the program's key stakeholders and identifies their expectations and concerns for the program. Also, it ensures their commitment and support of the program. It is essential to understand and address the stakeholders' expectations and concerns to

leverage them to support the program's business case and its continuation throughout its life cycle.

B. STAKEHOLDER ANALYSIS CHART

This is a spreadsheet that contains the necessary information for each identified program stakeholder. See the accompanying "Stakeholder Management Matrix."

C. STAKEHOLDER COMMUNICATIONS APPROACH

This section describes the methods that will be used to communicate with the various stakeholders associated with the program.

D. STAKEHOLDER COMMITMENT

This section describes the approach the team will use to ensure stakeholder commitment to the program.

E. APPROVALS

This section contains the written approval of the program stakeholder management plan by the program sponsor, program manager, program management office, members of the governance board, and other stakeholders.

SIGNATURES AND DATE APPROVAL OBTAINED

Program manager
Program sponsor
Program management office director
Governance board chairperson
Governance board member 1
Governance board member 2
Governance board member N
Stakeholder 1
Stakeholder 2
Stakeholder N

Stakeholder Management Matrix

Stakeholder Name	Contact Information	Area or Phase of Concern	Level of Involvement or Participation (Low, Moderate, or High)	Primary Concerns or Issues	Specific Requirements	Expectations	Responsible Team Member

Considerations

Remember that stakeholders may be internal to the performing organization or external to it.

Examples of *internal* stakeholders include:

- **Performing organization:** The group that will perform the work of the program through its various projects.
- **Program director or executive sponsor:** The person who has executive ownership of the program and its policies and is responsible for creating an environment for program success. This person may be part of the selection committee for the program and may provide input as the program's business case is developed and the program charter is prepared.
- **Program management office:** May provide tools and templates to assist in identifying stakeholders and may be responsible for preparing the plan.
- **Program governance board:** Will be involved in the program once it is initiated and until it is complete, and may wish to review the plan to ensure it meets expectations and identifies the key stakeholders.
- **Program sponsor:** The person who provides funding for the program and is its champion.
- **Portfolio manager:** The individual responsible for assisting the organization's board responsible for program selection, prioritization, and continuation.
- **Program manager:** The individual responsible for managing the program.
- **Various project managers:** The individuals working in the program responsible for managing the projects within the program.
- **Program and project team members:** The individuals responsible for performing project and program activities.

Examples of *external* stakeholders include:

- Regulatory groups
- Consumer groups
- Environmental groups
- Customers/public

Steps to Consider in Preparing the Plan

1. The first step is to identify the various stakeholders associated with the program and their expectations. Build on the stakeholder identification document and the stakeholder inventory. Recognize that stakeholder interests vary, and will vary over the life of the program, and include items such as:
    - Direct or indirect program benefits
    - Adverse impact the program could cause

- Competition with this program for resources
- Interest in, but not a stake in, the program
- Need for cooperation from the program
- Need to comply with organizational policies and procedures
- Need to comply with regulatory policies and procedures
- Support or opposition to the program
- Governance of the program
- Influence over the program

2. Use a variety of methods to identify stakeholders. Consider methods such as:
   - Brainstorming
   - Expert interviews and judgment
   - Delphi approaches
   - Planning meetings
3. Identify stakeholder expectations. The program's mission is complemented by assessing, compiling, and documenting stakeholders' individual concerns and expectations and obtaining their support. The mission statement then establishes the direction of the program and sets a baseline for action and direction.
4. Prioritize the stakeholder expectations in terms of those individuals who have a major interest in or influence over the program. Recognize that interests and influences may be positive or negative. Each stakeholder may have different ideas as to which factors in the program are the most significant. In addition, each stakeholder may have different tolerances for risks associated with the program.
5. Recognize that the plan will be progressively elaborated as the program continues and should be reviewed and updated on a regularly scheduled basis.

Component Stakeholder Management Guidelines

Since programs consist of projects and nonproject work, they too have stakeholders and interface with their own stakeholders, but also likely interface with stakeholders at the program level. The program can help the components by suggesting sources of information such as the Project Management Body of Knowledge (PMBOK®), providing program-unique guidance, and defining appropriate contact boundaries. These guidelines are developed in the plan program stakeholder management process in the *Standard for Program Management*—Second Edition (2008).

Component Stakeholder Management Guidelines Instructions

Purpose: Stakeholder management is equally important at the component (project and nonproject work) level as it is at the program level.

Each component will have stakeholders who will impact and influence the component. One recommended practice is for the program management team to issue stakeholder management guidelines to its components. In the Project Management Institute's *Standard for Program Management*—Second Edition (2008), these guidelines are an output to the plan program stakeholder management process. They are an input to the manage component interfaces process.

This document presents some guidelines for consideration as to how each component should effectively manage its stakeholders for component and program success. These guidelines should be reviewed periodically and updated as required:

1. As each component begins, the component manager and his or her team should identify relevant stakeholders and determine their level of interest in the component and influence over it. They may wish to interview stakeholders or to survey them as part of the identification process. They should document the results of their stakeholder identification.
2. The component managers should maintain an ongoing list of these stakeholders and should meet with them periodically to address their issues and concerns. They should use a stakeholder register, similar to the one used at the program level.
3. The component manager should ensure that the stakeholders receive the information they need regarding the status of the component, as stated in the component's program communications management plan. Information should be distributed according to the information distribution process.
4. The component managers should ensure that the information provided to the stakeholders meets their needs and should request feedback from them. Stakeholders, for example, may request other information about project performance, and this request may show a need to more actively engage the stakeholder and to update the information that is provided.
5. Component managers should work with the program management team to prepare the program stakeholder management plan. A joint planning session also is recommended as stakeholders involved with one component may also be involved with other components, and these stakeholders then should receive higher priority at the program level in the program stakeholder management plan, stakeholder inventory, and stakeholder management strategy.
6. Component managers should inform the program manager about any issues they have with their stakeholders, as these issues may affect other components or the entire program.
7. If the component manager cannot resolve the stakeholder issues, he or she should ask the program manager for assistance and resolve the issues in a timely way.

8. Periodically, component managers should meet as a group to review these guidelines with the program manager and his or her team.
9. The guidelines should be reviewed when the work of the component is complete and is transitioned to an operational unit, or if the work of the component is terminated for any reason.
10. When new components are added to the program, the program management team should meet with the component manager to review these guidelines, explain their purpose, and solicit any suggestions for improvement.
11. Based on these feedback sessions, it may be necessary to revise these guidelines. If so, a member of the program management team should be assigned to implement these changes and inform the component managers of the updated guidelines.
12. The guidelines should be accessible by any member of the team.

Stakeholder Register

As you maintain the stakeholder list throughout the program, you use the stakeholder register whether in spreadsheet or database form. Since this list may be more widely distributed, it does not contain all the columns in the similar stakeholder inventory, some of which are likely extremely sensitive in nature. This register is prepared in the identify program stakeholders process in the *Standard for Program Management*—Second Edition (2008).

Stakeholder Register Instructions

Purpose: The stakeholder register is one of the first documents prepared in the program. It is used as part of the business case for the program, is refined during the planning process as the stakeholders are identified, and then is updated as the program planning continues and during program execution. It can be an appendix to the program stakeholder management plan and also to the program communications management plan. It is designed as a table, and a description of its contents follows.
1. **Name:** List the name of the stakeholder.
2. **Position:** List the stakeholder's position in the program. Typical examples are:
   a. Program director
   b. Program manager
   c. Project managers
   d. Program sponsor
   e. Customers
   f. Program team members
   g. Project team members

h. Functional/department managers
   i. Funding organization
   j. Project office director
   k. Project management office director
   l. Portfolio manager
   m. Members of the program's governance board
   n. Suppliers
   o. Government agencies
   p. Competitors
   q. Groups (environmental, consumer, or other types of groups affected by the program)
   r. Others (people in other programs or other organizational units that may require similar resources or may have goals that conflict with or complement those of the program)
3. **Contact information:** List contact information for each stakeholder: phone numbers (office and cell), location, and email. For government agencies, competitors, and groups, list the name and contact details of the principal representatives with an interest in the program.
4. **Areas of influence:** State whether the stakeholder has a high level of influence concerning the program. It typically is based on the stakeholder's level of power and authority. Consider a ranking scale such as the following:
   a. 5 = Major influence throughout the program life cycle; should be consulted regularly and should meet regularly with the program management team.
   b. 4 = Involved at certain phases during the program; should be informed of progress regularly.
   c. 3 = Involved at only one phase of the program's life cycle; should be informed of progress regularly in the area of interest but infrequently at other times.
   d. 2 = Somewhat interested in the program; should be kept informed of the progress of the program from time to time.
   e. 1 = Requires limited notification as to the progress of the program.
5. **Program opinion:** List whether the stakeholder is considered to be a strong supporter of the program, a neutral party, or someone who does not believe the program should be pursued. Consider a ranking scale such as the following:
      5 = Strong program advocate
      4 = Supporter
      3 = Neutral
      2 = Limited interest in the program
      1 = Does not believe the program should be pursued

6. **Program impact:** State whether the stakeholder will be directly or indirectly impacted by the outcome of the program. Consider a ranking scale such as the following:
   5 = Direct impact
   4 = Somewhat impacted
   3 = Neutral
   2 = Limited impact
   1 = No impact
7. **Management strategy:** State the approach the program management team plans to use to work with this stakeholder. Consider a RACI chart such as the following:
   A = Approves all key documents and decisions as required
   C = Consulted before a decision is made and receives a preliminary draft of documents before they are in final form
   I = Informed of progress and can receive documents upon request
   R = Responsible for a critical area in the program
8. **Information requirements:** State the stakeholder's information requirements. Consider an approach such as the following:
   5 = Receives all issued reports and requests others as needed
   4 = Receives all issued reports
   3 = Receives monthly reports
   2 = Receives quarterly reports
   1 = Receives press releases or general program information
9. **Responsible team member:** State the name and contact information of the program team member who will be the principal point of contact for work with this stakeholder.
10. **Issues identified:** List any issues this stakeholder identifies during the course of the program and the date.
11. **Resolution and date:** List how these issues were resolved and the date.
12. **Notes:** Use this field for any additional notes about the stakeholder.

Stakeholder Inventory

While the stakeholder inventory (Figure 5.6) contains all of the information in the stakeholder register, it also contains a wealth of other information that is often sensitive in nature. If this information is in a database, the stakeholder register could be a report of only the first few columns in the stakeholder inventory, but careful data security measures must then be in place. It also is prepared in the identify program stakeholder process in the *Standard for Program Management*—Second Edition (2008).

The Program Setup Phase ■ 83

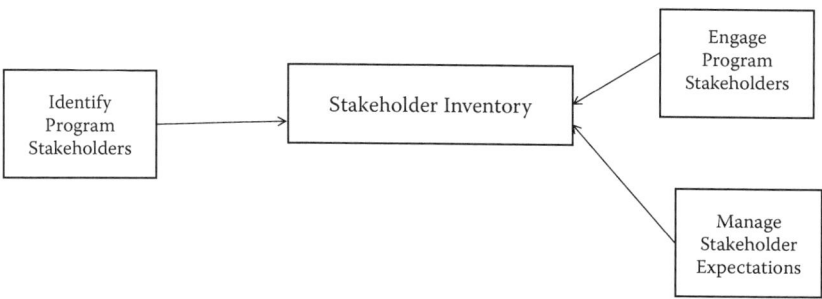

Program Management Life Cycle: Program Initiation and Program Setup

Figure 5.6 Stakeholder inventory.

Stakeholder Inventory Instructions

The stakeholder inventory will include the following:

Purpose: A brief introductory statement defining the purpose of the stakeholder inventory, such as:

> The stakeholder inventory is part of the program's commitment to effective stakeholder management. It provides a summary of each stakeholder's involvement in the program, his or her possible responses, any identified issues, and possible mitigation strategies.

Different stakeholders will have an interest in or influence over the program at different times. During the pre-program preparations phase in the life cycle, initial stakeholder identification begins.

Then, during the identify program stakeholders process, a stakeholder inventory should be prepared, which builds on this initial stakeholder identification. It should complement the program stakeholder management plan and stakeholder register, and it supports the stakeholder management strategy since stakeholder management is a key theme in program management and is essential for program success.

The stakeholder inventory is prepared during the program's planning process, but it is an iterative document that should be reviewed periodically during meetings of the program management team and the governance board and updated as new stakeholders are identified throughout the program.

In the Project Management Institute's *Standard for Program Management—Second Edition* (2008), the stakeholder inventory is an output from the identify program stakeholders process. It is an input to the following processes:

- Engage program stakeholders
- Manage stakeholder expectations

Stakeholder categories: To set up the inventory, use categories for the program's stakeholders based on those included in the initial stakeholder identification as well as in the program stakeholder management plan. This section should list the categories that will be part of the inventory. It also should consider the various roles of the stakeholders, both internal and external.

Stakeholder influence: For each category, determine the stakeholder's level of influence concerning the program. This section should describe how the stakeholder will be impacted by the program and how the stakeholder will influence it. A matrix can be prepared. A possible example follows the template.

Possible stakeholder responses: Using the categories and the level of stakeholder influence in the program, this section lists possible responses to various changes that may affect the program or specific areas of interest to the stakeholders. For example, some stakeholders may be more concerned about different areas than others, such as:

- Program benefits
- Program deliverables
- Program funding/financial management
- Schedule
- Governance issues
- Communications issues
- Intellectual property
- Vendor issues
- Level of risk
- Issue resolution
- Internal and external influences
- Resources

This section then describes the areas of greatest interest to specific stakeholders so possible responses can be prepared should a change occur. Negative impacts should be determined in order that the response then can address them quickly to minimize any adverse impacts to the program.

Potential mitigation strategies: This section describes the potential mitigation strategies to consider should an area of interest be affected. These strategies are further defined in the stakeholder management strategy document.

Approvals: This section contains the written approval of the stakeholder inventory by the program sponsor, program manager, program management office, members of the governance board, and others as appropriate.

Stakeholder Inventory Template

<Insert Program Name>
Stakeholder Inventory

Program name:	
Program manager:	PM's email address here as a hyperlink
Program sponsor:	
Proposed start date:	
Proposed end date:	
Prepared by:	
Revision history:	
Business unit:	

A. PURPOSE

A brief introductory statement defining the purpose of the stakeholder inventory, such as:

> The stakeholder inventory is part of the program's commitment to effective stakeholder management. It provides a summary of each stakeholder's involvement in the program, his or her possible responses, any identified issues, and possible mitigation strategies.

_____
_____
_____

B. STAKEHOLDER CATEGORIES

This section lists the stakeholder categories that will be part of the inventory.

_____
_____
_____

C. STAKEHOLDER INFLUENCE

This section defines the influence level of each of the stakeholders and shows how the stakeholder will be affected by the program.

D. POSSIBLE STAKEHOLDER RESPONSES

This section uses the categories and the stakeholder's influence on the program and lists possible responses to various changes that may affect the stakeholder's specific areas of interest.

E. POTENTIAL MITIGATION STRATEGIES

This section describes the potential mitigation strategies to consider should an area of interest be affected. These strategies are further defined in the stakeholder management strategy document.

F. APPROVALS

This section contains the approval of the stakeholder inventory by the program manager, program sponsor, program management office, members of the governance board, and others as required.

SIGNATURES AND DATE APPROVAL OBTAINED

Program manager _____

Program sponsor _____

Program management office director _____

Governance board chairperson _____

Governance board member 1 _____

Governance board member 2 _____

Governance board member N _____

Stakeholder 1 _____

Stakeholder 2 _____

Stakeholder N _____

Matrix Example

Stakeholder	Interests	Program Impact	Possible Responses	Possible Mitigation Strategies	Priority
Program sponsor	Program benefits	High	Benefit reports	Corrective action	1
Governance board members	Program benefits Strategic objectives	High	Regular meetings Status reports	Decisions Corrective action	1
Functional managers	Resources	Medium	Meetings Program charter	Escalate to governance board	3
Team members	Program responsibilities	Low	Status reports	Responsibility assignment matrix	5

Stakeholder Management Strategy

Having identified and analyzed your stakeholders, it then is important to devise strategies for mitigating potential problems and maximizing the desirable potential impacts. Yes, this is a lot like risk management, PMBOK® style, or the stakeholder management strategy in the PMBOK®, but with a higher-level and more specific focus.

Stakeholder Management Strategy Instructions

The stakeholder management strategy includes the following:

Purpose: A brief introductory statement defining the purpose of the stakeholder management strategy, such as:

The stakeholder management strategy is part of the program's commitment to effective stakeholder management. It contains guidelines to manage the impact of the program on its stakeholders.

Different stakeholders will have an interest in or influence over the program at different times. During the pre-program preparation stage in the life cycle, initial stakeholder identification begins.

Next, in the plan program stakeholder management process, a stakeholder management plan is prepared. Then, during the identify program stakeholders process, a stakeholder register, stakeholder inventory, and stakeholder management plan are prepared.

The stakeholder management strategy focuses on the ways the program management team will actively engage stakeholders in the program and will work to distill any negative attitudes that any stakeholders may have about the program and to ensure the stakeholders are united in working together toward program success. This strategy is needed because of the complexities of many programs, the changes to be realized by the program, and the interdependencies among program components and possibly other programs and projects under way in the organization. Additionally, programs tend to have more stakeholder involvement given the benefits to be provided by the program.

It is an iterative document that should be reviewed regularly by the program management team and the governance board as new stakeholders become involved in the program at different phases of the life cycle or as other stakeholders have new interests in the program.

Stakeholder engagement: Stakeholder management is a key to successful program management. The program management team must work to ensure all stakeholders are engaged in the program and are supportive of it. This section describes how the program management team will ensure stakeholders are actively supporting the program so that any possible negative impacts can be easily resolved.

Stakeholder mitigation strategies: When stakeholders do have issues concerning the program, strategies are required to mitigate these negative impacts. This section describes the strategies the program management team will use to work with these stakeholders. For example, since programs represent organizational change, it may be appropriate for the program management team to conduct training so affected stakeholders understand why the program is being conducted so they can best adjust to the resulting changes from it. It also may be appropriate to prepare job aids for use once the program is transferred to ongoing operations to best handle the impact of the program on stakeholders. These job aids could include specific descriptions of processes to follow, guidelines to consider, and quick reference guides that are readily available.

Stakeholder feedback: The program management team also must ensure that stakeholders have embraced the changes and that the mitigation strategies that have been prepared are effective. This section describes how the program management team will obtain feedback from stakeholders concerning these mitigation strategies to see if changes are required. It also will state the need for change orders as appropriate and whether the changes will result in the need to update any other program documents and specific responsibility to implement the changes as necessary.

Approvals: This section contains the written approval of the stakeholder management strategy by the program sponsor, program manager, members of the governance board, and others as appropriate.

Stakeholder Management Strategy Template

<Insert Program Name>
Stakeholder Management Strategy

Program name:	
Program manager:	PM's email address here as a hyperlink
Program sponsor:	
Proposed start date:	
Proposed end date:	
Prepared by:	
Revision history:	
Business unit:	

A. PURPOSE

A brief introductory statement defining the purpose of the stakeholder management strategy, such as:

> The stakeholder management strategy is part of the program's commitment to effective stakeholder management. It contains guidelines to manage the impact of the program on its stakeholders.

_____
_____
_____

B. STAKEHOLDER ENGAGEMENT

This section describes how the program management team will ensure stakeholders are actively supporting the program so that any possible negative impacts can be easily resolved.

_____
_____
_____

C. STAKEHOLDER MITIGATION STRATEGIES

This section describes the strategies the program management team will use to work with stakeholders when the stakeholders have issues with the program to minimize any negative impacts.

_____
_____
_____

D. STAKEHOLDER FEEDBACK

This section describes how the program management team will obtain feedback from stakeholders concerning the mitigation strategies to see if changes are required.

_____
_____
_____

E. APPROVALS

This section contains the approval of the stakeholder management strategy by the program manager, program sponsor, members of the governance board, and others as required.

SIGNATURES AND DATE APPROVAL OBTAINED

Program manager	_____
Program sponsor	_____
Program management office director	_____
Governance board chairperson	_____
Governance board member 1	_____
Governance board member 2	_____
Governance board member N	_____
Stakeholder 1	_____
Stakeholder 2	_____
Stakeholder N	_____

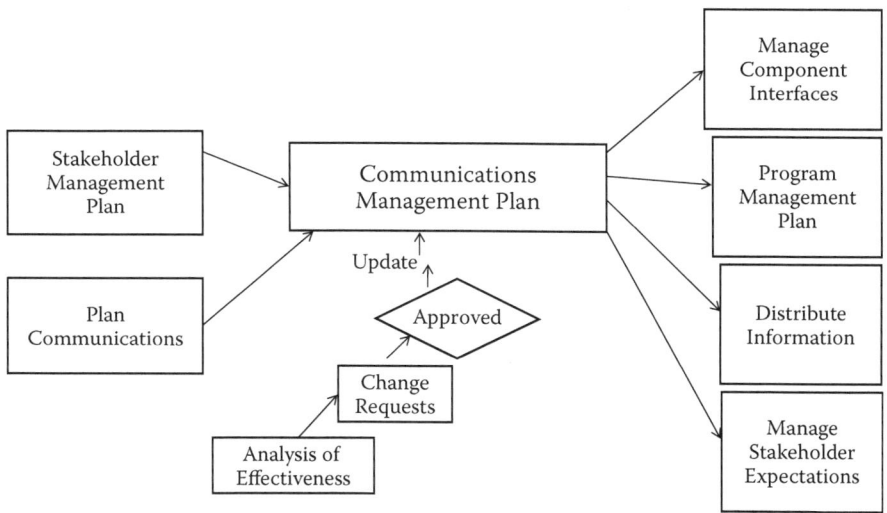

Figure 5.7 Communications management plan.

Program Communications Management Plan

Lots of internal and external stakeholders will be interested in what you are doing and how the program is progressing. The *Standard for Program Management—Second Edition* (2008) is not kidding when it says you need to decide how much of which information is sent to whom, how, and how often. For example, if you give just a little more information than a particular stakeholder needs—airing issues that you know will ultimately be resolved—you could wind up spending too much of your time answering questions about matters some stakeholders do not need to worry about yet. On the other hand, transparency demands that bad news gets to the right people in a timely manner. A balance is in order, and that is part of the art of program management. For example, failure to have a publishing schedule will mean missed deadlines for reports. Your program communications management plan (Figure 5.7) addresses these issues and more. It is prepared in the plan communications process in the *Standard for Program Management—Second Edition* (2008).

Program Communications Management Plan Instructions

The program communications management plan includes the following:

Purpose: A brief introductory statement defining the purpose of the program communications management plan, such as:

> The program communications management plan describes the process of determining the information and communications needs of the project stakeholders and states which stakeholders need what information, to what granularity, when they need it, how it will be given to them, and by whom.

This plan builds on the stakeholder management plan, which is developed earlier in the program. In fact, once the program communications management plan is approved, the stakeholder management plan can become an appendix to it. Effective communications are essential for program success. Program communications create a bridge between the various stakeholders in the program, connecting various cultural and organizational backgrounds, different levels of expertise, and various perspectives and interest in program execution. Although the plan is drafted early in the program, it is an iterative document that should be further refined as the program moves through the phases of the life cycle, especially since its development may entail the need to create additional deliverables. If the latter is the case, then the program work breakdown structure, program schedule, and program budget also will require updates.

It is prepared in the plan communications process in the *Standard for Program Management*—Second Edition (2008). The stakeholder management plan is an input to the plan. Outputs are to manage the component interfaces process, the program management plan, the distribute information process, and the manage stakeholder expectations process.

Stakeholder communications requirements: This section builds on the stakeholder management plan as it describes the communications requirements of the program stakeholders. These requirements are defined by combining the type and format of the information needed with an assessment of the value of the information. It is important to ensure that program resources are expended only on communications that lead to program success, or where a lack of information may lead to program failure.

Information to be communicated: This section describes the information to be communicated, including language, format, content, and level of detail. Like many plan elements, this information will not be completely known at the outset. While all stakeholders require information about the program, the information needs of stakeholders vary greatly and may change during various program phases in the life cycle. To be effective, the information must be communicated in the right format, at the right time, and with the right impact. Efficiency also is important, as it focuses on providing only the information that is needed.

- **Program team member responsibilities:** This section states which program team member is primarily responsible for the communications requirements of each of the program stakeholders.
- **People to receive the information:** This section describes the specific people or organizational units that will receive each type of information that will be communicated. This section may change based on the stage of the process in the program life cycle, as different groups will have different levels of interest. Not everyone needs to communicate with everyone else; however, people do require information based on their roles and responsibilities in the program and their specific areas of interest.
- **Methods or technologies to use to convey the information:** This section describes the methods to use to transfer information to the program stakeholders. Methods range from brief conversations to extended meetings, or from one-page reports of progress to detailed status reports. To prepare this section consider factors such as the urgency of the need for the information, the available technology, the expected program staffing, the program duration, and the program environment.
- **Frequency of information to be provided:** This section describes the frequency of information to be provided to each of the program stakeholders. Some stakeholders will require information on a daily basis, while others may only need program information before a stage gate review of the governance board or steering committee.
- **Escalation process for communications issues:** This section describes how communications issues will be escalated from project managers or program team members to the program manager, or from the program manager to the sponsor or to the governance board or steering committee. It should include time frames to resolve any issues at each level.
- **Methods to update the program communications management plan:** This section describes the specific methods to use to update the program communications management plan as the program ensues. It is important to ensure that stakeholders receive the required information. If a number of issues surface that require escalation, this can serve as a trigger to update the plan. Similarly, if new stakeholders have an interest in the program, it may be appropriate to update the plan.
- **Glossary of common terminology:** Each program has certain terms that are used by the various program stakeholders. Similarly, standard program management terms also are used. The same acronym may have vastly different meanings in different organizations. This section contains a glossary of common terms that stakeholders can use who are interested in the program to ensure there are no misunderstandings that can lead to communications breakdowns.
- **Guidelines for meetings and email:** Meetings and email are common methods to distribute program information. This section describes how meetings are to be held: whether they are formal or informal or collocated or e-meetings.

It states the need for an agenda for each meeting, for minutes to be taken and distributed, and for action items or issues to be recorded and reviewed at subsequent meetings. This section also describes guidelines for the use of email. It is important to ensure that guidelines are set as to how to identify critical program information, a specific timetable as to when a response is required, when an email should be sent to the entire program team or to only key team members, manual or automated archiving processes, and the need for confidentiality and security requirements for certain information in emails.

Approvals: This section contains the written approval of the program communications management plan by the program sponsor, program manager, program management office, members of the program board or governance board, and other stakeholders.

Program Communications Management Plan Template

<Insert Program Name>
Program Communications Management Plan

Program name:	
Program manager:	PM's email address here as a hyperlink
Program sponsor:	
Actual start date:	
Approved end date:	
Program no.:	
Revision history:	
Business unit:	

A. PURPOSE

A brief introductory statement defining the purpose of the program communications management plan, such as:

> The program communications management plan describes the process of determining the information and communications needs of the program stakeholders and states which stakeholders need what information, when they need it, how it will be given to them, and by whom.

B. STAKEHOLDER COMMUNICATIONS REQUIREMENTS

This section describes the communications requirements of the program stakeholders. They are defined by combining the type and format of the information needed with an assessment of the value of the information.

C. INFORMATION TO BE COMMUNICATED

This section describes the information to be communicated, influencing language, format, content, and level of detail. The information needs of program stakeholders vary greatly and may change during the various program phases in the life cycle.

D. PROGRAM TEAM MEMBER RESPONSIBILITIES

This section states which program team member is responsible for the communications requirements of each program stakeholder.

E. PEOPLE TO RECEIVE THE INFORMATION

This section describes the specific people or organizational units that will receive each type of information that will be communicated. People require information based on their roles and responsibilities in the program and their specific areas of interest.

F. METHODS OR TECHNOLOGIES TO USE TO CONVEY THE INFORMATION

This section describes the methods to use to transfer information to the program stakeholders. Consider items such as the urgency of the need for the information, the available technology, expected program staffing, program duration, and the program environment.

G. FREQUENCY OF INFORMATION TO BE PROVIDED

This section describes the frequency of information to be provided to each of the program stakeholders, as some may require only infrequent communications and others may require information on a daily basis.

H. ESCALATION PROCESS FOR COMMUNICATIONS ISSUES

This section describes how communications issues will be escalated from project managers or project team members to the program manager, and from the program manager to the program sponsor or to the governance board or steering committee. It should include time frames to resolve any issue at each level.

I. METHODS TO USE TO UPDATE THE PROGRAM COMMUNICATIONS MANAGEMENT PLAN

This section describes the specific methods to use to update the program communications management plan as the program ensues. It is important to ensure stakeholders receive the required information, and stakeholders will change over the life of the program.

J. GLOSSARY OF COMMON TERMINOLOGY

This section contains a glossary of common terms that are used by the program stakeholders and standard program management terms to ensure there are no misunderstandings that can lead to communications barriers.

K. GUIDELINES FOR MEETINGS AND EMAIL

This section describes how meetings are to be held and their specific format. It states the need for an agenda for each meeting, for minutes to be taken and distributed, and for action items or issues to be recorded and reviewed at subsequent meetings. It also describes guidelines for the use of e-mail to state critical program information, a specific timetable in which a response is required, when email should be sent to the entire team or to only key team members, and the need for confidentiality and security requirements for certain information in emails.

_____

_____

_____

L. APPROVALS

This section contains the approval of the program communications management plan by the program sponsor, program manager, program management office, members of the program board or governance board, and other key stakeholders.

SIGNATURES AND DATE APPROVAL OBTAINED

Program manager _____

Program sponsor _____

Program management office director _____

Governance board chairperson _____

Governance board member 1 _____

Governance board member 2 _____

Governance board member N _____

Stakeholder 1 _____

Stakeholder 2 _____

Stakeholder N _____

Communications Log

Your program cannot be sure of consistent and uniform information without a communications log. It consists of meeting minutes, emails, reports and memos, presentations, etc. It too is prepared in the plan communications process in the *Standard for Program Management*—Second Edition (2008). In today's environment, it is usually implemented in a Web portal or perhaps a database.

Communications Log Instructions

Purpose: The communications log is used throughout the program to document program communications to the various program stakeholders. It also is used to show other communication items that were not in the program communications management plan but were requested by stakeholders, and how the stakeholders received the needed information. These data then are used to determine whether changes to the program communications management plan are warranted. This log is prepared by a program team member or the program manager.

This communications log complements the program communications management plan.

The communications log is designed as a table, and a description of its contents follows:

1. **Communications requirement:** List the stakeholder communications requirement as described in the program communications management plan.
2. **Type of communication:** State the type of communication. Examples include upcoming meetings, meeting agendas, status reports, memos, press releases, risk log, program issues register, benefit register, program schedule, financial reports, meeting minutes, formal reports, lessons learned, newsletters, etc.
3. **Frequency:** State how often the specific type of communication is to be prepared. Examples include daily, weekly, monthly, quarterly, at the end of a phase gate or program review, at the end of an audit, according to schedule milestones, when deliverables are completed, at the end of the program, etc.
4. **Prepared by:** List the person who prepared the communications item and his or her contact information.
5. **Delivered to:** List the people who received the communications item and their contact information.
6. **Delivery method:** State how the communication was delivered, e.g., email, posted in a discussion forum or in a blog, hard copy, newsletter, demonstrations, brochures, etc.
7. **Date:** State the date the communications item was delivered.
8. **Feedback measures:** State the approach used by the program management team to determine if the communications item was considered effective by the recipients, such as an interview, phone call, email, or survey. Use this column to determine whether the communications item was considered effective and addressed the stakeholder's requirements to see if any changes are needed.

9. **Communications request:** Describe any requests for unscheduled communications by program stakeholders.
10. **Requested by:** List who requested the communications item and his or her contact details.
11. **Prepared by:** State who prepared the needed information and his or her contact details.
12. **Recipients:** State who received the information and his or her contact details.
13. **Delivery method:** State how the information was delivered.
14. **Date:** State the date the communications item was delivered.
15. **Notes:** Use this field for any additional notes about the communications item.

Communications Strategy

According to the *Standard for Program Management*—Second Edition (2008), the communications strategy is comprised of the stakeholder register, the "stakeholder engagement log" (presumably the communication log since most communications are with stakeholders), and the program communications management plan. This communications strategy is prepared in the plan communications process.

Communications Strategy Instructions

The communications strategy includes the following:

Purpose: A brief introductory statement defining the purpose of the communications strategy, such as:

The communications strategy ensures that stakeholders receive the information they need about the program and that their issues and concerns are resolved in a timely and appropriate way.

Communications are especially important on programs given the numerous stakeholders involved, the high level of interest in the outcomes of the program in terms of achieving benefits, and the link between the program's objectives and the organization's strategic objectives.

The communications strategy is the document that incorporates the stakeholder register, stakeholder management plan, stakeholder management strategy, and the program communications management plan. These documents can be attached to this strategy.

It is prepared as an output of the plan communications process, in *Standard for Program Management*—Second Edition (2008), but it is an iterative document and should be reviewed on a periodic basis to ensure that stakeholders receive the information they need in a timely way and that the information provided is relevant and accurate. It also is used to ensure that any stakeholder issues and concerns are addressed and resolved as appropriate.

Organization's communications strategy: If the organization has a communications strategy, it should be noted in this section. The section also should state whether this strategy is to be used without change or whether tailoring is needed to meet the specific program requirements. If this strategy is to be used without any changes, there is no need to complete the rest of this template except for the approvals section.

Constraints: This section documents those items that may limit the program team's communications options. Examples are stakeholders who are located in different geographic areas to ensure they are not affected adversely when virtual meetings are held; the need to use a common language for communications, such the standard English vocabulary of four thousand words; an inability to access common systems because of the lack of software compatibility; and the use of different technical capabilities.

Assumptions: This section describes those items that are considered to be true, real, or certain concerning the communications strategy. Examples may be regulatory requirements, changes in technology, the need to consult with advisory boards, media involvement at certain phases of the program, involvement of consumer groups, terms and conditions and other confidential clauses in contracts, and organizational requirements.

Information transfer from components to the program: This section states the format and process the components will use to transfer information from the component to the program and how often information will be transferred. It also describes the mechanisms to ensure that the information that is transferred is timely and accurate. To ensure stakeholders receive needed information, major component milestones should be addressed as part of the program's master schedule, and information should be provided when these milestones are met.

Assessment of potential communications channels: This section states the potential communications channels in the program given the number of stakeholders. The program manager then can determine who needs to communicate with whom and how often communications should occur in order that there is an optimal exchange of information with stakeholders.

Resolution of stakeholder issues and concerns: This section describes the methods to be used to resolve any stakeholder issues and concerns. It describes how component managers will escalate issues to the program manager. It states the items the program manager can resolve on his or her own and the process to use to escalate items to the governance board for resolution.

Approvals: This section contains the written approval of the communications strategy by the program sponsor, program manager, program management office, members of the governance board, and others as appropriate.

Communications Strategy Template

<Insert Program Name>
Communications Strategy

Program name:	
Program manager:	PM's email address here as a hyperlink
Program sponsor:	
Proposed start date:	
Proposed end date:	
Prepared by:	
Revision history:	
Business unit:	

A. PURPOSE

A brief introductory statement defining the purpose of the communications strategy, such as:

> The communications strategy ensures that stakeholders receive the information they need about the program and that their issues and concerns are resolved in a timely and appropriate way.

_____
_____
_____

B. ORGANIZATION'S COMMUNICATIONS STRATEGY

This section states whether the organization's communications strategy will be followed in the program.

_____
_____
_____

C. CONSTRAINTS

This section documents those items that may limit the program team's communications options.

D. ASSUMPTIONS

This section describes those items that are considered true, real, or certain concerning the communications strategy.

E. INFORMATION TRANSFER FROM COMPONENTS TO THE PROGRAM

This section states the format and process the components will use to transfer information from the component to the program and how often information will be transferred. It describes mechanisms to ensure the information that is transferred is timely and accurate.

F. ASSESSMENT OF POTENTIAL COMMUNICATIONS CHANNELS

This section states the potential communications channels in the program given the number of stakeholders.

G. RESOLUTION OF STAKEHOLDER ISSUES AND CONCERNS

This section describes the methods to be used to resolve any stakeholder issues and concerns.

H. APPROVALS

This section contains the approval of the communications strategy by the program manager, program sponsor, program management office, members of the governance board, and others as required.

SIGNATURES AND DATE APPROVAL OBTAINED

Program manager _____

Program sponsor _____

Program management office director _____

Governance board chairperson _____

Governance board member 1 _____

Governance board member 2 _____

Governance board member N _____

Stakeholder 1 _____

Stakeholder 2 _____

Stakeholder N _____

Program Resource Plan

While most resources and cost are probably at the component (project and non-project work) level and are thus managed there, the program level employs most or all of some resources for program management and governance. Necessary plans for efficiency and timeliness are in the program resource plan (Figure 5.8). It is prepared in the develop program infrastructure process in the *Standard for Program Management*—Second Edition (2008).

Program Resource Plan Instructions

The program resource plan includes the following:

> **Purpose:** A brief introductory statement defining the purpose of the program resource plan, such as:
>
> > The program resource plan describes the resources required to manage the program. It includes methods to monitor and track resource use.
> >
> > These program resources include more than human resources and consist of materials, tools, equipment, facilities, and finances that will be used

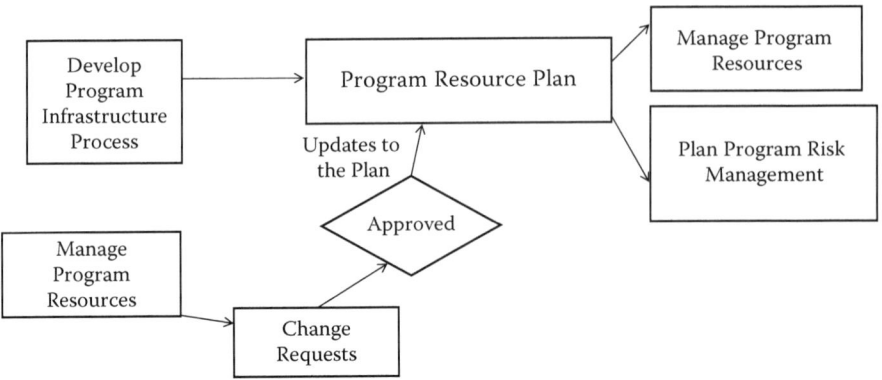

Program Management Life Cycle: Program Setup

Figure 5.8 Program resource plan.

in the program. It also is important to recognize that this plan addresses resource use at the program level, not at the individual component level. Although the plan is drafted early in the program, it is an iterative document that should be further refined, especially since the preliminary requirements regarding the resources probably will change as the program progresses.

In the Project Management Institute's *Standard for Program Management—Second Edition* (2008), the program resource plan is an output from the develop program infrastructure process and is an input to manage program resources and plan program risk management processes. This plan may require updates as a result of the manage program resources process.

Internal and external required resources: This section describes specific internal and external, when appropriate, resources required for program success. It presents costs for each of these needed resources to assist in overall financial management and in determining the program's financial framework.

Organizational influences: This section defines various organizational influences that can impact the program team. It describes key procurement and personnel policies that may affect the acquisition of needed resources for the program. Also, it notes guidance on the appropriate use of program resources, such as depreciation or release of purchased equipment, sharing resources with other parts of the organization, or recurring costs of resources that are leased.

Methods to meet resource requirements: This section describes when and how resource requirements will be met in the program. It describes whether resources will be obtained internally or through procurements. It also describes the need to follow the issue escalation process should the program manager have difficulty acquiring needed resources to support the program.

Resource calendars: This section describes the necessary time frames for use of the program resources. These calendars can assist in development of the overall program schedule.

Tracking and monitoring: This section describes the methods to be used to track and monitor resource use throughout the program's life cycle. Since change is inevitable in all programs, the need for certain resources may change, especially as new components become part of the program, and other components are transitioned or terminated.

Approvals: This section contains the written approval of the program resource plan by the program sponsor, program manager, program management office, members of the governance board, and other stakeholders.

Program Resource Plan Template

<Insert Program Name>
Program Resource Plan

Program name:	
Program manager:	PM's email address here as a hyperlink
Program sponsor:	
Actual start date:	
Approved end date:	
Program no.:	
Revision history:	
Business unit:	

A. PURPOSE

A brief introductory statement defining the purpose of the resource management plan, such as:

> The program resource plan describes the resources required to manage the program. It includes methods to monitor and track resource use.

___
___
___

B. INTERNAL AND EXTERNAL REQUIRED RESOURCES

This section defines specific internal and external, when appropriate, resources required for program success. It also presents costs for each of these resources.

C. ORGANIZATIONAL INFLUENCES

This section defines various organizational influences that can impact the program team's resource requirements, such as personnel and procurement policies and procedures, guidance regarding depreciation or release of equipment, sharing resources within the organization, and recurring costs of leased resources.

D. METHODS TO MEET RESOURCE REQUIREMENTS

This section describes when and how resource requirements will be met in the program.

E. RESOURCE CALENDARS

This section describes the needed time frames for use of the program resources.

F. TRACKING AND MONITORING

This section describes the methods to be used to track and monitor resource use throughout the program's life cycle.

G. APPROVALS

This section contains the approval of the program resource plan by the program sponsor, program manager, program management office, members of the governance board, and other key stakeholders.

SIGNATURES AND DATE APPROVAL OBTAINED

Program manager _____

Program sponsor _____

Program management office director _____

Governance board chairperson _____

Governance board member 1 _____

Governance board member 2 _____

Governance board member N _____

Stakeholder 1 _____

Stakeholder 2 _____

Stakeholder N _____

Program Requirements Document

Unlike many of the documents described in the *Standard for Program Management*—Second Edition (2008), requirements documents have been around for many years. We chose not to cover this document in detail, except to emphasize the fact that both program requirements and component requirements must be included, where program requirements are much higher in level. Component requirements, on the other hand, are written only to such a level that the component can begin work. The requirements document (Figure 5.9) is prepared in the develop program requirements process in the *Standard for Program Management*—Second Edition (2008).

Program Requirements Document Instructions

The program requirements document includes the following:

> **Purpose:** A brief introductory statement defining the purpose of the program requirements document, such as:

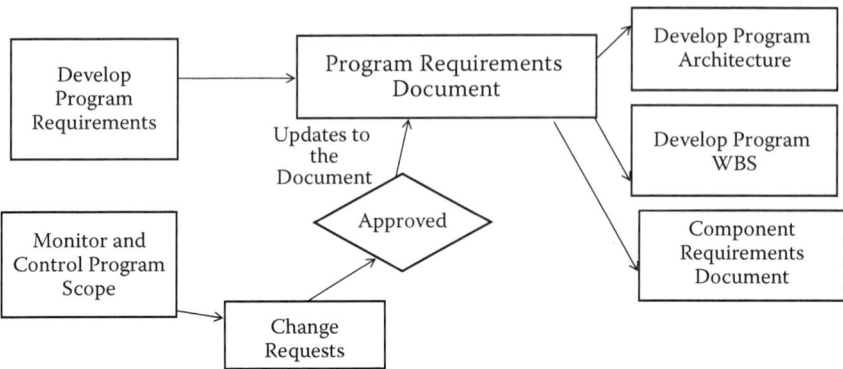

Program Management Life Cycle: Program Setup

Figure 5.9 Program requirements document.

The program requirements document describes the high-level requirements to ensure that the program delivers its expected benefits.

The program requirements document serves as the basis for the component requirements document, which is used to develop the technical requirements for each of the component's deliverables. It identifies and details program specifications and specific outcomes to be achieved by the program during implementation.

The program requirements document should be prepared once program goals and objectives are defined. It builds on the requirements listed in the business case, the scope statement, and the program road map. Programs must ensure that a detailed process is followed as this document is developed, since it is imperative for successful program implementation.

In the Project Management Institute's *Standard for Program Management*—Second Edition (2008), the program requirements document is an output of the develop program requirements process. It is an input to the develop program architecture and develop program work breakdown structure processes. Updates to this document may result from the monitor and control program scope process.

Requirements management process: This section describes how the project manager and his or her team will develop the program requirements in sufficient detail to ensure they address all program components. It describes roles and responsibilities of program management team members and states the level of detail to be provided in the program requirements.

Requirements gathering tools: This section describes the specific requirements gathering tools the program management team will use as it develops the program requirements. Examples include the use of brainstorming, interviews, focus groups, questionnaires, and surveys as the program management team actively engages its stakeholders in this process.

Requirements analysis process: This section then describes the approach the program management team will follow to ensure that the requirements it has identified are complete. It describes the decomposition process the team will follow to take the high-level requirements into ones that can be further detailed by each component.

Requirements review process: This section states how the program management team will review the requirements that have been developed to ensure they are consistent, accurate, and complete. It describes specific approaches that may be used, such as various reviews, both informal and formal. It notes how the team will verify that best practices were followed and describes whether subject matter experts will be used in the reviews. It also states the level of customer involvement and that of the senior managers in the organization.

Requirements validation and verification: This section describes methods to be used to validate and verify the requirements that have been developed in order to ensure that they support the program's business case and have been decomposed to the level required for implementation. It then describes how the products of the program will be verified against the requirements and the acceptance process that will be followed both at a detailed and at a system level. It states the extent of any testing to be used, inspections to be conducted, or other approaches that will be followed.

Approvals: This section contains the written approval of the requirements document by the program sponsor, program manager, program management office, members of the governance board, and any other key stakeholders as appropriate.

Program Requirements Document Template

<Insert Program Name>
Requirements Document

Component name:	
Program name:	
Program manager:	PM's email address here as a hyperlink

Program sponsor:	
Actual start date:	
Approved end date:	
Program no.:	
Revision history:	
Business unit:	

A. PURPOSE

A brief introductory statement defining the purpose of the requirements document, such as:

> The program requirements document describes the high-level requirements to ensure that the program delivers its expected benefits.

B. REQUIREMENTS MANAGEMENT PROCESS

This section describes the process the program management team will follow to develop the program requirements in sufficient detail to ensure all program components are addressed. It describes team member roles and responsibilities and states the level of detail to be provided in the program requirements.

C. REQUIREMENTS GATHERING TOOLS

This section describes the specific requirements gathering tools the program management team will use.

D. REQUIREMENTS ANALYSIS PROCESS

This section describes the approach of the program management team to ensure the requirements it has identified are complete.

E. REQUIREMENTS REVIEW PROCESS

This section states how the program management team will review the requirements to ensure they are consistent, complete, and accurate. It describes specific reviews that will be held, and attendees at these reviews and their roles.

F. REQUIREMENTS VALIDATION AND VERIFICATION

This section describes methods to validate and verify the requirements to ensure they support the program's business case and have been decomposed to the necessary level. It states how products will be verified against the requirements and the acceptance process to follow.

G. APPROVALS

This section contains the approval of the program requirements document by the program sponsor, program manager, program management office, members of the governance board, and other key stakeholders as required.

SIGNATURES AND DATE APPROVAL OBTAINED

Program manager	_____
Program sponsor	_____
Program management office director	_____
Governance board chairperson	_____
Governance board member 1	_____
Governance board member 2	_____
Governance board member N	_____
Stakeholder 1	_____
Stakeholder 2	_____
Stakeholder N	_____

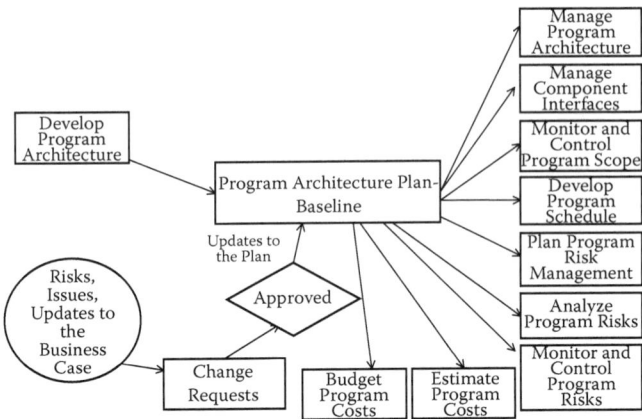

Figure 5.10 Program architecture plan—baseline.

Program Architecture Plan—Baseline

The program architecture plan, while in the exposure draft of the *Standard for Program Management*—Second Edition (2008), has been removed from the final edition. We have kept it here as a reminder of the program-level architecture considerations, but we appended the word *baseline* to its name, indicating that its nature is indeed a baseline, rather than a plan to produce a baseline. This baseline (Figure 5.10) is prepared in the develop program architecture process in the *Standard for Program Management*—Second Edition (2008).

Program Architecture Plan—Baseline Instructions

The program architecture plan—baseline includes the following:

Purpose: A brief introductory statement defining the purpose of the architecture plan—baseline, such as:

The architecture plan—baseline describes the structure of projects and other components in the program as it relates to delivery of the capabilities necessary to ensure the program realizes its expected benefits.

The architecture plan—baseline sets the stage for the development of the program work breakdown structure, as it shows the technical relationships among the various components of the program. It builds on the initial program requirements and defines the structure of the program components and their interactions and dependencies. As the plan is prepared, it may be appropriate to conduct some trade-off analyses of different architecture approaches since different approaches will have different cost implications.

This plan then is used to show where the program is expected to be at a certain time, how it will get to this point, and how stakeholders will know the program is successful. Serving to provide direction to manage the relationships across the various program components, this plan provides a consistent architecture. It also shows how the projects and nonproject work in the program will deliver the capabilities needed to achieve the program's benefits. It also helps in providing direction as the program's initial cost estimates are prepared.

Once the plan is approved, an architecture baseline is established. In the Project Management Institute's *Standard for Program Management*—Second Edition (2008), this baseline is an output of the develop program architecture process. It is an input to the following processes:

- Manage program architecture
- Manage component interfaces
- Monitor and control program scope
- Develop program schedule
- Plan program risk management
- Analyze program risks
- Monitor and control program risks
- Estimate program costs
- Budget program costs

This plan is an iterative document and should be reviewed periodically by the program management team, other key stakeholders, and the members of the governance board, as the work of the program continues throughout the various phases in its life cycle, especially when there are schedule, financial, and other program changes. If there are changes, a change request form should be prepared and processed. These changes may result in a need to update the architecture plan—baseline and may affect various projects in the program.

Program structure: This section describes the structure of the program in terms of its various components. The section discusses each component's characteristics, timing, deliverables, and interfaces and states how the components relate to one another in terms of dependencies. It shows the order in which the program's incremental benefits are planned for delivery. Various components will relate to one another in different ways. It is then used to establish a baseline so changes to it can be actively tracked and monitored to ensure that risks or threats to the program and its components are minimized.

Management approach: This section describes the approach the program management team plans to use to manage the relationships among the program components, both projects and nonproject work, so the architecture is consistent as deliverables are completed, and benefits are realized, in order that changes to the baseline are not required. It describes roles and responsibilities of the program management team and the project managers to not only develop the program architecture but also to keep it up to date. The program management team may need to perform trade-off analyses since different architectures will have different schedule and financial considerations.

Change management: Because changes are inevitable in programs, and because components will be added during the program's life cycle and other components will be completed or terminated at various times, this section describes the process to follow to update the architecture plan—baseline as required. Issues that occur during the program also may result in a need to update this plan. Change requests should be submitted following the program's change control process. As the change requests are analyzed and possibly approved, it may be apparent that changes to the program's architecture also may affect the schedule, financial status, product deliverables, and program documents as appropriate. These changes then may lead to the need to update the program management plan.

Approvals: This section contains the written approval of the architecture plan—by the program sponsor, program manager, program management office, members of the governance board, and any other key stakeholders as appropriate.

Program Architecture Plan—Baseline Template

<Insert Program Name>
Architecture Plan

Program name:	
Program manager:	PM's email address here as a hyperlink
Program sponsor:	
Actual start date:	
Approved end date:	
Program no.:	
Revision history:	
Business unit:	

A. PURPOSE

A brief introductory statement defining the purpose of the architecture plan—baseline such as:

> The architecture plan—baseline describes the structure of projects and other components in the program as it relates to delivery of the capabilities necessary to ensure the program realizes its expected benefits.

_____
_____
_____

B. PROGRAM STRUCTURE

This section describes the structure of the program in terms of its various components. It discusses each component's characteristics, timing, deliverables, and interfaces and states how the components relate to one another in terms of dependences. It shows the order in which the program's incremental benefits are planned for delivery.

_____
_____
_____

C. MANAGEMENT APPROACH

This section describes the approach the program management team plans to use to manage the relationships among the program components and describes the key roles and responsibilities of the team to develop the architecture and to keep it up to date.

_____
_____
_____

D. CHANGE MANAGEMENT

This section describes the process to follow to update the architecture plan—baseline as required.

_____
_____
_____

E. APPROVALS

This section contains the approval of the architecture plan—baseline by the program sponsor, program manager, program management office, members of the governance board, and other key stakeholders as required.

SIGNATURES AND DATE APPROVAL OBTAINED

Program manager   _____

Program sponsor   _____

Program management office director   _____

Governance board chairperson   _____

Governance board member 1   _____

Governance board member 2   _____

Governance board member N   _____

Stakeholder 1   _____

Stakeholder 2   _____

Stakeholder N   _____

Task Responsibility Matrix

This item is known as a Responsible, Accountable, Consult, Inform (RACI) chart in the PMBOK®. It performs exactly the same function in program management but includes only program-level tasks. As a tool and technique used in the develop program WBS process in the *Standard for Program Management*—Second Edition (2008), it is referred to as a task responsibility matrix.

Program WBS

An abundance of references address the topic of work breakdown structure (WBS) generation, so we do not discuss this topic here. A salient point, however, is that the program WBS typically includes only one or two levels of each project's WBS—only enough to enable project tracking, monitoring, and control at the program level. The program WBS is prepared in the develop program WBS process in the *Standard for Program Management*—Second Edition (2008).

Work Breakdown Structure Matrix

The U.S. Department of Defense publication MIL-HDBK-881A defines a work breakdown structure matrix to be essentially a "contract WBS." That is, it is the WBS that a project within the program would use, omitting program-level items. Since this is often done by a contractor, the term *contract WBS* is often used. For more details, see MIL-HDBK-881A or any treatise on project WBS generation.

This matrix is prepared in the develop program WBS process in the *Standard for Program Management*—Second Edition (2008).

Quality Management Plan

The quality management plan establishes minimum standards for quality planning, quality control, and quality assurance for the program's components, as well as responsibilities for quality assurance and control at the program level. It is prepared in the plan program quality process in the *Standard for Program Management*—Second Edition (2008).

Quality Management Plan Instructions

The quality management plan will include the following:

Purpose: A brief introductory statement defining the purpose of the quality management plan, such as:

The quality management plan describes the program's quality requirements that cross the various components of the program. It also provides requirements to assist the program components as project managers in the program prepare their quality management plans.

It should be noted that the program's quality management plan does not replace the quality management plans to be prepared by each of the project managers working in the program. Instead, its purpose is to specific quality standards and policies, as well as oversights, designed to ensure that the program realizes the benefits it is to achieve. This plan also serves to ensure that there is consistent application of specific quality requirements across the various components (projects and other work) in the program.

It is prepared in the plan program quality process in the *Standard for Program Management*—Second Edition (2008).

Organizational quality standards: This section states the performing organization's quality standards and policies. It also should note quality standards and policies of the program's customers. If the program is a joint venture, the program management team will need to set specific standards and policies to be followed in the program. Note that standards are established norms, methods, policies, and practices. The quality policy sets forth the intended direction of the organization with regard to quality.

Overview of the program's benefits: This section presents an overview of the benefits the program is designed to achieve. It can show a link to the program's benefits realization plan. With a complete understanding of the scope and nature of the benefits from the program, the program manager then can more effectively design appropriate quality standards and measures.

Quality planning tools and techniques: This section describes the tools and techniques the program management team will use as they prepare the program's quality management plan. Examples of tools and techniques that may be used include cost-benefit analysis, benchmarking, checklists, and determination of the total cost of program quality.

Requirements for quality planning, quality assurance, and quality control for the program's components: This section describes the minimal requirements each of the program's components must follow concerning quality planning, quality assurance, and quality control. It specifies the minimal quality standards and testing standards for the components. The purpose is to ensure that the quality management activities of the program components support the overall quality policy and standards at the program level.

Program-level roles and responsibilities: This section describes roles and responsibilities at the program level for quality assurance and quality control. Quality assurance responsibilities may include audits of the program's overall commitment to quality management or an audit of a specific component's quality management activities to ensure appropriate standards are used, and there is compliance as required with regulations. These responsibilities also focus on continuous process improvement for the program. Quality control responsibilities may include methods to monitor and record results of executing activities to assess performance and to recommend preventive or corrective actions. Note that both quality assurance and quality control are performed throughout the program.

Quality metrics: This section describes quality metrics that will be used in quality assurance and quality control. These metrics assist in comparing actual practices to planned practices to ensure program requirements are met successfully, and rework is not required. These metrics show compliance as well with the program's standards and any applicable regulations.

Approvals: This section contains the written approval of the quality management plan by the program sponsor, program manager, program management office, members of the program board or governance board, and other stakeholders.

Quality Management Plan Template

<Insert Program Name>
Quality Management Plan

Program name:	
Program manager:	PM's email address here as a hyperlink

Program sponsor:	
Actual start date:	
Approved end date:	
Program no.:	
Revision history:	
Business unit:	

A. PURPOSE

A brief introductory statement defining the purpose of the quality management plan, such as:

> The quality management plan describes the program's quality requirements that cross the various components of the program. It also provides requirements to assist the program components as project managers in the program prepare their quality management plans.

___
___
___

B. ORGANIZATIONAL QUALITY STANDARDS

This section states the performing organization's quality standards and policies. It also should note the customer's quality standards and policies. If the program is a joint venture, the program management team will need to set these standards and policies.

___
___
___

C. OVERVIEW OF THE PROGRAM'S BENEFITS

This section presents an overview of the benefits the program is to achieve in order to more effectively design program quality standards and metrics. A link to the program benefits realization plan may be included.

___
___
___

D. QUALITY PLANNING TOOLS AND TECHNIQUES

This section describes the tools and techniques the program management team will use as they prepare the program's quality management plan.

E. REQUIREMENTS FOR QUALITY PLANNING, QUALITY ASSURANCE, AND QUALITY CONTROL FOR THE PROGRAM'S COMPONENTS

This section describes the minimal requirements each of the program's components must follow concerning quality planning, quality assurance, and quality control in order that the quality management activities of the program components support the overall quality policy and standards at the program level.

F. PROGRAM-LEVEL ROLES AND RESPONSIBILITIES

This section describes roles and responsibilities at the program level for quality assurance and quality control. These roles and responsibilities are performed throughout the program.

G. QUALITY METRICS

This section describes quality metrics that will be used in quality assurance and quality control at the program level to ensure program requirements are met successfully, rework is not required, and there is compliance with the program's standards and any applicable regulations.

H. APPROVALS

This section contains the approval of the quality management plan by the program sponsor, program manager, program management office, members of the governance board, and other key stakeholders.

SIGNATURES AND DATE APPROVAL OBTAINED

Program manager _____

Program sponsor _____

Program management office director _____
Governance board chairperson _____
Governance board member 1 _____
Governance board member 2 _____
Governance board member N _____
Stakeholder 1 _____
Stakeholder 2 _____
Stakeholder N _____

Risk Management Planning Meeting Agenda

Documents such as the risk management plan and more are generated at risk management planning meetings. This agenda should be of significant help in assuring success in this critical endeavor. This agenda is used in the plan program risk management process in the *Standard for Program Management*—Second Edition (2008).

Risk Management Planning Meeting Agenda Instructions

All programs will have risks, and risk management planning is an important component to continually assess the program for risks that are opportunities to pursue as well as possible threats to the program. A key tool and technique in the process is a risk management planning meeting with a variety of program stakeholders to determine the program's risk management activities and to prepare the risk management plan.

Typical participants include the program manager, members of the program management team, a risk management specialist in the organization, the director of the program management office, and the portfolio manager. The program manager should review the stakeholder identification template and the stakeholder management plan and decide whether or not to invite other stakeholders to the meeting.

Prior to the meeting, participants should receive copies of the program brief, business case, stakeholder management plan, program charter, program road map, architecture plan, scope statement, program work breakdown structure, governance plan, and resource management plan. The program manager should consult the organization's knowledge management repository for any lessons learned from previous or ongoing projects or programs that may be helpful to this program concerning risk management. If component projects have been under way before inclusion in the program and have prepared a risk management plan, the project manager should provide them to attendees. If there are existing templates in the organization for use in risk management, participants should receive them prior to the planning meeting.

An agenda for these meetings is as follows:

PARTICIPANTS (NAMES/ORGANIZATION)

Date: _____

Time: _____

Place: _____

Program overview: The program manager presents a brief high-level overview of the program as to why the program was undertaken and where it stands in the program management life cycle. After the first meeting in which the risk management plan is prepared, he or she should provide a short summary of the last meeting held and should provide participants with the latest program risk register.

Program risk management activities: The risk management planning meeting defines the risk management activities to be followed in the program. During this meeting, participants determine the following:
- Specific risk categories that are expected to affect the program
- A risk breakdown structure
- Standard definitions for risk levels, probability, and impact to be followed throughout the program
- A probability/impact matrix
- Risk identification checklists
- A method to follow to assess component-level risks for their effect on the program and to see if there are any interdependencies
- The use of modeling techniques
- The need for the use of independent experts to periodically review risk management activities
- Items to be included in the risk management plan
- Items to be included in the risk register

Risk management responsibilities: There are a number of responsibilities associated with risk management, which include:
- Authority level for decisions regarding risks that affect the program
- Maintenance of the risk register
- Updates to the risk management plan
- Preparation of agendas and minutes from risk reviews
- Use of risk management software
- Including risk items on the program's schedule and updating them as needed
- Including risk as part of the program's budget and updating requirements as needed

Program risk management plan: This plan defines the program's approach to risk management, and its contents are described in a separate template.

Decisions: This section documents the decisions made during this meeting.

SIGNATURES OF PARTICIPANTS

Program manager   _____
Participant 1   _____
Participant 2   _____
Participant N   _____

Lessons Learned Review Agenda

Agendas assure orderly and complete coverage of essential matters. We have included a suggested agenda for your lessons learned reviews, assisting in the population of the lessons learned database, and used in the plan program risk management process in *Standard for Program Management*—Second Edition (2008).

Lessons Learned Review Agenda Instructions

Lessons learned are collected throughout the program for use on future program activities and in other programs and projects under way in the organization. They are documented in the lessons learned register and should be accessible to members of the program management team and others given appropriate access rights. Ideally, they should be part of a knowledge management system in the organization.

To complement the lessons learned register, and to support the plan program risk management, identify program risks, and monitor and control program risks processes, where these reviews are tools and techniques in the Project Management Institute's *Standard for Program Management*—Second Edition (2008), reviews should be conducted periodically.

Typical participants in a lessons learned review include the program manager, members of the program management team, a knowledge management specialist in the organization, the director of the program management office, and the portfolio manager. The program manager should review the stakeholder identification inventory and the stakeholder management plan and decide whether or not to invite other stakeholders to the meeting.

Prior to the meeting, participants should receive copies of the lessons learned register.

An agenda for these meetings is as follows:

PARTICIPANTS (NAMES/ORGANIZATION)

Date: _____
Time: _____
Place: _____

Program overview: The program manager presents a brief high-level overview of the program as to why the program was undertaken and where it stands in the program management life cycle. After the first meeting, he or she should provide a short summary of the last meeting held and should ensure each participant has the latest lessons learned register.

Discussion of the types of lessons learned: The program manager should lead a discussion concerning the types of lessons learned during the meeting using the classification system in the lessons learned register. The purpose is to see whether the classification system is helpful or whether categories should be added or deleted.

Use of lessons learned: The program manager next leads a discussion as to the usefulness of lessons learned in terms of exploiting possible opportunities. The discussion also concentrates on responses to any negative items so preventive action can be taken so they do not occur in the future.

Risk management processes: The program manager also asks the group about the usefulness of these reviews in terms of the various risk management processes where lesson learned reviews are a recommended tool and technique.

Suggestions and recommendations: The program manager asks the group for any suggestions or recommendations concerning the lessons learned process so it is more useful to the program and other initiatives in the organization. These suggestions are documented in the program's decision log.

Decisions: This section documents the decisions made during this meeting.

SIGNATURES OF PARTICIPANTS AND DATE

Program manager _____

Director of the program management office _____

Portfolio manager _____

Knowledge management specialist _____

Participant 1 _____

Participant 2 _____

Participant N _____

Lessons Learned Database

Many items in the *Standard for Program Management*—Second Edition (2008) are referred to as registers and may, of course, be stored in databases. The lessons learned records are referred to as a database. Here is a suggested format, no matter the storage medium.

Lessons Learned Database Instructions

Purpose: Lessons learned are collected throughout the program. This register is used to document lessons learned in the program and may be used to support a best practices library, knowledge repository, or lessons learned database.

Lessons learned include both weaknesses to correct and be aware of for future programs and projects, and opportunities to be pursued in this program and in other programs and projects in the organization. The program management team should review them regularly, and the program manager should discuss lessons learned with the governance board at program review meetings for applicability to other programs and projects under way in the organization. At the end of the program, the lessons learned register should be part of the program's archives. It should also become part of the organization's knowledge management repository, as these lessons learned are part of the organization's assets and are a compilation of knowledge gained for use on future programs and projects.

In the Project Management Institute's *Standard for Program Management*—Second Edition (2008), lessons learned are an output of the approve component transition process, and a lessons learned database is a tool and technique used in the distribute information process.

Lessons learned updates are outputs of the following processes:

- Distribute information
- Monitor and control program risks

Lessons learned reviews are tools and techniques used in the following processes:

- Plan program risk management
- Identify program risks
- Monitor and control program risks

The lessons learned register is designed as a table, and a description of its contents follows.

1. **Lesson learned number:** Assign an identification number to the lesson learned.
2. **PWBS number:** Link the lesson learned to the corresponding program package in the program work breakdown structure.
3. **Description:** Provide a description of the lesson learned. Set up a classification system such as:

a. Technical
b. Managerial
c. Policy
d. Procedure
e. Process
  i. Program management
  ii. Stakeholder management
  iii. Governance board
  iv. Audits
  v. Reviews
  vi. Project management
f. Cause of variance from a plan
g. Corrective action used and its impact
h. Effectiveness of selected risk response
  i. Lack of a need to implement a fallback plan
  ii. Lack of subsidiary risks as a result of implementing the response
  iii. Contingency plan implemented and its impact
i. Issue resolution
j. Benefit realized
k. Best practice
l. Business skills
m. Unforeseen risk
n. Product improvement
o. Service improvement
p. Evaluation criteria
q. Qualified seller
r. Contract terms and conditions
s. Reason for contract termination

4. **Supporting details:** List supporting details as appropriate.
5. **Key words:** Provide some key words for use as metadata tags for future searching for information that may be contained as part of this lesson learned, especially when it becomes part of the organization's knowledge management repository and the program's archives.
6. **Submitted by:** List the person who submitted the lesson learned and provide contact information. Note that the lesson learned could be submitted as part of a review by the governance board or as a recommendation in a program audit.
7. **Date:** State the date the lesson learned was added to the register.
8. **Program life cycle phase:** List the phase in the program life cycle that involves the lesson learned.
9. **Affected program processes:** List the program management processes affected by the lesson learned. For example, a lesson learned may be an output of one program management process and an input to another.

10. **Program documents affected:** State the program documents affected by the lesson learned and whether any require updates. If updates are needed, state the program management team member who is responsible and the date the documents are to be updated.
11. **Use in the program:** State whether the lesson learned was used later in the program if applicable.
12. **Date submitted to the knowledge management repository or archives:** If the organization has a knowledge management repository, state the date this lesson learned was submitted to it so it can be used by other programs and projects in the organization. Once submitted, the lesson learned becomes a source of historical information for use by other programs and projects.
13. **Date submitted to archives:** State the date the lessons learned register was submitted to the program's archives.
14. **Notes:** Use this field for any additional notes about the lesson learned.

Program Risk Management Plan

Programs must have a disciplined way to deal with risks. This plan, while a living document throughout the program, would normally remain somewhat static, defining the processes that populate and manage the risk register, generate risk response plans, contingency plans, etc. It is prepared in the plan program risk management process in the *Standard for Program Management*—Second Edition (2008).

Program Risk Management Plan Instructions

The program risk management plan includes the following:

Purpose: A brief introductory statement defining the purpose of the risk management plan, such as:

The risk management plan describes the process of determining how to approach, plan, and execute the program risk activities.

This plan recognizes that risks are a series of events that, if they occur, may have a positive or a negative impact on the program. At the program level, risks tend to occur from external factors or from individual components. If they are due to risks at the component level, the program management team must assess them for impact to other components or to the entire program. The program management team must ensure that the level, type, and visibility of risks are appropriate to the specific program since some programs may require greater attention to risk management than others, especially programs that are new in numerous aspects to the organization, are considered complex, and involve new technologies and systems.

In the *Standard for Program Management*—Second Edition (2008), it is an output of the plan program risk management process. It is an input to the following processes:

- Identify program risks
- Analyze program risks
- Plan program risk responses
- Monitor and control program risks

Updates to the plan may result from the monitor and control program risks process.

Risk management approach: This section describes how the program management team will handle risk management in the program. It states the methodology to be followed, tools and techniques to be used, and any other data sources, such as a knowledge repository or lessons learned database, that may be helpful. It also describes whether a risk management planning meeting will be held, and if so, who will attend, and specific roles and responsibilities. If an organization-wide risk management approach is in place, it notes whether or not it will be followed or whether changes to it are warranted. It also describes how proposed changes will be identified and managed in order that they do not pose additional risks to the program. It notes the process for the program manager to learn of changes at the project level that may affect other projects in the program or the overall program in order that the program management team can then review these changes for possible new risks.

Program risk categories: This section describes specific categories of risks that may affect the program. Typically these categories may include external environmental risks, such as new regulations or standards or strategic issues; program-level risks, such as ones involving program stakeholders, the governance board, and how the program components are organized; project-level risks, while managed by the project manager, that may affect other components in the program; operational-level risks, such as ones that involve transition of the program benefits into the overall operations of the organization or to the customer or possible new systems in the organization that may affect program benefits; portfolio-related risks, since the portfolio level defines the organization's strategic intent, which then may affect the overall priority of the program in terms of resources; and benefit-related risks, which involve the impact of risks from the component level to the overall delivery of program benefits. If a risk breakdown structure is prepared, it should be attached to this plan.

Roles and responsibilities: This section describes the roles and responsibilities of the program management team regarding risk management planning, identification, analysis, response planning, monitoring, and control. It may be appropriate on certain projects to designate a member of the core team to focus on risk management at the program level and to work with the various project managers to review risks at the project level and to conduct project risk audits. This section describes how risks will be escalated from component managers to the program manager, and from the program manager, as appropriate, to the governance board, to describe specific roles and responsibilities at each level. It also addresses roles and responsibilities for risk management of intercomponent risks and for analysis of root causes of these risks in order that an appropriate risk response can be provided.

Probability and impact matrix: This section describes definitions of probability and impact for use on the program. These definitions can be related to the program's objectives or to the program's expected benefits. Numeric and nonnumeric approaches can be used. This matrix then serves as a table in which to show specific combinations of risk probability and risk impact that are then considered to be high, medium, or low in terms of importance to help plan appropriate risk responses. This matrix serves to help prioritize those risks that require the greatest attention from the program management team.

Risk management budget: This section describes the budget or contingency that will be set aside to focus on risk management throughout the program life cycle. It therefore provides a cost estimate for risk management at the program level to be used to determine the funding and resources required. It also describes the process to follow when it is necessary to allocate contingency reserve in order to respond to program-level risks.

Risk management schedule: Although risk management is a continual activity throughout the program, this section describes the specific risk management activities that should be included in the program's schedule. Items such as when a program risk management planning meeting, program risk reviews or audits, and analysis of lessons learned from risk management initiatives in the program are planned are examples of activities to be part of the schedule.

Stakeholder tolerances for risk: This section describes the tolerance level of the key program stakeholders in terms of risk. The stakeholder analysis and stakeholder register can be used as this section is prepared, and interviews can be conducted with key stakeholders. The purpose is to show those stakeholders in terms of their influence on the program in generating and responding to program risk based on their tolerance for risk. It considers the culture of the organization in terms of its approach to risk management.

Risk reporting: This section describes the content and format for the program's risk register, which will be used throughout the program for risk reporting and to assist in risk identification, analysis, response planning, and risk monitoring and control. It also describes communication approaches to be used in the program with the various stakeholders and the governance board concerning risks.

Risk tracking: This section describes the process to track identified risks and to recognize any new risks that may affect the program. It also describes how the program's risk management process will be audited and the frequency of the audits to be conducted. It describes the process for documenting lessons learned based on the program's risk management activities.

Approvals: This section contains the written approval of the risk management plan by the program sponsor, program manager, program management office, members of the program board or governance board, and other stakeholders.

Program Risk Management Plan Template

<Insert Program Name>
Risk Management Plan

Program name:	
Program manager:	PM's email address here as a hyperlink
Program sponsor:	
Actual start date:	
Approved end date:	
Program no.:	
Revision history:	
Business unit:	

A. PURPOSE

A brief introductory statement defining the purpose of the risk management plan, such as:

> The risk management plan describes the process of determining how to approach, plan, and execute the program risk activities.

_____

_____

_____

B. RISK MANAGEMENT APPROACH

This section describes how the program management team will handle risk management in the program. It states the methodology to be followed, tools and techniques to be used, and any other data sources that may be helpful. It also notes whether a risk management planning meeting will be held. It further describes how proposed changes will be identified and managed in order that they do not pose additional risks to the program.

C. PROGRAM RISK CATEGORIES

This section describes specific categories of risks that may affect the program. If a risk breakdown structure is prepared, it should be attached to this section.

D. ROLES AND RESPONSIBILITIES

This section describes the roles and responsibilities of the program management team regarding risk management planning, identification, analysis, response planning, monitoring, and control. It also describes how risks will be escalated from component managers to the program manager, and from the program manager, as appropriate, to the governance board, to describe roles and responsibilities at each level. It shows roles and responsibilities for intercomponent risks and for analysis of root causes of these risks.

E. RISK MANAGEMENT BUDGET

This section describes the process to be followed to prepare a risk management cost estimate that then will be used for a risk management budget or contingency throughout the program life cycle. It describes the process to follow when it is necessary to allocate contingency reserve in order to respond to program-level risks.

F. RISK MANAGEMENT SCHEDULE

This section describes the specific risk management activities that should be included in the program's schedule.

G. STAKEHOLDER TOLERANCES FOR RISK

This section describes the tolerance level of the program stakeholders in terms of risk to show those stakeholders based on their level of influence on the program in generating and responding to program risk. It also considers the organization's culture regarding risk management.

H. RISK REPORTING

This section describes the content and format for the program's risk register. It also describes communication approaches to be used in the program with the various stakeholders and the governance board concerning risks.

I. RISK TRACKING

This section describes the process to follow to track identified risks and to recognize any new risks that may affect the program. It also describes how the program's risk management process will be audited and the frequency of the audits, as well as the process to document lessons learned based on the program's risk management activities.

J. APPROVALS

This section contains the approval of the risk management plan by the program sponsor, program manager, program management office, members of the program board or governance board, and other key stakeholders.

SIGNATURES AND DATE APPROVAL OBTAINED

Program manager	_____
Program sponsor	_____
Program management office director	_____
Governance board chairperson	_____
Governance board member 1	_____

Governance board member 2	_____
Governance board member N	_____
Stakeholder 1	_____
Stakeholder 2	_____
Stakeholder N	_____

Program Risk Register

The risk register (Figure 5.11) is a critical program decision-making tool. It combines in one place the needed decision criteria such as the likelihood, status, and impact of program risks. It is first prepared in the identify program risks process in the *Standard for Program Management*—Second Edition (2008).

Program Risk Register Instructions

Purpose: The risk register is used throughout the program. Its use begins when a risk is identified and continues until all risks have been closed or are no longer considered a threat or opportunity to the program. It complements the program risk management plan but does not replace it.

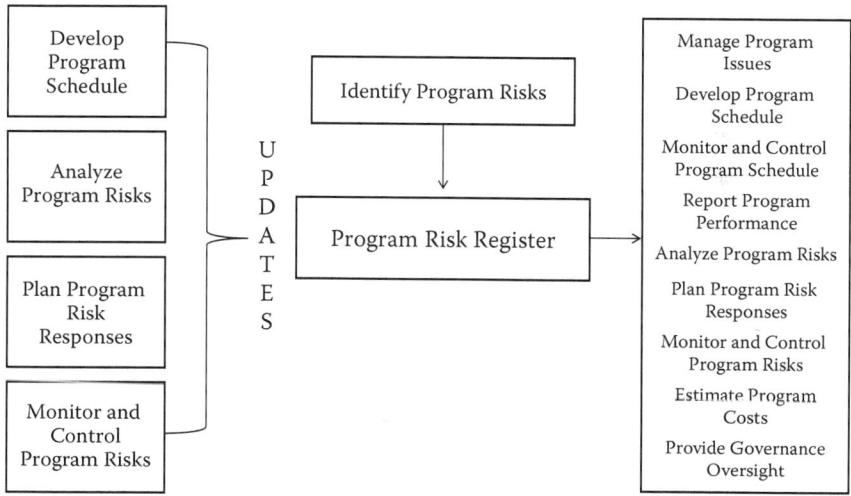

Program Management Life Cycle: Program Setup and Delivery of Program Benefits

Figure 5.11 Program risk register.

With continuous use of the risk register throughout the program, and monitoring the impact and probability of occurrence of a program risk, the program management team can monitor possible risks and use proactive actions to prevent their occurrence. Such an approach can be effective in ensuring the risk responses have the desired effect.

Resolution of certain risks may be handled by the risk owner; others may need to be escalated to the program manager or to the governance board. The decision as to which risk response to use and when to close a risk may require involvement from other stakeholders. Change requests to various items in the program may lead to a need to revise the risk register or to add newly identified risks to it. Even though the program has an issue register, it does not replace the need for a risk register.

In the Project Management Institute's *Standard for Program Management*—Second Edition (2008), the risk register is an input to the following processes:

- Manage program issues
- Develop program schedule
- Monitor and control program schedule
- Report program performance
- Analyze program risks
- Plan program risk responses
- Monitor and control program risks
- Estimate program costs
- Provide governance oversight

It is an output from the identify program risks process.

Updates to the risk register are outputs from the following processes:

- Develop program schedule
- Analyze program risks
- Plan program risk responses
- Monitor and control program risks

The risk register is designed as a table, and a description of its contents follows:

1. **Risk identification number:** Assign an identification number to the risk.
2. **PWBS number:** Link the risk to the corresponding program package in the program work breakdown structure.
3. **Risk description:** Describe the risk and why it is significant to the program.
4. **Identified by:** List the person who identified the risk and provide contact information.
5. **Date:** State the date the risk was identified and added to the register.
6. **Risk type:** Describe the type of risk. Follow the categories established in the risk management plan.

7. **Root cause:** Describe the program-level root cause of the risk in order to determine potential responses. Doing so can also help group risks into causes for analysis and review and avoid potential future program risks.
8. **Probability/impact:** State the probability/impact of the risk to the program. Use a probability/impact matrix.
9. **Risk owner:** Identify a member of the program management team to be responsible for the risk and to track it until it is resolved and closed. Provide contact information for the owner.
10. **Symptoms/warning signs:** Identify various triggers or warning symptoms to alert the program management team that the risk might occur. For example, poor morale on the program management team might indicate that the program's resources may be affected as people may choose to leave the program for other opportunities.
11. **Proposed response:** State the proposed risk response. Examples include:
    - Negative risks or threats:
        - Avoid
        - Transfer
        - Mitigate
        - Accept
    - Positive risks or opportunities:
        - Enhance
        - Exploit
        - Share
        - Accept

    Note that if a risk is accepted, a contingency plan will be required. Follow the process outlined in the risk management plan in the risk management budget section in allocating contingency reserve to respond to program-level risks. Describe the budget and schedule activities needed to implement the response. Follow the template for the contingency plan.
12. **Actual response:** If the risk does in fact occur, indicate which response strategy was selected. If it was not the planned response, describe why for purposes of lessons learned.
13. **Approved by:** State who approved the risk response. Examples include:
    a. Risk owner
    b. Program manager
    c. Governance board
14. **Date:** State the date the risk response was approved.
15. **Subsequent impacts:** State any subsequent impacts as a result of the risk response. Examples include the need to use a fallback plan if the response was not effective, residual risks that remain and may affect the program at a later time after the response was implemented, and the identification of subsidiary risks as a result of implementing the response. Use the risk register to state any residual or secondary risks as appropriate.

16. **Date closed:** State the date the risk was closed.
17. **Notes:** Use this field for any additional notes about the risk.

Probability/Impact Matrix

The probability/impact matrix is used to determine the overall priority of each risk in the risk register to the program. It also serves as way to communicate the importance of the risk to program stakeholders, as a red, yellow, green approach may be helpful as part of this matrix.

Risk probability describes the degree of uncertainty, while risk impact states the magnitude of the effect the risk will have on program objectives. The example in the table presents one approach to consider. It also relates to the variances based on stakeholder tolerances for risks as described in the risk management plan.

Probability/Impact Matrix

Impact	Probability				
	Very High	*High*	*Medium*	*Low*	*Very Low*
Catastrophic	Very High	High	Moderate	Moderate	Low
Critical	High	High	Moderate	Low	Very Low
Marginal	Moderate	Moderate	Low	Very Low	None
Negligible	Moderate	Low	Very Low	None	None

Probability		Risk Impact to +Cost, +Schedule, + Resources, –Performance/Benefits	
Very High	90–100%	Catastrophic	> 10% Variance
High	60–89%	Critical	< 10% Variance
Medium	30–59%	Marginal	< 5% Variance
Low	10–29%	Negligible	Marginal Impact
Very Low	0–9%	Little to None	Little to None

In preparing the matrix, consider items such as:

- The time the risk is expected to occur
- Whether the risk is expected to occur at a certain phase in the program's life cycle
- Whether the probability or the impact is expected to change over time

- Whether there is a date after which the risk is expected not to affect the program
- The ease of managing and controlling the risk
- The completeness of the description of the risk in the risk register
- The level of vulnerability to the project should the risk occur
- Whether the cause of the risk is due to the program or to other events

Update and review the probability/impact matrix as risk responses are implemented, risks are closed, and new risks are added to the register. Note the results of the probability/impact matrix in the risk register.

Contingency Plan

The most serious program risks need at least a preliminary plan that can be implemented should they occur. Not having a contingency plan for an occurring risk is serious and possibly a threat to overall program success. The contingency plan is prepared in the plan program risk responses process in the *Standard for Program Management*—Second Edition (2008).

Contingency Plan Instructions

The contingency plan will include the following:

Purpose: A brief introductory statement defining the purpose of the contingency plan, such as:

The contingency plan describes the impact on the program for those risks in the risk register that require such a plan.

This plan complements the program risk management plan and the risk register. It is prepared only for those risks in which a contingency plan is warranted and is part of risk monitoring and control. It is used for unknown risks that cannot be managed proactively and also for those identified risks in which the response strategy is to actively accept the risk. Time, money, and resources then will be required if this is the case, regardless if the risk is a threat to the program or an opportunity. The program management team uses these contingency plans to assess impacts across the program and to see if any of them are interrelated to mitigate risk activities that could affect the program components.

When a contingency plan is implemented, it will require a change request and should be handled as part of the program's integrated change control system.

Trigger conditions: Each risk should have certain triggers or warning signs associated with it. This section lists these triggers, which then will result in executing the contingency plan, such as missing a key milestone.

Cost impact: Each contingency plan requires a cost estimate. This section states the needed budget to implement the contingency plan and considers the associated impacts on the schedule, resources, and deliverables as the estimate is prepared.

Schedule impact: If there is a need to implement a contingency plan, it will affect the program's schedule. This section describes this impact and shows the need to update or change duration estimates of key activities or to change or add milestones as appropriate.

Required resources: If a contingency plan is executed, resources will be required. This section states these necessary resources.

Responsibilities: This section describes the responsibilities associated with implementing the contingency plan. It describes the various stakeholders and their level of involvement. It states the primary point of contact on the program management team.

Approvals: This section contains the written approval of the contingency plan by the program manager and other stakeholders as required.

Contingency Plan Template

<Insert Program Name>
Contingency Plan

Program name:	
Program manager:	PM's email address here as a hyperlink
Program sponsor:	
Actual start date:	
Approved end date:	
Program no.:	
Last updated:	
Unit:	

A. PURPOSE

A brief introductory statement defining the purpose of the contingency plan, such as:

> The contingency plan describes the impact on the program for those risks in the risk register that require such a plan.

B. TRIGGER CONDITIONS

The risk register lists those risks for which a contingency plan will be needed. This section describes the triggers or warning symptoms associated with these risks.

C. COST IMPACT

This section describes the cost estimate if the contingency plan is to be implemented.

D. SCHEDULE IMPACT

This section describes the effect on the schedule if the contingency plan is implemented, as duration estimates may require change, and milestones may need to be added or deleted.

E. REQUIRED RESOURCES

This section states the necessary resources to implement the contingency plan.

F. RESPONSIBILITIES

This section describes the responsibilities associated with implementing the contingency plan and states the primary point of contact on the program management team.

G. APPROVALS

This section contains the written approval of the contingency plan by the program manager and other stakeholders as required.

SIGNATURES AND DATE APPROVAL OBTAINED

Program manager　　　　　　_____

Stakeholder 1　　　　　　　_____

Stakeholder 2　　　　　　　_____

Stakeholder N　　　　　　　_____

Change Request Form

Change requests (Figure 5.12) are inevitable, and there are more change forms than there are organizations. The key here is that this form should be focused at the *program* level. This document is prepared in the plan program risk responses process in the *Standard for Program Management*—Second Edition (2008). It also is prepared in the approve component intiation and manage program benefits processes.

Change Request Form Instructions

Purpose: The change request form is used throughout the program. It is inevitable that programs will have changes throughout the program life cycle. The

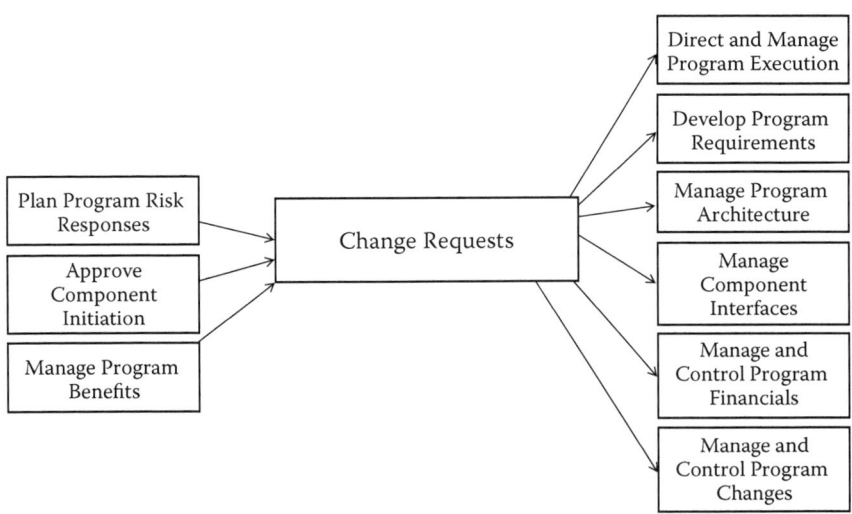

Figure 5.12 Change requests.

component projects also will have changes. Each project should manage its changes and use a change request form as well once a change is identified.

This change request form complements the program's change management plan and change request log.

The change request form is designed as a table, and a description of its contents follows:

1. **Change identification number:** Assign a change number to the change request.
2. **PWBS number:** Link the change to the corresponding program package in the program work breakdown structure.
3. **Change description:** Describe the change and why it is significant to the program.
4. **Requested by:** List the person who requested the change and provide contact information.
5. **Date:** State the date the change was requested.
6. **Change type:** Describe the type of change. Use the types in the change management plan, such as one involving technical aspects or the program's scope, schedule, cost, or contracts.
7. **Notes:** Use this field for any additional notes about the change.

Change Request Form

Change Identification Number	PWBS Number	Change Description	Requested by	Date	Change Type	Notes

Schedule Management Plan

The program must have discipline and control in maintenance of its official schedule. The schedule management plan describes how this discipline will be achieved and is prepared in the develop program schedule process in the *Standard for Program Management*—Second Edition (2008).

Schedule Management Plan Instructions

The schedule management plan will include the following:

Purpose: A brief introductory statement defining the purpose of the schedule management plan, such as:

The schedule management plan identifies an agreed-upon sequence of component deliveries (projects and nonproject work) to enable them to be planned and managed. It sets forth a scheduling methodology, states the scheduling tool to be used, and sets the format and criteria for monitoring and controlling the program schedule.

This plan provides the program management team and stakeholders with an approach to how the schedule will be managed throughout the program. It enables the program manager to identify any risks associated with the schedule and any component issues that may need to be escalated for resolution. A common understanding among program stakeholders is required as to how to clearly define the program's schedule status. Although the plan is drafted early in the program, it is an iterative document that should be further refined in each phase of your program.

In the Project Management Institute's *Standard for Program Management—Second Edition* (2008), the schedule management plan is an output of the develop program schedule process.

Program schedule constraints: This section describes constraints, both internal and external, that may affect the program schedule. Examples include funding, resource availability, technical considerations, contracts, predetermined milestones, environmental issues, other external dependencies, and other factors in the program environment.

Delivery of incremental benefits: Since the purpose of a program is to deliver benefits that might not be realized if the projects in the program were managed individually, this section of the plan provides a description of the order in which the incremental benefits should be delivered. It also contains component milestones to show when program benefits are expected to be realized.

Schedule management software: This section states the schedule management software to be used in the program, as it helps to manage and control the schedule throughout the program life cycle. The software tool to be used should be appropriate to the scope and complexity of the program.

Program funding schedule: This section describes the funding schedule for the program's revenue and expenses. Money payable to contractors or for other program expenses, for example, cannot be paid unless it is available to the program. Schedule activities may need to occur at the latest possible start in order to defer expenses until as close as possible to when the funding will be available.

Schedule tracking and monitoring methods: This section describes the methods to use to track and monitor schedule performance according to the master program schedule. Methods to track and monitor all high-level component and program activities and milestones against planned timelines should be stated. If earned value is to be used, it should be stated in this section, including the method to use to report progress.

Schedule metrics: This section describes how schedule progress is to be measured in the program. For example, if the schedule is behind by 10%, does this mean the overall schedule is red, yellow, or green? This section describes what will be measured and how status will be reported against these metrics.

Approvals: This section contains the written approval of the schedule management plan by the program sponsor, program manager, program management office, members of the governance board, and other stakeholders.

Schedule Management Plan Template

<Insert Program Name>
Schedule Management Plan

Program name:	
Program manager:	PM's email address here as a hyperlink
Program sponsor:	
Actual start date:	
Approved end date:	
Program no.:	
Revision history:	
Business unit:	

A. PURPOSE

A brief introductory statement defining the purpose of the schedule management plan, such as:

> The schedule management plan identifies an agreed-upon sequence of component deliveries (projects and nonproject work) to enable them to be planned and managed. It sets forth a scheduling methodology, states the scheduling tool to be used, and sets the format and criteria for monitoring and controlling the program schedule.

B. PROGRAM SCHEDULE CONSTRAINTS

This section describes constraints, both internal and external, that may affect the program schedule.

C. DELIVERY OF INCREMENTAL BENEFITS

This section describes the order in which the incremental benefits of the program are to be delivered. It also contains component milestones to show when program benefits are expected to be realized.

D. SCHEDULE MANAGEMENT SOFTWARE

This section states the schedule management software to be used in the program, as it helps to manage and control the schedule throughout the program life cycle.

E. PROGRAM FUNDING SCHEDULE

This section describes the funding schedule for the program's revenue and expenses.

F. SCHEDULE TRACKING AND MONITORING METHODS

This section describes the methods to use to track and monitor schedule performance according to the master program schedule. If earned value is to be used, it is stated in this section along with the method to use to report progress.

G. SCHEDULE METRICS

This section describes how schedule performance is to be measured in the program. It states what will be measured and how status will be reported against these metrics.

_____

_____

_____

H. APPROVALS

This section contains the approval of the schedule management plan by the program sponsor, program manager, program management office, members of the governance board, and other key stakeholders.

SIGNATURES AND DATE APPROVAL OBTAINED

Program manager	_____
Program sponsor	_____
Program management office director	_____
Governance board chairperson	_____
Governance board member 1	_____
Governance board member 2	_____
Governance board member N	_____
Stakeholder 1	_____
Stakeholder 2	_____
Stakeholder N	_____

Program Financial Plan

The program financial plan is part of the program financial management knowledge area. It helps deal with the myriad challenges that arise in the financial management arena, some of which can be fatal if not properly managed. It is prepared in the develop program financial plan process in the *Standard for Program Management*—Second Edition (2008).

Program Financial Plan Instructions

The program financial plan will include the following:

> **Purpose:** A brief introductory statement defining the purpose of the financial plan for the program, such as:

The financial plan documents all the program's financial aspects, as it describes the funding schedules and milestones, baseline budget, contact payments and schedules, financial reporting processes and mechanisms, and financial metrics.

This plan takes into account items such as risk reserves, potential cash flow problems, international currency rate fluctuations, future interest rate increases or decreases, local laws as appropriate, trends in the cost of materials and supplies, and contract incentives and penalty clauses. It also describes any funds to be retained in contracts as invoices are submitted for payment in those situations in which the contract terms and conditions contain a clause that specifies that a certain percent of the price will be retained and paid once the contract has been completed. It is necessary to recognize that programs may have multiple sources of funding, tend to be long in duration, may have multiple contractors, and may involve international work. Many of the environmental factors that affect this plan may be outside of the program manager's direct control. Further, although the plan is drafted early in the program, it is an iterative document that should be further refined as the program progresses through the life cycle.

In the Project Management Institute's *Standard for Program Management—Second Edition* (2008), the program financial plan is an output of the develop program financial plan process. It is an input to the monitor and control program financials process.

Financial framework and goals: This section identifies the overall financial environment for the program, as it pinpoints funds to be expended at key milestones and helps to ensure that money is spent efficiently with the least waste possible.

Funding constraints: This section describes methods to receive program funding since it is rare that 100% of the required funding is provided when the program is initiated. It describes release of funds at specific milestones or on an annual or fiscal year basis. Other examples of constraints are if it is a global project, whether payment is to be made in local currencies; future changes in material prices; or, for contracts, the percent of payment that is to be retained until the contractor's work is complete.

Program operational costs: This section describes the specific costs associated with the operation of the program. It includes infrastructure costs, such as required facilities and systems, or the costs associated with the program management office, including human resources.

Format and criteria for cost estimating: This section describes the various tools and techniques to be used to estimate the costs associated with the program in order that an overall cost estimate for the program can be prepared. Typically, the cost estimate will be prepared in stages given the duration and complexity of the program. Once the cost estimate is approved, it then becomes the basis for the program budget, as the budget baseline is the target for measuring overall financial progress.

Program payment schedule: This section identifies the schedule and milestones where funding for the program is received from the funding organization. This section is needed because program funds typically are spent in advance of receipt of revenues or benefits realization.

Program financial metrics: This section describes the specific financial metrics for the program by which the program's benefits are measured. These metrics are necessary because as changes to schedules and costs occur to the program, these metrics are used against those set at the time the program was approved to help determine whether or not it should be continued. Examples of metrics for consideration are funds expended against total funds available, earned value measurements, the use of contingency and management reserves, return on investment versus that stated in the business case, and the payback period versus that stated in the business case.

Methods for financial monitoring and control: This section describes the approach to be used to identify factors that may create changes to the financial baseline, methods to monitor the environment for changes that may affect the financial plan, ways to monitor the disbursement of funds to contractors, methods to identify impacts to program components from overruns or underruns, methods to manage the program's infrastructure, and methods to communicate the financial situation to the program stakeholders.

Remaining budget allocations: This section describes the process to return any remaining budget allocations to the overall program budget. It is a consideration during the close program procurement process when all approved payment requests have been processed.

Approvals: This section contains the written approval of the financial plan by the program sponsor, program manager, program management office, members of the governance board, and other stakeholders.

Program Financial Plan Template

<Insert Program Name>
Financial Plan

Program name:	
Program manager:	PM's email address here as a hyperlink
Program sponsor:	
Actual start date:	

Approved end date:	
Program no.:	
Revision history:	
Business unit:	

A. PURPOSE

A brief introductory statement defining the purpose of the financial plan, such as:

> The financial plan documents all the program's financial aspects as it describes the funding schedules and milestones, baseline budget, contact payments and schedules, financial reporting processes and mechanisms, and financial metrics.

_____

_____

_____

B. FINANCIAL FRAMEWORK AND GOALS

This section identifies the overall financial environment for the program as it pinpoints funds to be expended at key milestones and helps ensure money is spent efficiently with the least waste possible.

_____

_____

_____

C. FUNDING CONSTRAINTS

This section describes the methods by which program funding will be received since it is rare that 100% of the required funding will be available at the time the program is initiated. Other financial constraints also are included in this section.

_____

_____

_____

D. PROGRAM OPERATIONAL COSTS

This section describes the specific costs associated with the operation of the program, such as infrastructure costs—facilities and systems—and costs associated with the program management office, including human resources.

E. FORMAT AND CRITERIA FOR COST ESTIMATING

This section describes the various tools and techniques to be used to estimate the costs associated with the program in order that an overall cost estimate for the program can be prepared.

F. PROGRAM PAYMENT SCHEDULE

This section identifies the schedule and milestones where funding for the program is received from the funding organization.

G. PROGRAM FINANCIAL METRICS

This section describes the specific financial metrics for the program by which the program's benefits are measured.

H. METHODS FOR FINANCIAL MONITORING AND CONTROL

This section describes the approach to use to identify factors that may create changes to the financial baseline, methods to monitor the environment for changes that may affect the financial plan, ways to monitor the disbursement of funds to contractors, methods to identify impacts to the program components from overruns and underruns, methods to manage the program's infrastructure costs, and methods to communicate the financial situation to program stakeholders.

I. REMAINING BUDGET ALLOCATIONS

This section describes the process to return any remaining budget allocations to the overall program budget, which may occur during the close procurement process.

_____

_____

_____

J. APPROVALS

This section contains the approval of the financial plan by the program sponsor, program manager, program management office, members of the governance board, and other key stakeholders.

SIGNATURES AND DATE APPROVAL OBTAINED

Program manager	_____
Program sponsor	_____
Program management office director	_____
Governance board chairperson	_____
Governance board member 1	_____
Governance board member 2	_____
Governance board member N	_____
Stakeholder 1	_____
Stakeholder 2	_____
Stakeholder N	_____

Financial Metrics

Program benefits are often based on financial results. Regardless, program financial performance is always important. Metrics facilitate critical "early warning" systems and are developed in the develop program financial plan process in the *Standard for Program Management*—Second Edition (2008) for use throughout the program.

This topic is covered as part of the program financial plan.

Procurement Management Plan

The procurement management plan (Figure 5.13), an output of plan program procurements in the *Standard for Program Management*—Second Edition (2008),

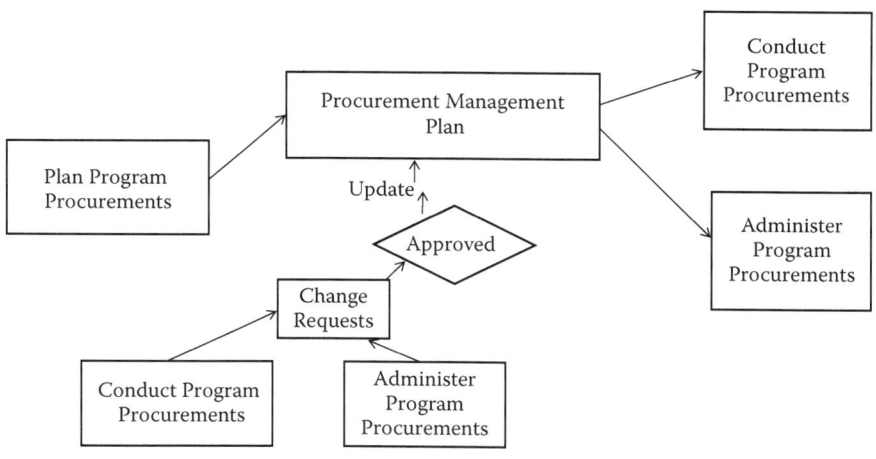

Program Management Life Cycle: Program Setup

Figure 5.13 Procurement management plan.

describes the procurement process, including what is to be procured and the means of arriving at a contract. It defers to the contracts management plan for the purpose of contracts administration and execution.

Procurement Management Plan Instructions

The procurement management plan includes the following:

> **Purpose:** A brief introductory statement defining the purpose of the procurement management plan, such as:
>
> The procurement management plan describes the process used to determine what to acquire, such as facilities, goods, materials, and external resources, based on product requirements and describes the contractual methods that will be used.
>
> This plan should be prepared early in the planning process, as the procurement process is critical to program success and benefits realization. Careful planning and analysis are required and cannot be understated in order that funding is used in the most effective way. Although the plan is drafted early in the program, it is an iterative document that should be further refined as the program moves through the phases of the life cycle, as it may require updates, especially during monitoring and controlling. It also may require updates because of changes in organizational strategy or because of risk responses,

which may lead to make-or-buy decisions. This plan also does not replace the procurement management plans to be prepared by the project managers in the program for their specific projects.

In the Project Management Institute's *Standard for Program Management—Second Edition* (2008), the procurement management plan is an output of the plan program procurements process. It is in an input to the conduct program procurements and administer program procurements processes. It may be updated as a result of the administer program procurements process.

Procurement planning approach: This section describes how the program management team will determine which items—facilities, goods, materials, and external resources—should be handled through the procurement process. It describes the make-or-buy process to follow and the various items that should be considered. These include external factors, market conditions, regulations, budget, and available suppliers. It also states the organization's capability to evaluate, procure, and then manage all items that are handled through procurements.

Required and available resources and sourcing decisions: This section describes the specific resources required for the program and whether or not they are available within the organization or need to be procured from external sources.

Required procurements: This section identifies the required procurements for the program. In preparing this section, planning is needed to ensure that there is an emphasis on shared resources across the program so that additional costs are not required later in the program life cycle.

Statements of work for each item to be procured: This section describes statements of work for each item to be procured. It is based on review of the program scope statement and the program work breakdown structure. It is noted that the statements of work are for items at the program level. It may be possible, and desirable, to group items to be procured as one procurement item in a single statement of work. These statements of work then guide the procurement process, as it may be different for the various items that will be procured. They serve to describe in specific detail the procurement item in order that prospective sellers can determine whether or not they can provide the required items. Information in the statement of work may include specifications, quantities required, quality levels, performance requirements, the period of performance, and other requirements as appropriate. This section also states how work will be managed for each item that is procured and whether the work will be done internally or externally.

Procurement documents: This section states the specific procurement documents that will be used for each item to be procured, such as request for proposal, request for quotation, or invitation to bid. The purpose is to structure these documents in a way that prospective sellers can prepare an accurate and complete response, and the program management team can then evaluate the responses easily. The documents should be ones that enable the prospective supplier to propose an alternative means of meeting the requirement if possible to provide greater flexibility.

Contract types: This section defines and documents the specific contract types that will be used. They will vary based on the nature of the procurement. While fixed-price, cost-plus, and time and materials contracts are typical, other vehicles such as basic ordering agreements, other umbrella-type contracts, leasing, and integrated volume discounts should be considered as appropriate.

Qualified seller lists: In order to expedite the procurement process, qualified seller lists may be appropriate. This section describes how these lists will be developed—by others in the organization, such as members of the procurement department, or by the program management team. It also states how information about qualified sellers will be obtained. A variety of tools and techniques can be used, such as requests for information, the Internet, advertising, directories, associations, and catalogs. This section also states whether on-site visits will be made as part of the process to develop these lists. It may be useful as well for the program management team to contact seller references to obtain information on past performance.

Proposals: This section describes the processes, procedures, and evaluation criteria that will be used to review proposals from potential sellers. It states who will be involved in evaluating the proposals that are received so that there is no bias in the process. The evaluation criteria may be limited to price for certain items or may be more complex for other items. If the latter, it is appropriate to consider whether prospective sellers understand the requirements, the management approach to be followed, the overall cost, the technical approach to be used, the people who will support the procurement, the schedule for deliverable items, the risk involved, past performance and references, intellectual property and proprietary rights, financial considerations, and warranties.

Approvals: This section contains the written approval of the procurement management plan by the program sponsor, program manager, program management office, members of the program board or governance board, and other stakeholders.

Procurement Management Plan Template

<Insert Program Name>
Program Procurement Management Plan

Program name:	
Program manager:	PM's email address here as a hyperlink

Program sponsor:	
Actual start date:	
Approved end date:	
Program no.:	
Revision history:	
Business unit:	

A. PURPOSE

A brief introductory statement defining the purpose of the procurement management plan, such as:

> The procurement management plan describes the process used to determine what to acquire, such as facilities, goods, materials, and external resources, based on product requirements and describes the contractual methods that will be used.

_____

_____

_____

B. PROCUREMENT PLANNING APPROACH

This section describes how the program management team will determine which items are to be handled as procurements. It describes the make-or-buy process to follow and the various items that should be considered. It also states the organization's capability to evaluate, procure, and then manage all the items that are procured externally.

_____

_____

_____

C. REQUIRED AND AVAILABLE RESOURCES AND SOURCING DECISIONS

This section describes the specific resources required for the program and whether or not they are available within the organization or need to be procured from external sources.

_____

_____

_____

D. REQUIRED PROCUREMENTS

This section identifies the required procurements for the program.

E. STATEMENTS OF WORK FOR EACH ITEM TO BE PROCURED

This section describes statements of work for each item to be procured. These statements of work guide the procurement process and describe in detail the specific procurement item. This section also states how work will be managed for each item that is procured and whether the work will be done internally or externally.

F. PROCUREMENT DOCUMENTS

This section states the specific procurement documents that will be used for each item to be procured.

G. CONTRACT TYPES

This section defines and documents the specific contract types that will be used based on the nature of the procurement item.

H. QUALIFIED SELLER LISTS

This section describes whether qualified seller lists will be used and how they will be developed. It describes the process that will be followed to obtain information on each of the possible sellers to be on the list.

I. PROPOSALS

This section describes the processes, procedures, and evaluation criteria that will be used to review proposals from potential sellers. It states who will be involved in the evaluation process so there is no bias in the process.

_____

_____

_____

J. APPROVALS

This section contains the approval of the procurement management plan by the program sponsor, program manager, program management office, members of the governance board, and other key stakeholders.

SIGNATURES AND DATE APPROVAL OBTAINED

Program manager	_____
Program sponsor	_____
Program management office director	_____
Governance board chairperson	_____
Governance board member 1	_____
Governance board member 2	_____
Governance board member N	_____
Stakeholder 1	_____
Stakeholder 2	_____
Stakeholder N	_____

Contracts Management Plan

The contracts management plan (Figure 5.14) builds on the procurement management plan, elaborating on contracts administration to ensure appropriate cost, quality, and schedule. It also is prepared during the plan program procurements process in the *Standard for Program Management*—Second Edition (2008).

Contracts Management Plan Instructions

The contracts management plan will include the following:

> **Purpose:** A brief introductory statement defining the purpose of the contracts management plan, such as:

The Program Setup Phase ■ 157

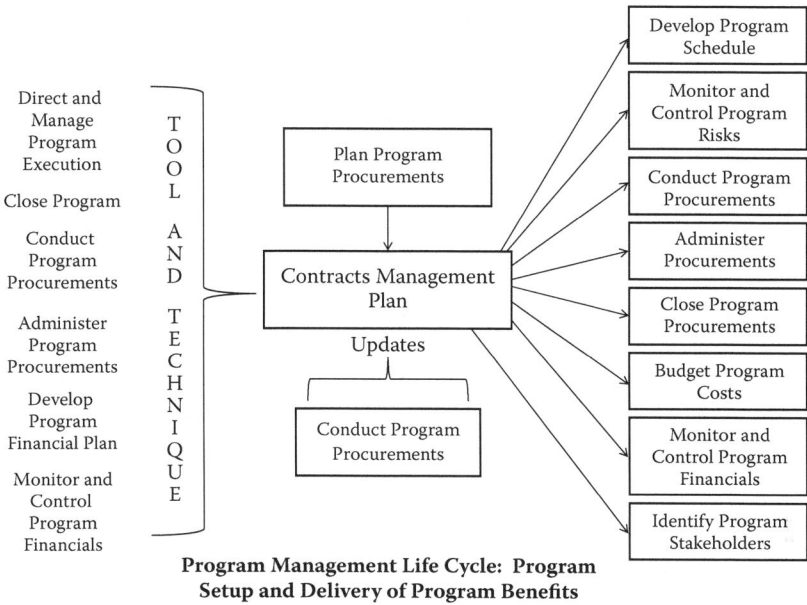

Figure 5.14   Contracts management plan.

The contracts management plan describes the process that will be followed to administer each of the program-level contracts to ensure that deliverables meet requirements concerning cost, schedule, and quality.

This plan builds on the procurement management plan, which is developed earlier in the program. In fact, once the contracts management plan is approved, it can become an appendix to the procurement management plan. It is an iterative document and should be reviewed periodically by the program management team, especially as contracts are closed, and new contracts are awarded to see if changes are warranted. This plan covers the contract administration activities throughout the life of the contract.

In the Project Management Institute's *Standard for Program Management—* Second Edition (2008), the contracts management plan is prepared as an output of the plan program procurements process. It is an input to the conduct program procurements process. Updates to this plan may result from the conduct program procurements process. Aspects of this plan are tools and techniques in many processes, including direct and manage program execution, close program, conduct program procurements, administer program procurements, develop program financial plan, and monitor and control program financials processes. Other items of this plan are inputs to the following processes: develop program schedule, monitor and control program risks, administer procurements, close program procurements, budget program costs, monitor and control program financials, and identify program stakeholders.

Roles and responsibilities: This section describes the roles and responsibilities of the program management team, the component managers, the procurement department, the legal department, and others in the organization concerning contract administration. It states the actions the program management team can take on its own without involvement from the procurement or legal departments. It also describes how the program management team will interface with the people on various projects in the program responsible for contract administration. Experts may also be needed, especially for global programs in which specific knowledge about contract laws in other countries will apply where the procurement will be awarded. Actions to be taken by whom if conditions outlined in the contract are not met are stated in this section.

Buyer-seller performance requirements: For overall program success, a partnership is needed between the buyer and the sellers. This section states the specific performance requirements each party should meet. For example, it describes the process to review each deliverable. While the deliverable due date is specified in the contract, the buyer should review it according to a predetermined schedule. The seller then should have a certain schedule in order to respond to needed changes if rework is required. Nontechnical factors, such as establishment of trust and excellent working relationships between the parties, also are critical to program success. The buyer enables the seller to complete the contract, pays the agreed-upon price, formally accepts the deliverable, and closes the contract. The seller completes the deliverable according to the contractual terms and conditions.

Monitoring and control: This section describes specific monitoring and controlling processes to be followed. It identifies the circumstances to consider if the contractual agreement is violated, to ensure that the deliverables meet requirements, to determine that the relationship between the buyer and seller ends as stipulated, and to ensure that any postprogram communications occur as specified.

Subcontract selection process criteria: Since many prime contractors in a program issue subcontracts, this section states the selection criteria for these subcontracts to ensure consistency in meeting overall program objectives and benefit expectations. If the subcontract involves an initiative in another country, consideration of local laws is necessary. Contractual terms and conditions should be specified for the subcontractors as appropriate.

Schedules: This section describes the process the program management team will use to coordinate the various schedules prepared by the program contractors and to ensure that these schedules are part of the program's master schedule. This section is required because the lack of delivery or performance of one contractor may affect the overall performance of the program and the delivery of the expected program benefits. It states how often revised schedules will be provided by the contractors, and the process to learn of any problems so corrective action can be taken as quickly as possible. It describes the tools and techniques to be used, as it may be beneficial for all the program contractors to use the same scheduling software for technical compatibility.

Meetings to be held with contractors: In many large programs, much of the work may be done by contractors. If this is the case in the program, this section would describe whether any meetings are planned to be held with the various contractors to better coordinate the work to be done and to resolve any conflicts that could occur during the process. The program management team then can use these meetings to coordinate and resolve any scheduling or other constraints.

Status reporting: This section describes the status reports to be provided by the various program contractors to describe progress in terms of achieving contractual objectives, and how the individual reports then will be merged into an overall program status report. It states the frequency in which the reports will be prepared and the format to be used. Ideally, each contractor should follow a standard format, which should include as a minimum schedule, budget, scope, risk, and quality metrics and approval status of program deliverables.

Contract performance review meetings: The section describes the items to be covered in contractor performance reviews and how often these meetings will be held. These meetings are useful not only to assess performance to date but also to determine if product pricing has changed significantly and requires revisions.

Change control: Change requests may be needed because of numerous factors, such as a change in overall strategy, a change in requirements, performance issues, etc. This section describes the process to follow when a change is needed to a contract in the program. It describes the contract change control system, as it states when change requests are required, the format to use to submit a change request, who must analyze requests for their impact on other aspects of the program, documentation requirements, and who is authorized to approve change requests. It also describes the process to use to notify the contractors when a change request has been approved or rejected.

Payment control: This section describes the payment control system that will be used to ensure that all invoices are processed in a timely fashion, that contract terms are followed, and that duplicate payments are not made. It describes the necessary approvals before a payment can be made.

Contract closure: This section describes the specific process the program team will use to close contracts and to determine that all contractual obligations have been met. It describes the specific documents to be reviewed, documents that will be archived, how lessons learned will be conducted, any performance reviews that may be held, contract closure audits that may be conducted, stakeholders to be notified, and any required follow-up work or warranties. This section also describes the process to follow if contracts are terminated early, such as documenting why the contract was terminated, determining the extent of the actual work that was performed, and updating contractual records.

Approvals: This section contains the written approval of the contracts management plan by the program sponsor, program manager, program management office, members of the program board or governance board, and other stakeholders.

Contracts Management Plan Template

<Insert Program Name>
Contracts Management Plan

Program name:	
Program manager:	PM's email address here as a hyperlink
Program sponsor:	
Actual start date:	
Approved end date:	
Program no.:	
Revision history:	
Business unit:	

A. PURPOSE

A brief introductory statement defining the purpose of the contracts management plan, such as:

> The contracts management plan describes the process that will be followed to administer each of the program-level contracts to ensure that deliverables meet requirements concerning cost, schedule, and quality.

_____

_____

_____

B. ROLES AND RESPONSIBILITIES

This section describes the roles and responsibilities of the program management team, the component managers, the procurement department, the legal department, and others in the organization concerning contract administration. It states the actions the program management team can take on its own without involvement from other groups and describes how the program management team will interface with the various people administering contracts at the project level. It describes whether the use of experts will be required.

C. BUYER-SELLER PERFORMANCE REQUIREMENTS

This section states the specific performance requirements of the buyer and the seller. It describes the process to follow in reviewing deliverables and the need for attention to nontechnical factors.

D. MONITORING AND CONTROL

This section describes specific monitoring and controlling processes to be followed. It identifies the circumstances to consider if agreements are violated, to ensure deliverables meet requirements, to see that the relationship between the buyer and seller ends as stipulated, and to see if postprogram communications occur as specified.

E. SUBCONTRACT SELECTION PROCESS CRITERIA

This section describes the selection criteria for any subcontracts by prime contractors to ensure consistency in meeting overall program objectives and benefit expectations. It specifies contractual terms and conditions to be included in the subcontracts as appropriate.

F. SCHEDULES

This section describes the process the program management team will use to coordinate the various schedules prepared by the program contractors and to ensure that these schedules are part of the program's master schedule. It states how often revised schedules will be provided by the contractors, and the process to learn of any problems so corrective action can be taken. It describes tools and techniques to be used for technical compatibility.

G. MEETINGS TO BE HELD WITH CONTRACTORS

This section describes whether any meetings are planned to be held with the various contractors to better coordinate the work to be done and to resolve any conflicts that could occur in the process.

H. STATUS REPORTING

This section describes status reports to be provided by the program contractors to describe progress in terms of achieving contractual objectives and how the individual reports will be merged into an overall program status report. It states the reporting frequency and the format to be used for the reports.

I. CONTRACT PERFORMANCE REVIEW MEETINGS

This section describes how often contractor performance will be reviewed by the program team and the items to be covered in a typical review.

J. CHANGE CONTROL

This section describes the contract change control system to be followed in the program, including notification to the contractors when a change request has been approved or rejected.

K. PAYMENT CONTROL

This section describes the payment control system to be used to ensure that invoices are processed in a timely way, that contract terms and conditions are followed, and that duplicate payments are not made. It describes the needed approvals before a payment is made.

___

L. CONTRACT CLOSURE

This section describes the process the program team will use to close contracts and to determine that all contractual obligations have been met. It also describes the process to follow if contracts are terminated early.

___

M. APPROVALS

This section contains the approval of the contracts management plan by the program sponsor, program manager, program management office, members of the program board or governance board, and other key stakeholders.

SIGNATURES AND DATE APPROVAL OBTAINED

Program manager _____
Program sponsor _____
Program management office director _____
Governance board chairperson _____
Governance board member 1 _____
Governance board member 2 _____
Governance board member N _____
Stakeholder 1 _____
Stakeholder 2 _____
Stakeholder N _____

Interface Management Plan

The interface management plan was included in the second edition exposure draft but has been removed in the final edition. We chose to keep it here for those programs that have complex interfaces and as a stimulus for consideration of the matters it addresses on smaller programs.

If multiple individuals are taking care of relations with a given external organization on the same matters, conflicts could result. Neglected interfaces with known stakeholders are almost always problematic. The interface management plan addresses these issues and more.

Interface Management Plan Instructions

The interface management plan includes the following:

Purpose: A brief introductory statement defining the purpose of the interface management plan, such as:

> The interface management plan identifies and maps interrelationships within the program, with other programs in the portfolio, and with factors outside of the program. It identifies interfaces in terms of ones that are organizational, technical, interpersonal, logistical, and political.
>
> It addresses internal and external interfaces as well as interdependencies and interrelationships. It then assists in identifying risks with these interrelationships throughout the management of the program. It describes roles and responsibilities for program interface management. Although the plan is drafted early in the program, it is an iterative document that should be further refined as the program moves through the life cycle.

Identification of organizational interfaces: This section defines each organizational interface in the program, such as the various departments or units within the organization to be involved in the program, the current relationships among them, and the informal and formal relationships among them. It also describes the relationship with the portfolio manager and the program management office.

Identification of technical interfaces: This section states the different disciplines and specialties that are needed to complete the program. It includes items such as software, subsystems, testing, and equipment that may need to be coordinated. It also should describe whether there are any transitions within the program management life cycle that may present challenges.

Identification of interpersonal interfaces: This section describes the formal and informal reporting relationships among members of the program team. It includes any cultural or language differences that may affect these working relationships and describes whether any levels of trust and respect already exist among team members. It also states customer-supplier relationships.

Identification of logistical interfaces: This section describes logistical interfaces, such as the use of virtual teams in the program and whether stakeholders are in different locations, time zones, or countries.

Identification of political interfaces: This section describes the individual goals and objectives of program stakeholders, to especially note whether people have informal power in areas of importance to the program. It lists any informal alliances that may exist.

Management approach for component interfaces: This section describes how interfaces between the various program components will be managed. Changes often can occur because of interfaces with various program components (projects and nonproject work), and a change to one component may affect another component in the program.

Management approach for interfaces with the program's governance board: This section describes the approach to follow to manage interfaces with other enterprises, such as customers, suppliers, and other parts of the organization, which are typically handled through work with the program's governance board.

Management approach for interfaces with other aspects of the program: This section describes how interface planning will be coordinated with other aspects of the program, such as with schedule development, human resource planning, communications planning, the program work breakdown structure, and risk management planning and analysis.

Roles and responsibilities for interface management: This section states the various roles and responsibilities for interface management in the program.

Approvals: This section contains the written approval of the interface management plan by the program sponsor, program manager, program management office, members of the governance board, and other stakeholders.

Interface Management Plan Template

<Insert Program Name>
Program Interface Management Plan

Program name:	
Program manager:	PM's email address here as a hyperlink
Program sponsor:	
Actual start date:	
Approved end date:	
Program no.:	
Revision history:	
Business unit:	

A. PURPOSE

A brief introductory statement defining the purpose of the interface management plan, such as:

The interface management plan identifies and maps interrelationships within the program, with other programs in the portfolio, and with factors outside of the program. It identifies interfaces in terms of ones that are organizational, technical, interpersonal, logistical, and political.

B. IDENTIFICATION OF ORGANIZATIONAL INTERFACES

This section defines each organizational interface in the program, such as the various departments or units within the organization to be involved in the program, the current relationships among them, and the informal and formal relationships among them.

C. IDENTIFICATION OF TECHNICAL INTERFACES

This section states the different disciplines and specialties that are needed to complete the program. It includes items such as software, subsystems, testing, and equipment that may need to be coordinated. It also should describe whether there are any transitions within the program management life cycle that may present challenges.

D. IDENTIFICATION OF INTERPERSONAL INTERFACES

This section describes the formal and informal reporting relationships among members of the program team, including any cultural or language differences that may affect these working relationships and any levels of trust and respect that already exist among team members. It also states customer-supplier relationships.

E. IDENTIFICATION OF LOGISTICAL INTERFACES

This section describes logistical interfaces, such as the use of virtual teams in the program and whether stakeholders are in different locations, time zones, or countries.

F. IDENTIFICATION OF POLITICAL INTERFACES

This section describes the individual goals and objectives of program stakeholders, to especially note whether people have informal power in areas of importance to the program. It lists any informal alliances that may exist.

G. MANAGEMENT APPROACH FOR COMPONENT INTERFACES

This section describes how interfaces between the various program components (projects and nonproject work) will be managed.

H. MANAGEMENT APPROACH FOR INTERFACES WITH THE PROGRAM GOVERNANCE BOARD

This section describes the approach to follow to manage interfaces with other enterprises, such as customers, suppliers, and other parts of the organization, which are typically handled through work with the program's governance board.

I. MANAGEMENT APPROACH FOR INTERFACES WITH OTHER ASPECTS OF THE PROGRAM

This section describes how interface planning will be coordinated with other aspects of the program, such as with schedule development, human resource planning, communications planning, the program work breakdown structure, and risk management planning and analysis.

J. ROLES AND RESPONSIBILITIES FOR INTERFACE MANAGEMENT

This section states the various roles and responsibilities for interface management in the program.

_____

_____

_____

K. APPROVALS

This section contains the approval of the interface management plan by the program sponsor, program manager, program management office, members of the governance board, and other key stakeholders.

SIGNATURES AND DATE APPROVAL OBTAINED

Program manager	_____
Program sponsor	_____
Program management office director	_____
Governance board chairperson	_____
Governance board member 1	_____
Governance board member 2	_____
Governance board member N	_____
Stakeholder 1	_____
Stakeholder 2	_____
Stakeholder N	_____

Staffing Management Plan

Although this plan is not part of the *Standard for Program Management*—Second Edition (2008), we believe it is an essential document for program management given the importance of acquiring, retaining, and releasing staff from the program.

Staffing Management Plan Instructions

The staffing management plan includes the following:

> **Purpose:** A brief introductory statement defining the purpose of the staffing management plan, such as:
>
> > The staffing management plan describes the timetable for staff acquisition and release from the program. It also includes identification of

roles and responsibilities, plans for recognition and rewards, compliance considerations, and safety issues.

It addresses availability of and competition for scarce human resources needed for the program. It designates roles and responsibilities required for program success. Although the plan is drafted early in the program, it is an iterative document that should be further refined, especially since the preliminary requirements regarding the people and competencies needed for the program are progressively elaborated as the program progresses.

Internal and external required resources: This section describes specific internal and external, when appropriate, human resources required for program success. Specific competencies are listed in this section. Competency refers to the skills and abilities required to complete program activities. The section lists the individuals and groups that may be part of the program organization and whether they are internal to the organization or external to it.

Organizational influences: This section defines various organizational influences that can impact the program team. It describes key personnel administration policies and procedures, standardized position descriptions, standardized performance plans, and the ability to acquire resources from groups external to the organization. It also specifically describes the assistance available to the program manager from the human resource department.

Program team roles and responsibilities: This section documents program team member roles and responsibilities so there is clarity of who is responsible for each program package in the program work breakdown structure. The objective is to ensure that the program team is aware of who is responsible for each of these program packages to ensure each one has an assigned owner, and duplicative work does not result. A role is defined as the portion of the program for which an individual is held accountable. Responsibility refers to the work the person is expected to perform in the program. A program organizational chart should be prepared and attached to the plan as a separate document. A resource assignment matrix also should be prepared.

Methods to meet human resource requirements: This section describes when and how human resource requirements will be met in the program. It describes how staff members will be acquired and whether or not the team will be virtual or collocated.

Resource calendars: This section describes the necessary time frames for members of the program team to join the program and begin their work, as well as when recruiting or acquisition activities will begin. A histogram of human resource requirements may be attached to this plan.

Staffing release: This section describes the method and timing of releasing staff members from the program team. Its purpose is to provide a smooth transition as staff members are released. Methods for identifying lessons learned for future program improvements can be part of this section of the plan as individuals move on to other assignments. Such a smooth transition can improve overall team morale.

Rewards and recognition: This section presents clear criteria for rewards and a planned system for their use on the program. Various types of available rewards are included in this section. The purpose of this section is to ensure there is a set timetable so recognition is not forgotten as program activities are completed.

Compliance requirements: This section describes strategies for compliance with various regulations, organizational policies, and human resource policies to be followed in the program. It also includes any safety policies and procedures.

Approvals: This section contains the written approval of the staffing management plan by the program sponsor, program manager, program management office, members of the governance board, and other stakeholders.

Staffing Management Plan Template

<Insert Program Name>
Staffing Management Plan

Program name:	
Program manager:	PM's email address here as a hyperlink
Program sponsor:	
Actual start date:	
Approved end date:	
Program no.:	
Revision history:	
Business unit:	

A. PURPOSE

A brief introductory statement defining the purpose of the staffing management plan, such as:

> The staffing management plan describes the timetable for staff acquisition and release from the program. It also includes identification of roles and responsibilities, plans for recognition and rewards, compliance considerations, and safety issues.

B. INTERNAL AND EXTERNAL REQUIRED RESOURCES

This section defines specific internal and external, when appropriate, human resources required for program success. It lists specific competencies that are needed.

_____
_____
_____

C. ORGANIZATIONAL INFLUENCES

This section defines various organizational influences that can impact the program team, such as personnel administration policies and procedures, standard position descriptions, standard performance plans, and the ability to acquire resources from external units.

_____
_____
_____

D. PROGRAM TEAM ROLES AND RESPONSIBILITIES

This section documents program team member roles and responsibilities for each program package in the program work breakdown structure. A program organization chart should be attached to this plan as a separate document. A resource assignment matrix also may be included.

_____
_____
_____

E. METHODS TO MEET HUMAN RESOURCE REQUIREMENTS

This section describes when and how human resource requirements will be met in the program. It states how staff members will be acquired and whether the team will be virtual or collocated.

_____
_____
_____

F. RESOURCE CALENDARS

This section describes the necessary time frames for members of the program team to join the program and begin their work. It also states when recruiting or acquisition activities will begin. A histogram may be attached to this plan.

_____
_____
_____

G. STAFFING RELEASE

This section describes the method and timing of releasing staff members from the program team so there is a smooth transition. It also includes methods to identify lessons learned as staff members move on to other assignments.

_____

_____

_____

H. REWARDS AND RECOGNITION

This section presents the criteria for rewards and a planned system for their use in the program. It helps to ensure there is a set timetable so recognition is not forgotten as program activities are completed.

_____

_____

_____

I. COMPLIANCE REQUIREMENTS

This section describes strategies for compliance with various regulations, organizational policies, human resource policies, and safety policies and approvals.

_____

_____

_____

J. APPROVALS

This section contains the approval of the staffing management plan by the program sponsor, program manager, program management office, members of the governance board, and other key stakeholders.

SIGNATURES AND DATE APPROVAL OBTAINED

Program manager	_____
Program sponsor	_____
Program management office director	_____
Governance board chairperson	_____
Governance board member 1	_____
Governance board member 2	_____
Governance board member N	_____
Stakeholder 1	_____

Stakeholder 2 _____

Stakeholder N _____

Program Transition Plan

Without transition, program benefits are, in most cases, simply forgotten or terminated. Without proper transition management for both the components and the program, the program is worthless.

Program Transition Plan Instructions

The program transition plan will include the following:

Purpose: A brief introductory statement defining the purpose of the program transition plan, such as:

The program transition plan describes the process that will be followed to deliver the final product to the customer or to transition it to another unit in the performing organization, such as a product support, customer support, or service management group, to ensure program benefits are sustained.

This plan serves to provide a smooth transition process. The objective is to ensure that the benefits from the program continue to be realized as long as possible. Once the transition activities are complete, program resources then are reallocated, and all program records are closed. It is an iterative document that may be refined as various program components are closed and transitioned to ongoing operational status or to the customer.

In the Project Management Institute's *Standard for Program Management—Second Edition* (2008), the transition plan is an output of the develop program management plan process. It is an input to the close program process.

Transition process: This section describes the program transition process to be followed. It states whether a program transition request must be prepared, its format, and approval requirements. It describes the need to evaluate all the subsidiary plans of the program management plan to see if requirements were met, to ensure that expected program benefits were realized, and to ensure that all program components have been closed. A schedule for the transition activities should be part of the overall program master schedule.

Component transition requests: Throughout the program, different components (projects and nonproject work) will finish before others. Each time a component is officially closed, a transition request should be prepared to transition the benefits from the component into ongoing operational status or to the customer. This section describes the process to prepare these requests, the format to be used, and the approval requirements. Typically, these activities are part of the last gate review for the component.

Documentation requirements: This section describes documentation to be prepared as part of the transition process. It also includes a description of any training to be provided or materials that may be needed. Often, transitions are formal contract-type activities; in other situations, a more informal process may be appropriate. A clear understanding of the specific items to be transitioned is required so there are no misunderstandings later in the process.

Roles and responsibilities: This section describes the roles and responsibilities of the program management team as well as the receiving organization in the transition process. The receiving organization ideally should be a participant in preparing the transition plan so there is a clear understanding of what will be handed to this unit and the process that will be followed.

Transition critical success factors: This section describes the critical success factors that are considered essential to ongoing benefits sustainment and assurance. It may include items such as continuing to meet product demands, adding value to the ongoing process that will be followed, having a customer or product support representative available, providing support if changes are required, and training support staff as needed.

Approvals: This section contains the written approval of the program transition plan by the program sponsor, program manager, program management office, members of the governance board, and other stakeholders.

Program Transition Plan Template

<Insert Program Name>
Program Transition Plan

Program name:	
Program manager:	PM's email address here as a hyperlink
Program sponsor:	
Actual start date:	
Approved end date:	
Program no.:	
Revision history:	
Business unit:	

A. PURPOSE

A brief introductory statement defining the purpose of the program transition plan, such as:

> The program transition plan describes the process that will be followed to deliver the final product to the customer or to transition it to another unit in the performing organization, such as a product support, customer support, or service management group, to ensure program benefits are sustained.

_____

_____

_____

B. TRANSITION PROCESS

This section describes the program transition process to be followed. It states whether a program transition request must be prepared, its format, and approval requirements.

_____

_____

_____

C. COMPONENT TRANSITION REQUESTS

This section describes the process to be followed to prepare a transition request each time a component is officially closed to transition the benefits from the component into ongoing operational status or to the customer.

_____

_____

_____

D. DOCUMENTATION REQUIREMENTS

This section describes the documentation to be prepared as part of the transition process. It also includes a description of any training to be provided or materials that may be needed.

_____

_____

_____

E. ROLES AND RESPONSIBILITIES

This section describes the roles and responsibilities of the program management team as well as the receiving organization in the transition process.

_____
_____
_____

F. TRANSITION CRITICAL SUCCESS FACTORS

This section describes the critical success factors that are considered essential to ongoing benefits sustainment and assurance.

_____

_____

_____

G. APPROVALS

This section contains the approval of the program transition plan by the program sponsor, program manager, program management office, members of the program board or governance board, and other key stakeholders.

SIGNATURES AND DATE APPROVAL OBTAINED

Program manager	_____
Program sponsor	_____
Program management office director	_____
Governance board chairperson	_____
Governance board member 1	_____
Governance board member 2	_____
Governance board member N	_____
Stakeholder 1	_____
Stakeholder 2	_____
Stakeholder N	_____

Program Management Plan

According to the *Standard for Program Management*—Second Edition (2008), the program management plan (Figure 5.15) includes the following subsidiary plans:

- Program road map
- Program schedule
- Program governance plan

The Program Setup Phase ■ 177

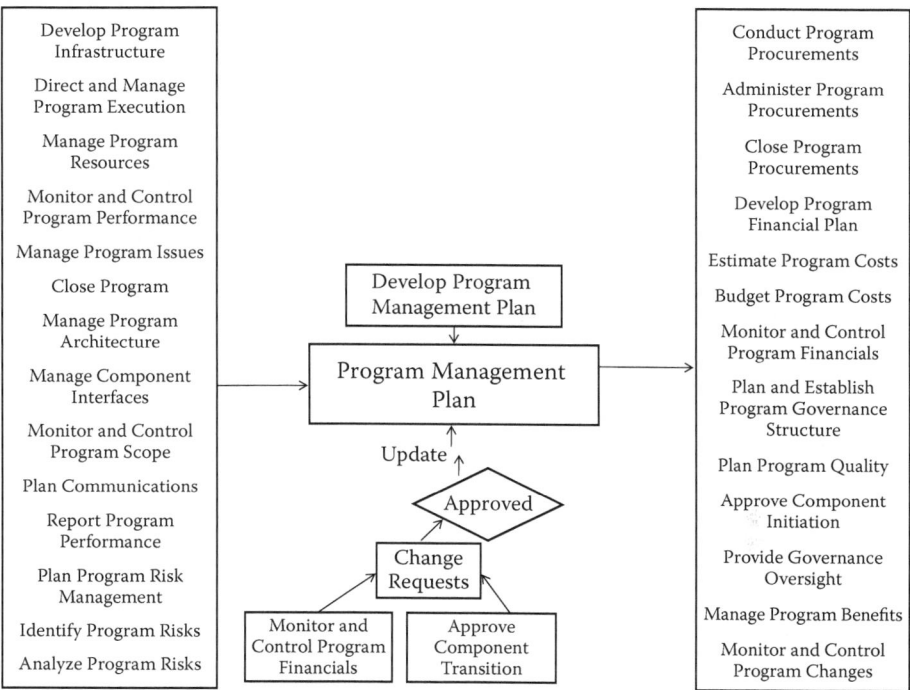

Program Management Life Cycle: Program Setup

Figure 5.15 Program management plan.

- Governance metrics
- Benefits realization plan
- Program stakeholder management plan
- Program communications management plan
- Program financial plan
- Contracts management plan
- Scope management plan
- Procurement management plan
- Quality management plan
- Program risk response plan
- Program risk management plan
- Schedule management plan

These items may be separate documents or some or all of them could be placed in a single volume, if desired, for smaller programs. In some cases, one of these plans could simply point to a standard organization plan.

Program Management Plan Instructions

The program management plan includes the following:

Purpose: A brief introductory statement defining the purpose of the program management plan, such as:

> The program management plan provides direction as to how the program will be managed, monitored and controlled, and closed; guides the allocation and use of program resources; and defines the program's deliverables and benefits.

Once the program management plan is approved, program execution begins. This plan contains the various subsidiary plans, and they can be set up as attachments to the program management plan, or they can be consolidated into a single document. Although this plan is prepared early in the program's life cycle, it is an iterative document that is expected to change throughout the program as the program progresses. It also is a starting point for project managers working on the program as they develop the plans for their specific projects, as it provides overall guidance. If the program begins after several components have been under way, the existing project plans should be reviewed as this plan is developed.

In the Project Management Institute's *Standard for Program Management*—Second Edition (2008), the program management plan is an output of the develop program management plan process. It is an input to the following processes:

- Develop program infrastructure
- Direct and manage program execution
- Manage program resources
- Monitor and control program performance
- Manage program issues
- Close program
- Manage program architecture
- Manage component interfaces
- Monitor and control program scope
- Plan communications
- Report program performance
- Plan program risk management
- Identify program risks
- Analyze program risks
- Conduct program procurements
- Administer program procurements
- Close program procurements

- Develop program financial plan
- Estimate program costs
- Budget program costs
- Monitor and control program financials
- Plan and establish program governance structure
- Plan program quality
- Approve component initiation
- Provide governance oversight
- Manage program benefits
- Monitor and control program changes

Updates to the program management plan are in the following processes:

- Monitor and control program financials
- Approve component transition

Program end result and schedule: This section describes the key program deliverables and their schedule for completion. It also describes the major program benefits. It provides background information, including why the program was initiated, and how it aligns with the organization's mission, vision, and values.

Program budget and cash flow requirements: This section contains information on the budget that is needed in order to complete the program. It describes cash flow requirements, referring to the financial management plan for details.

Program risks and issues: This section presents an overview of the key program risks, opportunities, and issues. It notes that details are included in the program risk management plan and risk register.

Program dependencies: This section describes the key dependencies between this program and other programs and projects under way by the organization.

Program assumptions: This section lists the assumptions or factors that the program management team considers to be true, real, or certain that are part of this plan. Subsidiary plans will describe some assumptions in greater detail as appropriate.

Program constraints: This section describes constraints, or restrictions or limits, that may affect overall program performance. These constraints are described in greater detail in some of the subsidiary program plans as appropriate.

Program management approach: This section describes the approach the program management team plans to follow as it executes the program and the methodology, tools, and techniques to be used. If the organization has an existing program management methodology, it states whether or not it will be used as is or whether it requires tailoring. It also describes how the program management team will work with component managers on the program, functional managers in the organization, the program's governance board, other stakeholders, and customers. It describes the metrics that will be used to help track and monitor the program to ensure deliverables are completed as planned, and expected benefits are realized. It shows how the various plans are integrated and coordinated at the program level. It also states how the program management team will document and use lessons learned throughout the program. Any supporting feasibility studies (technical, economic, ethical, social, environmental, etc.) should be attached to this section.

Program organization: This section states how the program will be organized. It describes the composition of the program management core team, the use of a program management office, and the interaction with the program's governance board.

Program management information system: This section describes the approach the program management team will use to collect and manage all program-related information. It shows the various tools and processes that will be used, such as software, documentation management, configuration management, earned value management, and the use of a program management office. It describes roles and responsibilities for use of this system and access privileges to it. This system is used for overall program performance monitoring and control, so this section also describes the specific reports that will be prepared and how they will be distributed, following the program communications management plan.

Schedule milestones and budget goals for program components: This section describes the high-level schedule milestones for each of the program's components (projects and nonproject work) and also includes the allocated budget for each component.

Tolerance ranges and decision making: Each organization has different levels of tolerance for variances in cost, scope, schedule, and risks and in how they will be handled. This section describes the level of tolerances for the program based on expectations of stakeholders and members of the program's governance board. It also states approvals required if the tolerance levels are exceeded. It discusses the various types of program decisions that are expected to be made by the program manager based on items in the program charter and the program manager's level of authority and accountability, and those that require escalation to the governance board. It states how the results of the decisions are communicated and managed, using the program communications management plan as a framework.

Updates to the program management plan: This section states when updates to the program management plan are required, such as when there are changes in the overall strategic direction of the organization, in the program's requirements, in organizational processes and procedures, or to the program's scope, schedule, cost, or quality baselines; unplanned circumstances; or risks that turn into issues that then require updates to the plan.

It describes the documentation management process to follow to update the plan and how key stakeholders will be notified that the plan has been updated. A formal change request should be prepared and approved before the plan is updated.

Approvals: This section contains the written approval of the program management plan by the program sponsor, program manager, program management office, members of the governance board, and other stakeholders.

Program Management Plan Template

<Insert Program Name>
Program Management Plan

Program name:	
Program manager:	PM's email address here as a hyperlink
Program sponsor:	
Actual start date:	
Approved end date:	
Program no.:	
Revision history:	
Business unit:	

A. PURPOSE

A brief introductory statement defining the purpose of the program management plan, such as:

> The program management plan provides direction as to how the program will be managed, monitored and controlled, and closed; guides the allocation and use of program resources; and defines the program's deliverables and benefits.

_____

_____

_____

B. PROGRAM END RESULT AND SCHEDULE

This section describes the key program deliverables and their schedule for completion. It also describes key program benefits and presents background information as to why the program was initiated.

C. PROGRAM BUDGET AND CASH FLOW REQUIREMENTS

This section contains information on the budget that is needed to complete the program and describes cash flow requirements, referring to the financial management plan for details.

D. PROGRAM RISKS AND ISSUES

This section presents an overview of the key program risks, opportunities, and issues. It notes that details are contained in the program risk management plan and risk response plan.

E. PROGRAM DEPENDENCIES

This section describes the key dependencies between this program and other programs and projects under way in the organization.

F. PROGRAM ASSUMPTIONS

This section lists the assumptions or factors that the project management team considers to be true, real, or certain that are part of this plan.

G. PROGRAM CONSTRAINTS

This section lists the constraints, or restrictions or limits, that may affect program performance.

H. PROGRAM MANAGEMENT APPROACH

This section describes the approach the program management team plans to follow as it executes the program, and the methodology, tools, and techniques to be used. It shows how the various plans are integrated and coordinated at the program level. Supporting feasibility studies, if applicable, are attached to this section.

I. PROGRAM ORGANIZATION

This section states how the program will be organized. It describes the composition of the program management core team, the use of a program office, the involvement of the program management office, and the interaction with the program's governance board.

J. PROGRAM MANAGEMENT INFORMATION SYSTEM

This section describes the approach the program management team will use to collect and manage all program-related information. It describes the various tools and processes that will be used and the roles and responsibilities for use of the system and access privileges to it. It states the performance reports to be prepared and how they will be distributed, following the program communications management plan.

K. SCHEDULE MILESTONES AND BUDGET GOALS FOR PROGRAM COMPONENTS

This section describes the high-level schedule milestones for each of the program's components and includes the allocated budget for each component.

184 ■ *Implementing Program Management: Templates for Success*

L. TOLERANCE RANGES AND DECISION MAKING

This section describes the tolerance levels for the program based on stakeholder expectations and those of the members of the governance board in terms of variances in cost, scope, schedule, and risk, and how the variances will be handled. It also states approval levels if the tolerance levels are exceeded. It describes the various types of program decisions the program manager is expected to make without the need to escalate them to the governance board. It describes how the results of these decisions will be communicated and managed, using the program communications management plan as a framework.

M. UPDATES TO THE PROGRAM MANAGEMENT PLAN

This section states when updates to the program management plan are required, the documentation process to follow to update the plan, and how key stakeholders will be notified that the plan has been updated.

N. APPROVALS

This section contains the approval of the program management plan by the program sponsor, program manager, program management office, members of the governance board, and other key stakeholders.

SIGNATURES AND DATE APPROVAL OBTAINED

Program manager _____

Program sponsor _____

Program management office director _____

Governance board chairperson _____

Governance board member 1 _____

Governance board member 2 _____

Governance board member N _____

Stakeholder 1 _____

Stakeholder 2 _____

Stakeholder N _____

Knowledge Management Plan

One of the most important assets of any organization is its corporate knowledge. This asset does not happen or grow accidentally. A knowledge management plan is therefore a key to success.

Knowledge Management Plan Instructions

The knowledge management plan includes the following:

Purpose: A brief introductory statement defining the purpose of the knowledge management plan, such as:

The knowledge management plan shows how knowledge management can improve the effectiveness and efficiency of overall program management, as it describes how people will be connected to one another in the program and to information generated throughout the course of the program.

This plan should be prepared early in the program because through a commitment to knowledge management (KM) by the program management team, greater efficiencies should result. People on the program team will be able to access information prepared by others with whom they may not have direct contact or even know. People also will be able to locate subject matter expertise that could help with key program issues. The emphasis is on use of KM to avoid reinvention, promote reuse, use less experienced staff on issues and problems for which solutions are available and staff members with greater expertise on areas in which innovative solutions are required, and provide the opportunity to eliminate redundancy in the program work environment.

The Project Management Institute's *Standard for Program Management*—Second Edition (2008) does not specifically recognize the knowledge management plan as an input, tool or technique, or output in any processes. However, the standard does note the importance of lessons learned and how they are collected and documented throughout the program, and lessons learned reviews are suggested in the plan program risk management process. The *Standard for Program Management*—Second Edition (2008) also notes the organization's knowledge bases. The develop program management plan and develop program infrastructure processes note a best practices library as an input. The plan and establish program governance process uses the best practices library as a tool and technique. Technical knowledge is a tool and technique in the develop program architecture process.

The lessons learned database is an input to the following processes:

- Plan program risk management
- Identify program risks
- Analyze program risks

Updates to the lessons learned database are an output of the monitor and control program risks process.

Knowledge transition is an output of the close program process.

Although the plan is prepared early in the program, it is an iterative document that should be reviewed and updated on a periodic basis.

Goals and objectives: This section lists the goals and objectives for KM in the program and describes how KM can contribute to the objectives of the program and the benefits to be realized. It may be that the program manager recognizes a need to quickly share information with his or her team, wishes to reduce the time required to locate information in documents and files, wants to reduce the time required to locate people with different areas of expertise on the team, or wants to avoid redundancy in the work that is done.

Roles and responsibilities: This section describes the key roles and responsibilities for KM in the program. A member of the program management team should have responsibility for KM activities, which would include preparing and updating the KM plan, ensuring that KM is a program package in the program work breakdown structure, determining the type of metadata tags to include on program artifacts, setting up a process so people can contribute knowledge assets or content to the program team, approving knowledge assets or content for publication, publishing the content, prioritizing the content that is contributed, communicating the availability of content to stakeholders and members of the program management team, determining access rights to the content that is published, reviewing blogs and discussion forums for examples of content to share, establishing and using debriefing tools as team members and contractors leave the program, and sharing content within the team and the organization.

Examples of approaches to consider as metadata tags include: authored by or prepared by, date, document type (form, presentation, plan, report, register, meeting minutes, lessons learned sessions, program reviews, and stage gate reviews), modified by, description, key topic (if not evident by the type of document), component involved, stakeholders involved, benefits affected, and metrics.

This member of the program management team with principal responsibility for KM may work with someone in the program management office. He or she also should set up a process to work with at least one other person on the team to ensure that the content that is contributed is of high quality and should be published. This KM team member also can determine whether the content requires updates or should be deleted, and should be responsible for knowledge transition to the program during the close program process.

Each member of the program management team, as well as customers and contractors, should identify knowledge assets or content and be able to contribute them.

Methods to communicate content availability within the program and within the organization include distribution lists, Web boards, Webinars, training sessions, discussion forums, blogs, podcasts, newsletters, white papers, collaboration rooms, document libraries, subscription notifications, and announcements.

Tools and techniques: This section describes the various tools and techniques to be used within the program team to share content that has been contributed. Examples of approaches include a program Web site, a shared drive, a collaboration room, a document library, and discussion forums.

Training and orientation sessions: This section describes whether any training and orientation sessions may be needed if people working on the program are not accustomed to active involvement in KM. Examples of items to be included in these sessions are ways to share information, approaches to contribute knowledge assets or content, ownership of content and intellectual property issues, the need for nondisclosure issues, and security.

Metrics: This section states how the effectiveness of the KM process in the program will be evaluated. Examples of items to consider include the contribution on a regular basis of useful content, the "hit" rates per knowledge asset or content, the actual use of contributed content, and the ability to locate key content quickly or key subject matter experts easily.

Rewards and recognition: If the organization does not actively practice KM, this section may be required to state how best to recognize and reward those members of the program team who are active in the KM process. Incentives may be needed so people regularly contribute knowledge assets and content and apply them to their work on the program as appropriate.

Approvals: This section contains the written approval of the knowledge management plan by the program sponsor, program manager, program management office, members of the governance board, and any other key stakeholders as appropriate.

Knowledge Management Plan Template

<Insert Program Name>
Knowledge Management Plan

Program name:	
Program manager:	PM's email address here as a hyperlink
Program sponsor:	
Actual start date:	
Approved end date:	
Program no.:	
Revision history:	
Business unit:	

A. PURPOSE

A brief introductory statement defining the purpose of the knowledge management plan, such as:

> The knowledge management plan shows how knowledge management can improve the effectiveness and efficiency of overall program management, as it describes how people will be connected to one another in the program and to information generated throughout the course of the program.

_____
_____
_____

B. GOALS AND OBJECTIVES

This section lists the goals and objectives for knowledge management (KM) in the program and describes how KM can contribute to the program's objectives and benefits to be realized.

_____
_____
_____

C. ROLES AND RESPONSIBILITIES

This section describes the key roles and responsibilities for KM in the program.

D. TOOLS AND TECHNIQUES

This section describes the various tools and techniques to be used by the program team to share content that has been contributed.

E. TRAINING AND ORIENTATION SESSIONS

This section describes whether any training and orientation sessions may be needed if people working on the program are not accustomed to active involvement in KM.

F. METRICS

This section states how the effectiveness of the KM process in the program will be evaluated.

G. REWARDS AND RECOGNITION

This section describes how members of the program team may be recognized and rewarded for their KM contributions.

H. APPROVALS

This section contains the approval of the knowledge management plan by the program sponsor, program manager, program management office, members of the governance board, and other key stakeholders as required.

Signatures and Date Approval Obtained

Program manager _____

Program sponsor _____

Program management office director _____

Governance board chairperson _____

Governance board member 1 _____

Governance board member 2 _____

Governance board member N _____

Stakeholder 1 _____

Stakeholder 2 _____

Stakeholder N _____

Chapter 6

The Delivery of Program Benefits Phase: Executing

> Good fortune is when opportunity meets with planning.
>
> — Thomas Alva Edison

Having said that plans are useless, but also that planning is tremendously important, now we talk about them coming together. But then we remember that as living documents, our plans and processes are designed to systematically evolve into desired reality.

It is useful to consider the delivery of program benefits phase, albeit just one phase, in two pieces—the executing part and the monitoring and controlling part. The bulk of program work is in the execution, the subject of this chapter.

Team Charter

A successful and motivated team is essential to success. A team can benefit greatly from a team charter, although it is not included in the *Standard for Program Management*—Second Edition (2008). This is true as it provides an agreed-upon model and standards for intrateam interactions not covered by other plans.

Program Management Life Cycle: Benefit Delivery

Figure 6.1   Audit report.

Team Charter Instructions

The team charter formalizes the program team members' roles and responsibilities. It provides guidelines for the team's operations. It describes the processes that the team will use to complete the program. It states the expectations to be met by the team members, such as the specific responsibilities regarding the program schedule. It includes procedures to resolve conflicts and describes how the team will plan the work, participate in making decisions, and communicate throughout the program. The team charter includes the following:

> **Purpose:** A brief introductory statement defining the purpose of the team charter, such as:
>
> The team charter states the team members' roles and responsibilities and provides guidelines for the team's operation throughout the life of the program. It describes actions and decisions the team can take on its own and escalation processes to follow as required.
>
> The team charter formalizes the program team members' roles and responsibilities. It provides guidelines for the team's operations. It describes the processes that the team will use to complete the program. It states the expectations to be met by the team members, such as the specific expectations regarding the program schedule. It includes procedures to resolve conflicts and describes how the team will plan the work, participate in making decisions, and communicate throughout the program.

Program commitment statement: This section describes the team's commitment to the program in terms of the team's desire to achieve the program's objectives and to be able to deliver the expected benefits of the program.

Program manager's role: The charter lists the program manager's name and describes how the team will interact with the program manager during the program. It contains specific roles and responsibilities of the various team members in terms of interaction with the program manager, recognizing that some team members will have more interaction than others.

Program sponsor's role: The charter lists the program sponsor's name and describes how the team will interact with the sponsor during the program.

Client's role: This section names the client and states how the program management team will interact with the client during the program.

Other stakeholders involved in the program: As described in the stakeholder management plan, a variety of stakeholders will be involved in the program at different times during the program's life cycle. This section describes the level of interaction of the program team members with the stakeholders during the program. A responsibility assignment matrix may be attached to this section.

Team performance objectives: This section describes specific performance objectives of the program team members during the program's life cycle. It links the performance objectives to the program's objectives.

Success measures: While there are overall success measures in terms of on time, within budget, and within specification delivery of the program's product, service, and result, this section describes specific success measures in terms of overall team performance.

Scope/boundaries of the team's work: This section builds on the scope management plan to describe any boundaries that may affect the work of the program team. It lists specific constraints and assumptions to be considered.

Deliverables: This section uses the program work breakdown structure and lists the various program packages. A responsibility assignment matrix may be attached to this section to show the roles and responsibilities of the program team members for the various deliverables.

Conflict management process: Recognizing that programs inevitably will have conflicts, this section describes a process to resolve conflicts that may exist among the team members. It notes how the team can resolve conflicts without the need to involve the program manager and states the process to follow if involvement from the program manager is required. It also describes how team members will learn of the conflict resolution. For example, if the conflict only involves a few team members, this section states whether the entire team should be included in the resolution method that is used.

Decision-making process: This section describes the process the team will follow to make program decisions. It states the types of decisions the team can make on its own without the need to involve the program manager and how these decisions will be communicated throughout the program and to relevant stakeholders according to the communications management plan. It also states when the program manager needs to be consulted before a decision is made and the circumstances when the team needs to escalate a decision to the program manager.

Administrative activities: Each program has a variety of administrative activities that must be performed for overall program success. This section states the roles and responsibilities of the team members in terms of these administrative activities. For example, it describes responsibilities in areas such as preparing agendas for various meetings, taking minutes, distributing action items, maintaining various logs and registers, updating plans and other documents, updating the knowledge management repository, and performing closeout tasks. A responsibility assignment matrix for these administrative activities may be attached to this section.

Issue escalation process: Issues are common in programs. In addition to use of the issue register to identify, track, monitor, and resolve issues, this section of the charter states the process the team will use to resolve issues on its own. It also states when issues should be raised to the program manager for consultation or for actual resolution.

Updates to the charter: This section states how often the charter will be reviewed to determine whether updates to it are required and who will be responsible for these updates. For example, if the conflict resolution process is not being followed or is not effective, the charter will require updates. As new members join the team, they may have ideas for changes to the charter, and as members leave the team, they should comment as to whether or not they feel changes to the charter are warranted.

Approvals: This section lists the approval of the team charter by the program sponsor, program manager, and each team member. When new team members join the team, they should sign the charter to indicate their commitment to it.

Team Charter Template

<Insert Program Name>
Team Charter

Program name:	
Program manager:	PM's email address here as a hyperlink
Program sponsor:	
Actual start date:	

Approved end date:	
Program no.:	
Revision history:	
Business unit:	

A. PURPOSE

A brief introductory statement defining the purpose of the team charter, such as:

> The team charter states the team members' roles and responsibilities and provides guidelines for the team's operation throughout the life of the program. It describes actions and decisions the team can take on its own and escalation processes to follow as required.

_____

_____

_____

B. PROGRAM COMMITMENT STATEMENT

This section describes the team's commitment to the program in terms of the team's desire to achieve program objectives and deliver the program's expected benefits.

_____

_____

_____

C. PROGRAM MANAGER'S ROLE

This section lists the program manager's name and describes how the team will interact with the program manager during the program.

_____

_____

_____

D. PROGRAM SPONSOR'S ROLE

This section states the program sponsor's role and describes how the team will interact with the sponsor during the program.

_____

_____

_____

E. CLIENT'S ROLE

This section names the client and states how the team will interact with the client during the program.

F. OTHER STAKEHOLDERS INVOLVED IN THE PROGRAM

This section describes the level of interaction of the program team members with the stakeholders during the program. A responsibility assignment matrix may be attached to this section.

G. TEAM PERFORMANCE OBJECTIVES

This section describes specific performance objectives of the team members during the program's life cycle to link these objectives to the overall program objectives.

H. SUCCESS MEASURES

This section describes specific success measures in terms of overall team performance.

I. SCOPE/BOUNDARIES OF THE TEAM'S WORK

This section describes any boundaries that may affect the work of the program team and lists specific constraints and assumptions to be considered.

J. DELIVERABLES

This section lists the various program packages in the program's work breakdown structure and shows the roles and responsibilities of the program team members to complete these deliverables. A responsibility assignment matrix may be attached.

_____
_____
_____

K. CONFLICT MANAGEMENT PROCESS

This section describes a process for use among the team to resolve conflicts without the need to involve the program manager and when involvement from the program manager is required. It also describes communication approaches to inform others of how conflicts were resolved.

_____
_____
_____

L. DECISION-MAKING PROCESS

This section describes the process the team will follow to make program decisions and states the types of decisions the team can make on its own without involvement from the program manager and when the program manager should be consulted or should make the decision. It describes how these decisions will be communicated following the communications management plan.

_____
_____
_____

M. ADMINISTRATIVE ACTIVITIES

This section states the roles and responsibilities of team members in terms of the program's administrative activities. A responsibility assignment matrix may be attached to this section.

_____
_____
_____

N. ISSUE ESCALATION PROCESS

This section states the process the team will use to resolve issues and when issues should be raised to the program manager for consultation or resolution.

O. UPDATES TO THE CHARTER

This section states how often the charter will be reviewed to assess its effectiveness and the process the team will follow to update it as needed.

P. APPROVALS

This section contains the approval of the team charter by the program sponsor, program manager, and each team member.

SIGNATURES AND DATE APPROVAL OBTAINED

Program manager _____

Program sponsor _____

Team member 1 _____

Team member 2 _____

Team member N _____

Audit Report

Audits provide important and more in-depth verification of actual program execution and performance. This report format can ensure completeness and consistency of the reports. They are prepared in the direct and manage program execution process.

Audit Report Instructions

The Audit Report (Figure 6.1) includes the following:

> **Purpose**—A brief introductory statement defining the purpose of the Audit Report such as:
>
> "The Audit Report presents an objective assessment of the performance of the program. The Report's findings and recommendations serve to enhance program effectiveness and ensure that the program benefits are being delivered as set forth in the benefit management plan and

that the program is being executed as stated in the program management plan."

Audits are common on programs. They are necessary for a number of reasons and should be viewed in a positive manner rather than considering them as necessary for compliance or for pinpointing specific problems and associating them to specific individuals. The Audit Report is an objective report of findings and provides recommended preventive or corrective actions to follow. It also is used to ensure program management processes are being followed and can be a way for checks and balances based on other views for governance decisions.

According to the In the Project Management Institute's *Standard for Program Management* - Second Edition (2008), the audit plan is an output to the Plan and Establish Program Governance Structure process and is an input to the Plan for Audits Process. The Audit Plan is an output of the Plan Program Audits Process and sets the stage for the report, which is an input to the following processes:

- Direct and Manage Program Execution
- Manage Program Issues

Background Information
   Time Period of the Audit: This section states the time the audit began and when the final report was prepared.
   Place: This section states where the audit was conducted.
   Audit Participants: This section states the names of the people on the audit team and provides their contact information for possible questions.
   Type of Audit: This section states the type of audit that was conducted: internal or external. Note whether the audit was conducted according to a schedule in the program's master schedule based on the Audit Plan or whether it was random.
   Reason for the Audit: This section describes why the audit was conducted such as to concentrate on a component that may be in trouble or because the overall program may be in trouble, to look at specific processes and procedures to see whether or not they are being followed, for compliance purposes with specific regulations or procedures, to examine the overall financial status of the program, to see if benefits are being realized as stated in the Benefits Realization Plan, or for other reasons.
   Program Areas Affected: This section describes the various areas of the program that were involved in the audit: e.g., the entire program or only certain components of it.
   Methodology: This section describes how the audit was conducted. For example, it notes whether documents were reviewed, interviews were held, surveys were used, focus groups were used, and/or other methods.

Findings: This section presents the findings from the audit. The findings should be presented in an objective way as they are the basis for the recommendations from the audit. They are the synthesis of all of the data that were reviewed. Findings should be carefully worded to reflect the audit team's observation, and they should be phrased as constructively presented problem statements. Appropriate background information that is needed to understand the findings should be included. Causes are observations that support the findings, and their identification is helpful in making constructive recommendations. Consequences list the problem results of a finding. Findings should represent issues for the entire program or for the components being audited and should have the broadest possible application.

Here is an example:

> *Finding (problem statement):* Each status report that is prepared involves development of completely new material.
> *Probable cause:* Reusable materials are not available.
> *Business consequence:* Reports that are prepared may not be completed on schedule or may not contain the information of interest to the program's stakeholders.
> *Recommendation:* Prepare a Communications Management Plan that describes the types of reports to prepare and provide to various program stakeholders and the data each report should include. Ask the Program Office to take the lead in providing a sample report template to use throughout the program.

In preparing findings, keep the specific audit goals and appraisal scope in mind. Avoid the following:

- Moot issues
- Findings based on hearsay alone
- Broad generalizations

Recommendations: This section states the recommendations based on the audit findings. Use categories if possible to group the recommendations and present them in priority order. If the audit is for compliance purposes, note if some of the recommendations are mandatory.

Appendices: Include appendices such as the following:

> **Persons Interviewed:** List the people who were interviewed during the audit and the date of each interview
> **Documents Reviewed:** List the documents that were reviewed during the audit

Approvals: This section contains the written approval of the Audit Report by the lead Auditor.

Audit Report Template

<Insert Program Name>
Audit Report

Program name:	
Program manager:	PM's email address here as a hyperlink
Program sponsor:	
Actual start date:	
Approved end date:	
Program no.:	
Revision history:	
Business unit:	

A. PURPOSE

A brief introductory statement defining the purpose of the Audit Report such as:

> "The Audit Report presents an objective assessment of the performance of the program. The Report's findings and recommendations serve to enhance program effectiveness and ensure that the program benefits are being delivered as set forth in the benefit management plan and that the program is being executed as stated in the program management plan."

B. BACKGROUND INFORMATION

This section provides background information about the audit. It should describe when the audit began and was completed; where the audit was conducted; who participated on the audit team, the type of audit that was conducted, the reason the audit was conducted, and the program areas involved in the audit.

C. METHODOLOGY

This section describes how the audit was conducted.

D. FINDINGS

This section presents the findings from the audit.

_____

_____

_____

E. RECOMMENDATIONS

This section states the recommendations based on the audit findings, in priority order, with notes if there are any mandatory recommendations if the audit was conducted for compliance purposes.

_____

_____

_____

F. APPENDICES

This section lists appendices such as the name of people who were interviewed and the documents that were reviewed.

_____

_____

_____

G. APPROVALS

This section contains the approval of the Audit Report by the lead Auditor.

SIGNATURES AND DATE APPROVAL OBTAINED

Lead Auditor   _____

Decision Log

Significant decisions should be recorded. Decisions and the "whys" of those decisions are sometimes forgotten, often leading to disastrous decision reversals, neglect of important reversals, or do-loop iterations of the same "new" decision. In some cases, your customer may force you to implement a poor decision, and this log is your chance to document that fact and your reservations. The latter case is sometimes known elsewhere in organizations as a memorandum for record. This log is prepared in the direct and manage program execution process of *Standard for Program Management*—Second Edition (2008).

Decision Log Instructions

Purpose: The decision log is used throughout the program by the program manager to document the major program decisions. In some organizations, it may be called a memorandum for record. The program manager should decide the level of detail to include in this log. The log is especially useful on large programs in which information about a particular decision made early in the program requires later review or where decisions are forced upon the program managers, for example, by the customer. The log also is helpful if someone else is assigned later as the program manager. The log should be part of the program's final records, as it can serve as an excellent source of lessons learned for future programs.

In the Project Management Institute's *Standard for Program Management*—Second Edition (2008), the decision logs are a tool and technique in the direct and manage program execution process. This decision log is designed as a table, and a description of its contents follows.

1. **Decision number:** Provide a number for the decision for tracking purposes.
2. **PWBS number:** Link the decision to a PWBS program package.
3. **Decision description:** Describe the actual decision and what is to be done. Provide sufficient detail for future use.
4. **Background information:** Provide background information as to why the decision was needed. Examples include escalated risk by a component manager to the program manager, or the program manager to the governance board, issue to be resolved, customer request for additional work to be done, lack of realization of benefits as described in the benefits realization plan, capacity problem, missed deliverable, need to add a new component to the program, need to terminate an existing component in the program, phase gate review, program performance review, or an audit recommendation.
5. **Decision maker:** List the decision maker and his or her contact information.
6. **Implementation date:** State the date the decision is to be implemented.
7. **Assigned to:** State the person who is responsible for implementing the decision and his or her contact information.
8. **Actual implementation date:** State the actual date the decision was implemented. Provide information if there is a variance between the actual date and the planned date.
9. **Notes:** Use this field for any additional notes about the decision.

Decision Log Template

Decision No.	PWBS No.	Decision Description	Background Information	Decision Maker	Implementation Date	Assigned to	Actual Implementation Date	Notes

Component Initiation Request

Programs consist of projects as well as management effort and infrastructure—known generically as components. Can just anyone at any time declare a new project to begin using up limited resources? Let's hope not! Business partners can even disagree on whether they agreed to start a project. Decisions regarding new components are best handled through a component initiation form so there is no uncertainty. This form is prepared in the direct and manage program execution process in the *Standard for Program Management*—Second Edition (2008).

Component Initiation Request Instructions

The component initiation request includes the following:

Purpose: A brief introductory statement defining the purpose of the component initiation request, such as:

The component initiation request describes the need, feasibility, and justification for the component to be part of the program.

Components include both projects and nonproject or operations work that is part of the program. In most cases, the program manager prepares the component initiation request with input from other key stakeholders and the program sponsor. It may be provided by the client or the funding organization. Approval by the governance board typically is required. It serves as the mandate for the component to be part of the program.

While some components already are under way when the program is initiated, other components will become part of the program at different phases in the life cycle, except during the closing phase. They are generally included in the program road map and the program management plan, with explicit criteria to show when components are to be initiated. As the work on the program ensues, other components that were not previously identified may be needed. The component initiation request is a document to secure formal approval for program components. Components to be part of the program must meet the organization's approved selection criteria. These criteria typically are stated in the program's governance plan. Once approved, a charter for the component is prepared and approved, a project manager or operations manager is assigned, and the work begins.

In the Project Management Institute's *Standard for Program Management*—Second Edition (2008), component initiation requests are an input to approve component initiation.

Component business case: Each component requires a business case to show how its expected benefits will be more significant if it is part of the program rather than managed as a stand-alone project or operational activity. This section describes the business case for the component. The component's expected results should complement those of the program and should be aligned with the organization's strategic plan and goals. The component also may be interrelated in various ways to other components in the program. Its financial indices must be detailed along with internal and external interfaces. If feasibility studies or alternative analyses were conducted, they should be noted in this section.

Project manager or operations manager: This section identifies the project manager or operations manager for the component and provides contact information.

Component sponsor: This section identifies the sponsor for the component and provides his or her contact information. In most cases the sponsor is the program manager.

Stakeholder communications: Once a component is approved to be part of the program, stakeholders will need to be notified. This section states those stakeholders who will have an active role with the component, will influence the outcome of the component, or will be interested in certain aspects of the component, and describes how these stakeholders will be notified of component approval.

Component governance structure: While the program has a governance management plan and uses a governance board, components also require a governance structure at the program level. This section states the processes and procedures to be used to monitor and track component progress. It describes gate reviews and performance reviews to be held and specifies status reports to be prepared at the component level. It also notes that audits may be conducted at scheduled and nonscheduled times.

Resource requirements: This section provides a high-level estimate of the resources required for the component. It may be necessary to transfer resources from existing components already under way in the program to the proposed component, especially if it has a higher priority than that of the existing work. This section states why the various resources are needed and when resources need to be available.

Change requests: Once a component is approved, change requests will be required. This section states the various change requests that will be needed for the specific component when it is approved.

Program documentation changes: Each time a new component is approved, program documents will require updates as noted by change requests. This section describes each of the program documents that will be updated and states the program team member who is responsible and when the updates are scheduled to be completed.

Approvals: This section contains the written approval of the component initiation request by the program manager, program sponsor, program management office, members of the program's governance board, or any other key stakeholders as appropriate.

Component Initiation Request Template

<Insert Program Name>
Component Initiation Request

Program name:	
Program manager:	PM's email address here as a hyperlink
Program sponsor:	
Proposed component start date:	
Proposed component end date:	
Date prepared:	
Revision history:	
Business unit:	

A. PURPOSE

A brief introductory statement defining the purpose of the component initiation request, such as:

> The component initiation request describes the need, feasibility, and justification for the component to be part of the program.

_____
_____
_____

B. COMPONENT BUSINESS CASE

This section describes the business case for the component and describes why it is more effective to include this component in the program rather than managing it as a stand-alone project or operational activity.

_____
_____
_____

C. PROJECT MANAGER OR OPERATIONS MANAGER

This section states the name of the project manager or operations manager and provides his or her contact information.

D. COMPONENT SPONSOR

This section identifies the sponsor for the component and provides contact information.

E. STAKEHOLDER COMMUNICATIONS

This section states those stakeholders who will be notified when the component initiation request is approved.

F. COMPONENT GOVERNANCE STRUCTURE

This section describes the governance structure for the program's components.

G. RESOURCE REQUIREMENTS

This section provides a high-level estimate of the resources required for the component and describes why they are needed and when they need to be available.

H. CHANGE REQUESTS

This section states the various change requests that will be needed when the component is approved.

I. PROGRAM DOCUMENTATION CHANGES

This section describes each of the program documents that will be updated when the component is approved, the program team member who is responsible for the update, and when it is expected to be completed.

J. APPROVALS

This section contains the approval of the component initiation request by the program manager, program sponsor, program management office, members of the program's governance board, and other key stakeholders as required.

SIGNATURES AND DATE APPROVAL OBTAINED

Program manager   _____

Program sponsor   _____

Governance board member 1   _____

Governance board member 2   _____

Governance board member N   _____

Stakeholder 1   _____

Stakeholder 2   _____

Stakeholder N   _____

Component Transition Request

As noted, various components will be initiated during a program. These components will transition to ongoing operations, such as to a product or customer support group, to customers, or to users at different times during the course of the program. The governance board will approve the requests to transition these components. This request is prepared in the direct and manage program execution process in the *Standard for Program Management*—Second Edition (2008), and the decision from the governance board is made during the approve component transition process.

Component Transition Request Instructions

The component transition request includes the following:

Purpose: A brief introductory statement defining the purpose of the component transition request, such as:

> The component transition request shows that the component's benefits have been realized, and the component should be transitioned to ongoing operations.

Components include both projects and nonproject or operations work that is part of the program. Different components will finish ahead of others as noted by completion of project deliverables, completion of program-level milestones, and achievement of benefits.

In most cases, the project manager or operations manager prepares the component transition request with input from other key stakeholders and the program manager. It may be provided by the client or the funding organization. The governance board typically approves this request. It serves as the mandate to ensure the knowledge, responsibilities, and benefits are ready to be handed over to ongoing operations.

It is noted that components also will transition from one phase in their life cycle to another. This form, though, is used for formal approval for component closure, rather than for approval to transition to the next phase in the life cycle, as that is covered as part of the program's governance procedures. This transition is the last phase in the component's life cycle.

This form is not used to terminate a component when it is apparent that the component does not support the program's objectives and does not contribute to the program's benefits; termination is handled by a termination request.

In the Project Management Institute's *Standard for Program Management—Second Edition* (2008), the component transition request is an output of the direct and manage program execution process. It is an input to the monitor and control program scope process and to the approve component transition process, as during the process, the decision to transition the component is made. In making this decision, the benefits realization report is consulted. Component closure notification is an input to the close procurement process to show additional procurements will not be required.

Reasons for request: This section describes the reasons for the transition request. For example, the component has achieved its specific benefits, it has completed all of its deliverables, or it has met all program-level milestones.

Resources released: Once the component transition request is approved, resources can be reallocated to other parts of the program or to the performing organization. This section states the available resources for planning purposes by the program manager, program sponsor, and portfolio manager, as appropriate.

Closure requirements: In order for the component to transition to ongoing operations, the program's closing policies and procedures must be met. This section states that all closure activities are complete, such as archiving records, returning customer property, and documenting lessons learned, as defined by the program management plan and governance plan.

Stakeholder communications: Each component will have its own stakeholders, in addition to stakeholders at the program level. This section describes how the affected or interested stakeholders will learn that the component is formally closed.

Change requests: Once a component is approved for transition, change requests will be required. This section states the various change requests that will be needed as a result of approval of the transition request.

Program documentation changes: This section states the requirements to update program-level documentation because of a component transition request, such as the program management plan, program resource plan, decision log, and program road map. It describes the program management team member who is responsible for updating the artifacts and the planned date the updates will be completed.

Project completion closure certificate: This section describes who will prepare the certificate noting that project completion has occurred and who must sign off on it once the transition request is approved.

Approvals: This section contains the written approval of the component transition request by the program manager, program sponsor, members of the program's governance board, or any other key stakeholders as appropriate.

Component Transition Request Template

<Insert Program Name>
Component Transition Request

Program name:	
Program manager:	PM's email address here as a hyperlink
Project or operations manager:	
Program sponsor:	
Component start date:	
Proposed component end date:	
Date prepared:	
Prepared by:	

A. PURPOSE

A brief introductory statement defining the purpose of the component transition request, such as:

> The component transition request shows that the component's benefits have been realized, and the component should be transitioned to ongoing operations.

_____

_____

_____

B. REASONS FOR REQUEST

This section describes the reasons for the transition request.

_____

_____

_____

C. RESOURCES RELEASED

This section states the resources that will be released once the transition request is approved in order that they may be used on other program components or elsewhere in the organization.

_____

_____

_____

D. CLOSURE REQUIREMENTS

This section describes the program's closure requirements for its components to ensure that all of them have been completed.

_____

_____

_____

E. STAKEHOLDER COMMUNICATIONS

This section states those stakeholders who will be notified when the component transition request is approved.

_____

_____

_____

F. CHANGE REQUESTS

This section describes the change requests that will be needed once the transition request is approved.

_____
_____
_____

G. PROGRAM DOCUMENTATION CHANGES

This section describes each of the program documents that will be updated when the component transition request is approved, the program management team member who is responsible for the update, and when it is expected to be completed.

_____
_____
_____

H. PROGRAM COMPLETION CLOSURE CERTIFICATE

This section states who will prepare the certificate noting the completion has occurred and who must sign off on it.

_____
_____
_____

I. APPROVALS

This section contains the approval of the component transition request by the program manager, program sponsor, members of the program's governance board, and other key stakeholders as required.

SIGNATURES AND DATE APPROVAL OBTAINED

Program manager	_____
Program sponsor	_____
Governance board member 1	_____
Governance board member 2	_____
Governance board member N	_____
Stakeholder 1	_____
Stakeholder 2	_____
Stakeholder N	_____

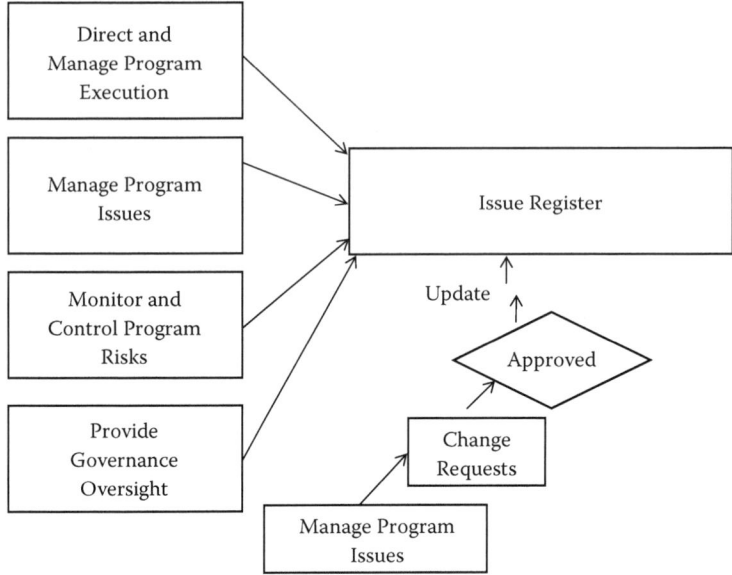

Program Management Life Cycle: Program Setup and Delivery of Program Benefits

---

Figure 6.2   Program issues register.

Program Issues Register

This register (Figure 6.2) provides a format for recording and reporting program issues and is prepared during the direct and manage program execution process in the *Standard for Program Management*—Second Edition (2008).

Program Issues Register Instructions

Purpose: The program issues register is used whenever there are program issues that require resolution. An issue is defined by the *Standard for Program Management*—Second Edition (2008) as an unplanned event, concern, or dispute. It may have consequences to the program's scope, schedule, cost, quality, and other areas as appropriate.

The program issues register, also known as an issue log, identifies each issue and then shows how it was resolved, and the people who were involved in the process. Issues may be identified by any program stakeholder. Issues at the program level may be ones that are escalated to the program manager for resolution by project managers. At the program level, the issues register shows whether an issue identified by a project manager affects other projects or nonproject work in the program. Regardless of the person who identified the issue, the issues register also shows whether the issue impacts other programs, projects, or work under way in the organization. Note that the issues register does not replace the need for a risk register.

Certain issues can be handled by the program manager; others require involvement by other stakeholders, or may need resolution by the governance board. Often, the decisions regarding program issues lead to the need to revise other planning documents or to take corrective actions. If this is the case, a change request should be used. Issue reviews should be conducted on a periodic basis, and the issues register is a key document when these reviews are held to show the status of identified issues and their resolution. The program issues register is designed as a table, and a description of its contents follows.

1. **Issue identification number:** Assign an identification number to the issue.
2. **PWBS number:** Link the issue to the corresponding program package in the program work breakdown structure.
3. **Issue description:** Describe the issue and why it is significant to the program.
4. **Identified by:** List the person who identified the issue and provide contact information.
5. **Date:** State the date the issue was identified and added to the register.
6. **Issue type:** Describe the type of issue. Examples include:
    a. Internal: Resources, schedule, scope, cost, quality, program architecture, contracts
    b. External: Environmental, political, ethical
7. **Root cause:** Describe the root cause of the issue in order to determine needed preventive action for the future and corrective action for this issue.
8. **Issue impact:** State the impact of the issue to the program. Examples include:
    a. Impacts other projects in the program
    b. Impacts other projects or programs under way in the organization
    c. Impacts the organization's strategic plan
    d. Impacts areas outside of the organization
9. **Issue owner:** Identify a member of the program management team to be responsible for the issue and to track it until it is resolved and closed. Provide contact information for the owner.
10. **Proposed resolution:** State the proposed resolution of the issue, such as the corrective action that is required. Recognize that the issue owner may need to work with the person who identified the issue and other stakeholders to determine an appropriate way to resolve the issue so it has minimal impacts to the program and other areas.

11. **Decision:** State whether the proposed resolution was approved, deferred, or rejected.
12. **Resolved by:** State who resolved the issue. Examples include:
    a. Issue owner
    b. Program manager
    c. Governance board

    Note whether the issue was resolved as proposed or whether a different approach was approved; if the latter, state the approach to resolve the issue.

    Recognize that a change request will need to be used to implement the resolution.
13. **Date:** State the date the issue was resolved.
14. **Subsequent impacts:** State any subsequent impacts as a result of resolving the issue. Examples include the need to modify the scope of the program, change processes and procedures used by the program, add resources, modify plans, modify program benefits, or change stakeholder expectations.
15. **Date closed:** State the date the resolution to the issue was implemented to close the issue.
16. **Notes:** Use this field for any additional notes about the issue.

Issue Register

Issue ID #	PWBS #	Issue Description	Identified By	Date	Issue Type	Root Cause	Issue Impact

Issue Owner	Proposed Resolution	Decision	Resolved By	Date	Subsequent impacts	Date Closed	Notes

Change Request Log

A detailed list of all changes, whether approved, rejected, deferred, or modified, must be maintained. It is prepared in the Distribute Information process in the *Standard for Program Management*—Second Edition (2008).

Change Request Log Instructions

Purpose: The change request log is used throughout the program to record changes as they are identified, and to describe the status of the request.

It is inevitable that programs will have changes throughout the program life cycle. The component projects also will have changes. Each project should manage its changes and report them to the program management team, especially if it seems as if the project change will affect the program. Changes should be tracked until they are approved, deferred, or rejected. Once a decision is made concerning the change, then the person who requested the change should be notified. If the change is implemented, its status should continue to be tracked through this log until the implementation is complete. It is important to ensure that the benefits to be realized through the program are not compromised by the change.

This change request log complements the program's change management plan. In the Project Management Institute's *Standard for Program*

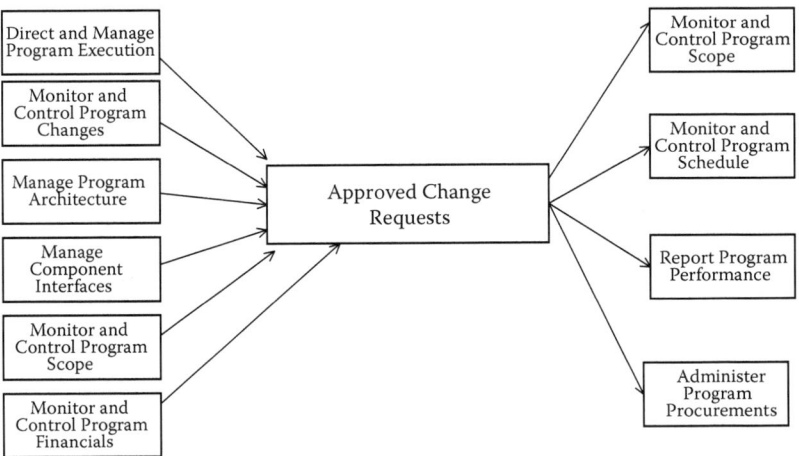

Program Management Life Cycle: Program Initiation, Program Setup, and Delivery of Program Benefits

Figure 6.3 Approved change requests.

Management—Second Edition (2008), the change request log is an input to the following processes:

- Distribute information
- Monitor and control program changes

Change request log updates are an output of the monitor and control program changes process.

Change requests are an input to the following processes:

- Direct and manage program execution
- Develop program requirements
- Manage program architecture
- Manage component interfaces
- Monitor and control program financials
- Monitor and control program changes

Change requests are an output of the following processes:

- Plan program risk responses
- Approve component initiation
- Manage program benefits
- Manage program issues

Approved change requests are an input to:

- Monitor and control program scope
- Monitor and control program schedule
- Report program performance
- Administer program procurements

Approved change requests are outputs from the following processes:

- Direct and manage program execution
- Monitor and control program changes
- Manage program architecture
- Manage component interfaces
- Monitor and control program scope
- Monitor and control program financials

The change request log is designed as a table, and a description of its contents follows:

1. **Change identification number:** Assign a change number to the change request.
2. **PWBS number:** Link the change to the corresponding program package in the program work breakdown structure.
3. **Change description:** Describe the change and why it is significant to the program.
4. **Requested by:** List the person who requested the change and provide contact information.
5. **Date:** State the date the change was requested and added to the log.
6. **Change type:** Describe the type of change. Use the types identified in the change management plan, such as one involving technical aspects or the program's scope, schedule, cost, or contracts.
7. **Priority/severity:** Describe the priority of the change request, such as emergency, urgent, high, medium, or low. Note the severity, such as catastrophic, major, minor, or an enhancement.
8. **Change impact:** State the impact of this change to the program. Note the configuration items identified in the change management plan that are affected.
9. **Cost:** Describe the expected cost of the change.
10. **Level of effort:** State the level of effort required to implement the change if it is approved. Note whether the program's schedule will require revision, the other program management processes that will require revision, and whether any new program components will be needed or existing components terminated.
11. **Feasibility:** Describe the feasibility of implementing the change, such as technical, environmental, economic, or ethical.
12. **Risk/opportunity:** Describe the risks associated with implementing the change to the program or the opportunity associated with implementing the change.
13. **Change owner:** Identify a member of the program management team to be responsible for ensuring that the change request is reviewed, that its impact on the program is analyzed, that it is submitted to the appropriate person for resolution, that once a decision is made on the change the decision is communicated to the requestor, and, if the change is approved, that this team member continues to track the change until its implementation is complete.
14. **Proposed resolution:** State the proposed resolution of the change after the change impact analysis has been conducted, such as approved, deferred, or rejected.
15. **Decision:** State whether the proposed resolution was finally approved, deferred, or rejected.

16. **Decision maker and actual resolution:** State who made the decision concerning the change request. Examples include:
    a. Change owner
    b. Program manager
    c. Change control board
    d. Governance board

    Note if the change is approved, whether the proposed implementation of it is to be followed or whether a different implementation process is to be used.

    If the decision was to defer the change, continue to keep it on the log until it is either approved or rejected.
17. **Date:** State the date the change request was approved, deferred, or rejected.
18. **Subsequent impacts:** State any subsequent impacts on other controlled or configuration items (see the change management plan) as a result of implementation of this change request.
19. **Date closed:** State the date the change was implemented.
20. **Notes:** Use this field for any additional notes about the change.

Change Request Log

Change ID #	PWBS #	Change Description	Requested By	Date	Change Type	Priority/ Severity	Change Impact	Cost	Level of Effort

Feasibility	Risk/ Oportunity	Change Owner	Proposed Resolution	Decision	Decision Maker and Actual Resolution	Date	Subsequent Impacts	Date Closed	Notes

Component Charter

A component charter is recommended since programs contain more than just projects.

Component Charter Instructions

Purpose: A brief introductory statement defining the purpose of the charter, such as:

> The component charter states the purpose of the component and shows how the component fits into the overall program. It also states the component manager's authority and responsibility and formally authorizes the component.

Components may be projects, nonproject work, or a set of projects and subprojects. Each component requires a charter before it begins work. It is prepared once the component is officially initiated. This charter then guides the work of the component and supports the overall program charter. Although it is prepared when the component is approved, it may need updates as work progresses during the life cycle or when other components are added to the program or are completed or terminated.

In the Project Management Institute's *Standard for Program Management—Second Edition* (2008), it is an input to the approve component initiation process and to the distribute information process.

If the component was under way before the program began and then became part of the program, its existing charter should be reviewed to see whether changes are required to support the program's vision, objectives, and benefits. During the program, status reports on the progress of each component are prepared.

Component objectives: Each component will have certain objectives. This section describes how the component's objectives support the overall program objectives.

Component expected benefits: Components provide benefits, and as they are managed in a program structure, the incremental benefits from all of the components typically are greater than if the component was managed individually as a project or as nonproject work. This section describes the benefits to be realized by the component and how the component's benefits fit within the program's benefits realization plan.

Component deliverables: This section lists specific deliverables in terms of products, services, and results to be provided by the component. The component requirements documents are inputs to the develop program WBS process. Scope statements for each component are considered during the plan program procurements process, with cost estimates an input to the conduct procurements process for the program. Component milestones are part of the program's schedule. Any risks associated with completing these deliverables should be identified for inclusion in the program's risk identification process, with component risk responses considered in the program's risk response process.

Component stakeholders: Since stakeholder management is essential for effective program management, this section lists the key stakeholders who may be involved in, have an interest in, or have an influence concerning the specific component. Component stakeholder management guidelines are an input to the manage component interfaces process, and they are developed during the plan program stakeholder management process.

Component constraints: Constraints are factors that limit the options of the project team. This section lists constraints that may affect the component.

Related program assumptions: Assumptions are factors that the project team considers to be true, real, or certain in planning the program. This section lists the assumptions that may affect the component.

Component manager's authority: The charter should name the component manager and describe his or her authority and responsibilities, especially in terms of being able to apply resources to the component.

Approvals: This section lists the approvals of the component charter by the component manager, program manager, program sponsor, members of the governance board, and other stakeholders as required.

Component Charter Template

<Insert Program Name>
Component Charter

Program name:	
Component manager:	Email address here as a hyperlink
Program manager:	
Program sponsor:	
Actual start date:	
Approved end date:	
Program no.:	
Revision history:	
Business unit:	

A. PURPOSE

A brief introductory statement defining the purpose of the component charter, such as:

> The component charter states the purpose of the component and shows how the component fits into the overall program. It also states the component manager's authority and responsibility and formally authorizes the component.

_____
_____
_____

B. COMPONENT OBJECTIVES

This section describes how the component's objectives support the overall program objectives.

_____
_____
_____

C. COMPONENT EXPECTED BENEFITS

This section describes the benefits to be realized by the component and states how the component's benefits fit within the program's benefits realization plan.

_____
_____
_____

D. COMPONENT DELIVERABLES

This section lists specific deliverables in terms of products, services, and results to be provided by the component.

_____
_____
_____

E. COMPONENT STAKEHOLDERS

This section lists the key stakeholders who may be involved in, have an interest in, or have influence concerning the specific component.

_____
_____
_____

F. COMPONENT CONSTRAINTS

This section lists the constraints that may affect the component.

_____
_____
_____

G. RELATED PROGRAM ASSUMPTIONS

This section lists any assumptions from the component that may affect the program.

_____
_____
_____

H. COMPONENT MANAGER'S AUTHORITY

This section names the component manager and describes his or her authority and responsibilities, especially in terms of being able to apply resources to the component.

_____
_____
_____

I. APPROVALS

This section lists the approvals of the component charter by the component manager, program manager, program sponsor, program management office, members of the governance board, and other stakeholders as required.

SIGNATURES AND DATE APPROVAL OBTAINED

Component manager	_____
Program manager	_____
Program sponsor	_____
Program management office director	_____
Governance board chairperson	_____
Governance board member 1	_____
Governance board member 2	_____
Governance board member N	_____
Stakeholder 1	_____
Stakeholder 2	_____
Stakeholder N	_____

Chapter 7

The Delivery of Program Benefits Phase: Monitoring and Controlling

> Drive thy business, let not that drive thee.
> —Benjamin Franklin

We now turn to the smaller but certainly no less important part of this phase—the business of monitoring and controlling. Strongly motivated to run our program rather than having it run us, we can put the following items to work.

Impact Analysis

This analysis tool is helpful in the overall process of monitoring and controlling the program as it facilitates the complete analysis and documentation of proposed changes. While the impact analysis referenced in the index, this item is not included in the *Standard for Program Management*—Second Edition (2008). Appearing quite useful in certain circumstances, we include it here.

227

Impact Analysis Instructions

The impact analysis includes the following:

> **Purpose:** A brief introductory statement defining the purpose of the impact analysis, such as:
>
> The impact analysis describes the factors involved in a program change and is used to explain the decision regarding the change request.
>
> The impact analysis provides information regarding the change decision, and it considers the program benefits associated with each change. It also is important to recognize that changes may be accepted, deferred, modified, or rejected. The impact analysis, therefore, supports the program's change management plan and change log. Decisions are communicated to stakeholders following the program communications management plan and information distribution process.
>
> The impact analysis is used in other aspects of the program and by various program components.
>
> **Type of change:** This section lists the type of change in order that its decision then can be communicated to the stakeholders who are interested. In completing this part of the template, the program management team should refer to the types of changes listed in the change management plan.
>
> **Factors involved in the change:** This section lists the factors involved in the change. For example, a change initially may be viewed as one that affects only one component in the program. When the change request form is prepared and it is analyzed, however, this change may be one that affects multiple components, deliverables, and program benefits. It also may affect other programs or projects under way in the organization. Additionally, it may affect some of the key processes and procedures used in program management in the organization.
>
> **Effect on common objectives:** This section lists the effect on common objectives at the program level because of the impact analysis. It considers both managerial and technical objectives. This section further considers the interdependencies between program components as well as the impact on the overall strategic objectives.
>
> **Change decision:** Based on the information provided, changes may be approved, deferred until a later date, modified, or rejected. The person or persons responsible for making the decision concerning the change also may request additional information. This section states the change decision.
>
> **Approving authority:** This section lists the person or persons who made the decision regarding the change. The program manager may make this decision

Delivery of Program Benefits Phase: Monitoring and Controlling ■ 229

on his or her own, it may be referred to the governance board, or it may be referred to a configuration management board or change control board.

Communication of the change decision: Based on the program communications management plan and the stakeholder management plan, certain stakeholders will have an interest in the impact analysis. This section describes those stakeholders who should be notified based on the topic of the change.

Change requests: As part of the impact analysis, change requests will need to be issued. Many of these changes, for example, will require updating the program management plan and perhaps the change management plan. They may require an update to the program work breakdown structure, schedule, financial plan, and others.

Approvals: This section contains the written approval of the impact analysis by the program manager, program sponsor, members of the governance board or similar group, and any other key stakeholders as appropriate.

Impact Analysis Template

<Insert Program Name>
Impact Analysis

Program name:	
Program sponsor:	
Program manager:	PM's email address here as a hyperlink
Actual start date:	
Approved end date:	
Program no.:	
Revision history:	
Business unit:	

A. PURPOSE

A brief introductory statement defining the purpose of the impact analysis, such as:

> The impact analysis describes the factors involved in a program change and is used to explain the decision regarding the change request.

___
___
___

B. TYPE OF CHANGE

This section provides a description of the type of change in order that its decision can be communicated to appropriate stakeholders.

_____
_____
_____

C. FACTORS INVOLVED IN THE CHANGE

This section lists the factors involved in the change.

_____
_____
_____

D. EFFECT ON COMMON OBJECTIVES

This section lists the effect on common objectives at the program level because of the impact analysis.

_____
_____
_____

E. TYPE OF CHANGE DECISION

This section states the change decision.

_____
_____
_____

F. APPROVING AUTHORITY

This section lists the person or persons who made the decision regarding the change.

_____
_____
_____

G. COMMUNICATION OF THE CHANGE DECISION

This section describes those stakeholders who should be notified based on the topic of the change.

_____
_____
_____

H. CHANGE REQUESTS

This section describes the need for any change requests based on the impact analysis.

_____

_____

_____

I. APPROVALS

This section contains the approval of the impact analysis by the program manager, program sponsor, members of the governance board, and any other key stakeholders.

SIGNATURES AND DATE APPROVAL OBTAINED

Program manager	_____
Program sponsor	_____
Governance board member 1	_____
Governance board member 2	_____
Governance board member N	_____
Stakeholder 1	_____
Stakeholder 2	_____
Stakeholder N	_____

Benefits Realization Report

This report specifies progress toward achieving benefits and correlates related expenditures. This report is important in the report program performance and manage program benefits processes in the *Standard for Program Management*—Second Edition (2008).

Benefits Realization Report Instructions

The benefits realization report includes the following:

> **Purpose:** A brief introductory statement defining the purpose of the benefits realization report, such as:
>
> > The benefits realization report describes the benefits realized to date to ensure that they are aligned with the program's business case and benefits realization plan.

Programs are established to achieve benefits that may not be realized if its components were managed individually. Benefits realization and benefits management together are keys to a successful program. Benefits have value when they are used in the organization. Stakeholders on every program are interested in the progress of the program in terms of its realization of benefits.

Since the program components will deliver benefits at different times, the benefits realization report needs to be prepared and issued on a regular basis so stakeholders are informed of progress and to see whether any corrective or preventive actions are required. The benefits realization report should track to the benefits realization plan.

In the Project Management Institute's *Standard for Program Management—Second Edition* (2008), it is an output of the report program performance process and complements the other outputs of this process, namely, status reports, forecasts, and communications messages. As an output of the manage program benefits process, it helps the program manager, program sponsor, and members of the governance board track benefits delivery.

The following are the recommended contents for the benefits realization report:

Background information:
   Program overview: This section presents a brief overview of the program in terms of the benefits that are expected to be realized based on the benefits realization plan and to ensure that the benefits remain aligned with the business case.
   Reporting period: This section states the reporting period for the report. A monthly report is recommended, with ad hoc communications as required when benefits are achieved before the report is formally issued.
   Prepared by: This section provides contact information for the program management team member who prepared the report.
Benefits realized during the reporting period:
   Quantitative benefits: This section states the quantitative benefits that were realized during the reporting period in conjunction with the program's business case and its objectives. It describes when the benefits realization starts in terms of transfer to ongoing operations. It also states quantifiable measures of success, such as an increase in productivity, market share, or profits; improvements over those of the competition; net present value; shareholder value added, return on investment; benefit-cost; extent of rework required; product conformance with requirements; and customer acceptance of deliverables.
   Qualitative benefits: This section states qualitative benefits such as customer satisfaction, team satisfaction, use of processes and procedures, value of program management tools used, strategic importance,

impact of the deliverables on the organization, validity of the program vision, effect of technology in terms of benefit achievement, and the involvement of team members in performance improvement initiatives. It is necessary to then describe these qualitative benefits in quantitative terms.

Benefits not realized during the reporting period: This section states those benefits that were expected to be realized during the reporting period but were not completed according to the benefits delivery schedule in the benefits realization plan. It describes any corrective actions that are required in order to meet the delivery schedule so that actions can be taken for successful benefits delivery. Corrective action may lead to the need to add new components, make revisions to existing components, or terminate a component.

New benefits: This section states any new benefits from existing components that now have led to a need to revise the benefits realization plan. It describes any interdependencies between these new benefits and those already identified in the plan. This section also states who is responsible to ensure that these benefits are realized and delivered as planned.

Approvals: This section contains the written approval of the benefits realization report by the program manager, program sponsor, members of the governance board, and any other key stakeholders as appropriate.

Benefits Realization Report Template

Background Information		
Program Overview	*Reporting Period*	*Prepared by*

Benefits Realized during the Reporting Period	
Quantitative Benefits	
Benefit Description	*Date Realized*

Qualitative Benefits	
Benefit Description	Date Realized

Benefits Not Realized during the Reporting Period	
Benefit Description	Planned Corrective Action

New Benefits	
Benefit Description	Assigned to

Approvals	
Program manager	Date
Program sponsor	Date
Program management office director	Date
Governance board chairperson	Date

Governance board member 1	Date
Governance board member 2	Date
Governance board member N	Date
Stakeholder 1	Date
Stakeholder 2	Date
Stakeholder N	Date

Governance Decision Register

The *Standard for Program Management*—Second Edition (2008) does not specify the format for recording governance decisions, but rather mentions several general formats, especially in the provide governance oversight process. The importance and impact of such decisions requires that they be clearly recorded and socialized. Here, we present one proposed format (Figure 7.1).

Governance Decision Register Instructions

Purpose: The governance decision register is used throughout the program by the governance board to document the program decisions made at each meeting of the board. It should be included with the minutes of the board and distributed to stakeholders as described in the governance management plan and the program communications management plan. This register then is reviewed at subsequent meetings of the governance board. It is also useful to show progress in terms of meeting the program's objectives and to ensure they remain aligned with the organization's strategic objectives. Each decision

Decision #	PWBS #	Board Meeting Date	Purpose of the Board Meeting	Decision Description	Background Information	Phase in the Life Cycle

Implementation Date	Assigned To	Actual Implementation Date	Notes

Figure 7.1 Governance decision register.

documented in the register is used to help improve overall program results. Change requests may be required based on the type of decision and its impact on the program. These decisions, for example, may lead to a need to revise the governance management plan and the program management plan.

The governance decision register is helpful should members of the governance board change during the life of the program. The decision register should be part of the program's final records, as it can serve as an excellent source of lessons learned for future programs.

In the Project Management Institute's *Standard for Program Management—Second Edition* (2008), governance decisions is an input to the distribute information processes and the governance decision register is an output of the provide governance oversight process.

This governance decision register is designed as a table, and a description of its contents follows:

1. **Decision number:** Provide a number for the decision for tracking purposes.
2. **PWBS number:** Link the decision to a PWBS program package.
3. **Board meeting date:** State the date of the governance board meeting.
4. **Purpose of the board meeting:** Describe the purpose of the board meeting, such as a phase gate review, overall program performance review, a meeting to initiate or terminate components, or an overall review of the effectiveness of the governance management plan.
5. **Decision description:** Describe the actual decision and what is to be done. Provide sufficient detail for future use.
6. **Background information:** Provide background information as to why the decision was needed. Examples include escalated risk, issue, or audit recommendation by the program manager to the governance board; a requirement for approval to move to the next phase in the program's life cycle; to determine changes to ensure expected benefits are being realized; to determine whether new components should be added to the program or existing components terminated; to determine whether changes are required in program management so that best practices are followed; or to ensure that the program's strategic objectives remain in alignment with the organization's strategic objectives.
7. **Phase in the program management life cycle:** List the phase in the program management life cycle for this meeting of the governance board.
8. **Implementation date:** State the date the decision is to be implemented.
9. **Assigned to:** State the person who is responsible for implementing the decision and his or her contact information.
10. **Actual implementation date:** State the actual date the decision was implemented. Provide information if there is a variance between the actual date and the planned date.
11. **Notes:** Use this field for any additional notes about the decision.

Delivery of Program Benefits Phase: Monitoring and Controlling ■ 237

Figure 7.2   Program performance report.

Program Performance Report

The *Standard for Program Management*—Second Edition (2008) talks of using the terms *performance report* and *status report* somewhat interchangeably. The Standard notes they are a common input and output to many processes in program management. Status reports often refer to areas such as finance and schedule, whereas performance reports tend to refer to higher-level matters, such as benefits, project closures, etc. Here, we use the term *performance report* (Figure 7.2).

Program Performance Report Instructions

Purpose: The program performance report provides a high-level status of program accomplishments and is distributed to various stakeholders in accordance with the program communications management plan. Stakeholders use this report for program monitoring and control and for general information as appropriate, given the stakeholder's level of interest and involvement in the program.

In the Project Management Institute's *Standard for Program Management*—Second Edition (2008), the program performance report is an input to the following processes:

- Direct and manage program execution
- Monitor and control program performance
- Manage program issues
- Provide governance oversight and manage program benefits
- Report program performance
- Monitor and control program risks
- Administer program procurements
- Close program procurements

It is an output from the following processes:

- Monitor and control program performance
- Distribute information
- Report program performance
- Monitor and control program schedules

Updates to the report are an output from the following process:

- Administer program procurements

The following describes the recommended items to be part of the performance report:

1. **Program name:** List the name of the program.
2. **Prepared by:** List the name of the person who prepared the report and his or her contact information.
3. **Date:** List the date the report was prepared.
4. **Program budget:** Provide information on the total program budget.
5. **Funds expended to date:** State the amount of funds that have been spent as of the date of the report.
6. **Business case:** Use this section for summary information about the program's business case.
    a. **Date of initial business case:** State the date the initial business case was prepared.
    b. **Changes needed and date:** Describe whether or not any changes were required to reflect changing conditions.
    c. **Assigned to:** List the person who is responsible for updating the business case and the date it is due.
7. **Benefit status:** Use this section for a summary of the status of the expected benefits to be realized by the program.
    a. **Benefit:** List the benefit and any corresponding number used for tracking purposes.
    b. **Description:** Provide a brief description of the benefit.

c. **Planned realization date:** State the date the benefit is expected to be realized.
d. **Actual realization date:** State the actual date the benefit was realized.
e. **Status:** Provide information as to the status. Consider a format such as green for on track, yellow for may not be realized as planned, and red for not expected to be realized.
f. **Notes:** Use this field for any additional notes or comments about the benefit.
8. **Deliverable status:** Use this section for a summary of the status of the program's deliverables.
   a. **Deliverable:** List the deliverable and any corresponding number used for tracking purposes.
   b. **Description:** Provide a description of the deliverable.
   c. **Planned date:** State the date the deliverable is expected to be complete.
   d. **Actual date:** State the actual date the deliverable was completed.
   e. **Status:** Provide information as to the status. Consider a format such as green for on track, yellow for may not be completed as planned, and red for not expected to be completed.
   f. **Notes:** Use this field for any notes or comments about the deliverable.
9. **Schedule status:** Use this section for a summary of the status of the program's schedule.
   a. **Milestone and date:** List the milestone and expected date.
   b. **Date completed:** List the date the milestone was finished.
   c. **Schedule revision:** Provide information as to whether a revision to the program's schedule is required.
   d. **Notes:** Use this field for any notes or comments about the milestone.
10. **Change request status:** Use this section for a summary of the program's change requests.
    a. **Description of the change request:** Provide a brief description of the change request. Include a number if used for tracking purposes.
    b. **Submitted date:** State the date the change request was submitted.
    c. **Status and date:** List whether the change request was approved, deferred, or rejected and the date. Also note whether any additional information was required.
    d. **Implementation date:** State the date the change request was implemented, if appropriate, and who was assigned to implement the change.
    e. **Notes:** Use this field for any notes or comments about the change request.
11. **Issue resolution status:** Use this section for a summary of program issues.
    a. **Issue:** Provide a brief description of the issue. Include a number if used for tracking purposes.
    b. **Assigned to:** State the person who is responsible for the issue and provide contact information.

c. **Proposed resolution and date:** Describe the proposed resolution and the date the issue is scheduled to be resolved.
d. **Actual resolution and date:** State the actual resolution and the date the issue was resolved.
e. **Notes:** Use this field for any notes or comments about the issue.

12. **Risk resolution status:** Use this section for a summary of program risks and the status of their resolution.
    a. **Risk:** Provide a brief description of the risk. Include a number if used for tracking purposes.
    b. **Proposed resolution:** State the proposed resolution for the risk following the risk response plan.
    c. **Assigned to:** State the person who is responsible as the risk owner and provide contact information.
    d. **Actual resolution and date:** State the actual resolution for the risk and the date.
    e. **Notes:** Use this field for any notes or comments about the risk.

13. **Resource issues:** Use this section for any information about project resources.
    a. **Description:** Provide a description of the resource requirement.
    b. **Proposed resolution:** If there is a problem in acquiring the resources, state the proposed resolution.
    c. **Assigned to:** State the person who is assigned to resolve the resource issue and provide contact information.
    d. **Actual resolution and date:** State the actual resolution and date.
    e. **Notes:** Use this field for any notes or comments about the resource issue.

14. **Escalated risks and issues:** Use this section for information about escalated risks and issues to the governance board or other stakeholders.
    a. **Description:** Provide a description of the escalated risk or issue.
    b. **Date escalated:** State the date the risk or issue was escalated.
    c. **Escalated to:** List the stakeholders who are to resolve the escalated risk or issue.
    d. **Resolution description and date:** State the actual resolution and the date.
    e. **Notes:** Use this field for any comments about the escalated risk or issue.

15. **Earned value metrics:** Use this section to report earned value metrics, as appropriate.
    a. **Schedule variance (SV):** Use this field for the schedule variance.
    b. **Cost variance (CV):** Use this field for the cost variance.
    c. **Schedule performance index (SPI):** Use this field for the schedule performance index.

d. **Cost performance index (CPI):** Use this field for the cost performance index.
   e. **Estimate at completion (EAC):** Use this field for the estimate at completion.
   f. **Estimate to complete (ETC):** Use this field for the estimate to complete.
   g. **To complete performance index (TCPI):** Use this field for the to complete performance index.
16. **Accomplishments during the reporting period:** Use this section to list key accomplishments during the reporting period and the date.
17. **Planned accomplishments before the next report:** Use this section to list planned accomplishments before the next report is due and list the planned date.
18. **Additional comments:** Use this field for any additional comments to include in the report.

Program Performance Report Template

Program Name	Prepared by	Date	Program Budget	Funds Expended to Date

Business Case		
Date of Initial Business Case	Changes Needed	Assigned to and Date

Benefit Status					
Benefit	Description	Planned Realization Date	Actual Realization Date	Status	Notes

Deliverable Status

Deliverable	Description	Planned Date	Actual Date	Status	Notes

Schedule Status

Milestone and Date	Date Completed	Schedule Revision	Notes

Change Request Status

Description of the Change	Submitted Date	Status and Date	Implementation Date	Notes

Issue Resolution Status

Issue	Assigned to	Proposed Resolution and Date	Actual Resolution and Date	Notes

Risk Resolution Status

Risk	Proposed Resolution	Assigned to	Actual Resolution and Date	Notes

Resource Issues

Description	Proposed Resolution	Assigned to	Actual Resolution and Date	Notes

Escalated Risks and Issues

Description	Date Escalated	Escalated to	Resolution Description and Date	Notes

Earned Value Metrics

SV	CV	SPI	CPI	EAC	ETC	TCPI

Accomplishments during the Reporting Period	
Accomplishment	*Date*

Planned Accomplishments before the Next Report	
Accomplishment	*Planned Date*

Additional Comments

Program Closure Recommendation

Program closure is clearly a major governance issue. Certain issues must be settled in the process, such as, for example, whether continuing benefits are transitioned to ongoing operations or become a part of another program. This template ensures that all appropriate issues are addressed. It is prepared in the provide governance oversight process in the *Standard for Program Management*—Second Edition (2008).

Program Closure Recommendation Instructions

The program closure recommendation includes the following:

Purpose: A brief introductory statement defining the purpose of the program closure recommendation, such as:

> The program closure recommendation states that all program benefits have been realized, and all deliverables have been completed, so the program can be officially closed.

The program manager prepares this recommendation and presents it to the governance board as the program then is at the last phase in its life cycle. Before the recommendation is prepared, the program manager should meet with each of the key stakeholders to ensure they support this recommendation. The governance board documents its approval to close the program in the governance decision register. This decision then is given to the program sponsor, who officially closes the program.

At this point, the program manager states that all components have been completed and have been closed according to the program's closure policies, all lessons learned have been documented, all documents have been archived, all resources have been reassigned, and any property provided by others has been returned.

The program manager provides metrics as part of the recommendation to show that expected program benefits have been realized, deliverables have been completed, and the program's objectives have been met.

Any work that may need to be done to transition the program to ongoing operations is described as part of the recommendation.

In the *Standard for Program Management*—Second Edition (2008), the program closure recommendation is an output of the provide governance oversight process. It is an input to the close program process.

Reasons for request: This section describes the reasons for the program closure recommendation. For example, it describes that the program's benefits have been realized, deliverables have been completed, and objectives have been met. The program manager may note any forecasts that have been prepared concerning the ongoing value of the benefits from the program.

Resources released: Once the program closure recommendation is approved, any remaining resources can be reallocated to other parts of the performing organization. This section states the available resources for planning purposes by the program sponsor and portfolio manager, as appropriate.

Disposition of property: This section states that any customer or performing organization property provided to the program has been returned.

Recommended changes: At the time the program officially is closed, during the lessons learned review session, the program management team may have noted some changes that could be beneficial to other programs and projects under way in the organization. This section describes any of these recommendations for consideration.

Continued benefits realization: This section describes requirements for any continued benefits realization once the program is closed, and the benefits are transitioned to either the customer, a product or customer support group in the organization, or another program under way in the organization. This section describes any ongoing activities that may be required to ensure the benefits continue to be realized and recommends any tracking or monitoring of these benefits as required.

Stakeholder communications: This section describes how the affected or interested stakeholders will learn that the program is formally closed.

Program completion closure certificate: This section describes who will prepare the certificate noting that program completion has occurred and who must sign off on it once the closure recommendation is approved.

Approvals: This section contains the written approval of the program closure recommendation by the program manager, program sponsor, members of the program's governance board, and any other key stakeholders as appropriate.

Program Closure Recommendation Template

<Insert Program Name>
Program Closure Recommendation

Program name:	
Program manager:	PM's email address here as a hyperlink
Program sponsor:	
Actual start date:	
Proposed closure date:	
Program no.:	
Revision history:	
Business unit:	

A. PURPOSE

A brief introductory statement defining the purpose of the program closure recommendation, such as:

> The program closure recommendation states that all program benefits have been realized, and all deliverables have been completed, so the program can be officially closed.

_____
_____
_____

B. REASONS FOR REQUEST

This section describes the reasons for the program closure recommendation.

_____
_____
_____

C. RESOURCES RELEASED

This section states the resources that will be released once the closure recommendation is approved in order that they may be used elsewhere in the organization.

_____
_____
_____

D. DISPOSITION OF PROPERTY

This section states that any customer or performing organization property provided to the program has been returned.

_____
_____
_____

E. RECOMMENDED CHANGES

This section describes any recommended changes in program management practices based on lessons learned in this program that could be beneficial for other programs and projects in the organization.

F. CONTINUED BENEFITS REALIZATION

This section describes requirements for any continued benefits realization once the program is closed, and the benefits are transitioned to a customer, a product or customer support group in the organization, or another program.

G. STAKEHOLDER COMMUNICATIONS

This section states those stakeholders who will be notified when the program closure recommendation is approved.

H. PROGRAM COMPLETION CLOSURE CERTIFICATE

This section describes who will prepare the certificate noting that program completion has occurred and who must sign off on it.

I. APPROVALS

This section contains the approval of the program closure recommendation by the program manager, program sponsor, members of the program's governance board, and other key stakeholders as required.

SIGNATURES AND DATE APPROVAL OBTAINED

Program manager _____

Program sponsor _____

Governance board member 1 _____

Governance board member 2 _____

Governance board member N _____

Stakeholder 1 _____

Stakeholder 2 _____

Stakeholder N _____

Risk Audit Report

The objectives and timing of risk audits can be specified in the audit plan. This is a suggested format for covering all the relevant points in a risk audit report. It is a tool and technique in the monitor and control program risks process in the *Standard for Program Management*—Second Edition (2008).

Risk Audit Report Instructions

The risk audit report includes the following:

Purpose: A brief introductory statement defining the purpose of the risk audit report, such as:

> The risk audit report presents an objective assessment of the program's risk responses according to the risk response plan and the overall risk management process used on the program according to the risk management plan. The report's findings and recommendations serve to enhance risk management effectiveness and ensure that the program is following the risk management plan.

Although program audits are conducted on a regular and ad hoc basis throughout the life cycle, risk audits also are recommended to ensure that risk processes and procedures are effective ones and to see if changes are needed so that risks do not turn into problems that impact overall benefits delivery. Risk audits complement the program audits and also the risk reviews that are held. They should be viewed in a positive manner rather than as necessary for compliance or for pinpointing specific problems and associating them to specific individuals.

In the *Standard for Program Management*—Second Edition (2008), the risk audit is a tool and technique used in the monitor and control risk process, as it is a part of normal reviews to be held at various times in the program's life cycle. These audits are planned and noted in the program's master schedule, although the program manager may feel a need to conduct them on an ad hoc basis. They focus on risks at the program level, as project managers may conduct them at the component level. A recommended best practice is for the audit team to review the risk management plan, the risk response plan, the risk register, and any minutes from risk reviews prior to the audit. The risk audit report is an objective report of findings and provides recommended preventive or corrective actions to follow. It also is used to ensure that program risk management and risk response processes are being followed.

The following are recommended contents for the risk audit report.

Background information:
    Time period of the audit: This section states the time the audit began and when the final report was prepared.
    Place: This section states where the audit was conducted.
    Audit participants: This section states the names of the people on the audit team and provides their contact information for possible questions.
    Type of audit: This section states the type of audit that was conducted—internal or external. Note whether the audit was conducted according to the program's master schedule as part of a program quality review or whether it was random.
    Reason for the audit: This section describes why the audit was conducted, such as to concentrate on a risk that occurred that was not part of the risk response plan and affected numerous program components, to evaluate the number of workarounds that were needed to address root causes, to determine whether the risk management planning process is effective or requires change, to determine whether new risk categories may be needed, especially as new components become part of the program and other components end, to assess whether the program stakeholders' tolerance for risks has changed, to determine whether the risk budget is adequate, to see whether the risk monitoring and tracking process is effective, and to determine whether stakeholders have requested any additional information other than that regularly reported on risks.
    Program areas affected: This section describes the various areas of the program that were involved in the audit, e.g., the entire program or only certain components of it.

Methodology: This section describes how the audit was conducted. For example, it notes whether documents were reviewed, interviews were held, surveys were used, focus groups were used, or other methods were used.

Findings: This section presents the findings from the audit. The findings should be presented in an objective way, as they are the basis for the recommendations from the audit. They are the synthesis of all of the data that were reviewed. Findings should be carefully worded to reflect the audit team's observation, and they should be phrased as problem statements. Appropriate background information that is needed to understand the findings should be included. Causes are observations that support the findings, and their identification is helpful in making constructive recommendations. Consequences list the problem results of a finding. Findings should represent issues for the entire program, or components, according to the scope of the audit, and should have the broadest possible application.

    Here is an example:

Finding (problem statement): Each risk review involves different participants, and many participants are not empowered to make decisions at the review.

Probable cause: Designated risk review attendees have not delegated the authority to others to make decisions when they cannot attend the review.

Business consequence: The risk reviews are not considered useful meetings, as decisions are not made as a result of the review.

Recommendation: Prepare and follow a risk review agenda. Have the governance board appoint members to attend each review that is held, and if the designated attendee is unable to attend a review, ensure that his or her replacement is empowered to make decisions at the meeting.

In preparing findings, keep the specific risk audit goals and appraisal scope in mind. Avoid the following:

- Moot issues
- Findings based on hearsay alone
- Broad generalizations

Recommendations: This section states the recommendations based on the audit findings. Use categories if possible to group the recommendations and present them in priority order. If the audit is for compliance purposes, note whether some of the recommendations are mandatory.

Appendices: Include appendices such as the following:

Persons interviewed: List the people who were interviewed during the audit and the date of each interview.

Documents reviewed: List the documents that were reviewed during the audit.

Approvals: This section contains the written approval of the risk audit report by the lead auditor.

Risk Audit Report Template

<Insert Program Name>
Risk Audit Report

Program name:	
Program manager:	PM's email address here as a hyperlink
Program sponsor:	
Actual start date:	
Approved end date:	

Program no.:	
Revision history:	
Business unit:	

A. PURPOSE

A brief introductory statement defining the purpose of the risk audit report, such as:

> The risk audit report presents an objective assessment of the program's risk responses according to the risk management plan and the overall risk management process used on the program. The report's findings and recommendations serve to enhance risk management effectiveness and ensure that the program is following the risk management plan.

_____
_____
_____

B. BACKGROUND INFORMATION

This section provides background information about the risk audit. It should describe when the audit began and was completed; where the audit was conducted; and who participated on the audit team, the type of audit that was conducted, the reason the audit was conducted, and the program areas involved in the audit.

_____
_____
_____

C. METHODOLOGY

This section describes how the audit was conducted.

_____
_____
_____

D. FINDINGS

This section presents the findings from the audit.

_____
_____
_____

E. RECOMMENDATIONS

This section states the recommendations based on the audit findings, in priority order, with notes on whether there are any mandatory recommendations if the audit was conducted for compliance purposes.

_____
_____
_____

F. APPENDICES

This section lists appendices such as the names of people who were interviewed and the documents that were reviewed.

_____
_____
_____

G. APPROVALS

This section contains the approval of the audit report by the lead auditor.

SIGNATURE AND DATE APPROVAL OBTAINED

Lead auditor   _____

Chapter 8

The Program Closure Phase

> While we often obsess over planning to start and run a program, we so often completely ignore its closure, and pay dearly for it in ongoing costs and lost lessons learned waiting to be learned again and again.
>
> **—Anonymous**

Like Primo in the movie *Analyze This,* if they hit us with "that closure thing," we need to be ready.

In the exhaustion after the heat of battle and with pressures to move on to the next frontier, closure too often gets slighted. Hundreds or thousands of dormant yet unclosed programs may lie around forever. In a vicious cycle, precious few lessons learned may be available to assist in starting up the next new frontier. Worse, expenses may continue to accrue because of unclosed contract matters.

Contract Closure Procedure

Focusing of course on program-level contracts, our format for this procedure gives form to the numerous contract closure considerations outlined in the *Standard for Program Management*—Second Edition (2008) as a tool and technique in the close program process.

Contract Closure Procedure Instructions

Purpose: Programs typically will use a variety of contractors or suppliers. This document describes a procedure to follow to close contracts that have been awarded. The purpose of this procedure is to close the contract according to the contract's terms and conditions and also according to the overall program management methodology.

In the Project Management Institute's *Standard for Program Management—Second Edition (2008)*, the contract closure procedure is a tool and technique in the close program and the close contracts processes.

This procedure should be reviewed periodically and updated as required.

1. As the contract closure process begins, first review the contracts management plan for any items that apply to closing contracts.
2. Next review the program management plan to see if it references any other items not covered in the contracts management plan.
3. Review the specific terms and conditions for closing contracts as outlined in the contract's terms and conditions. Note each one to ensure it is completed.
4. Review all other contract documentation, such as the following:
    a. Supporting schedules
    b. Unapproved contract changes
    c. Technical documentation prepared by the contractor
    d. Performance and status reports
    e. Invoices
    f. Payment records
    g. Warranties
    h. Results of inspections
    i. Results of audits
    j. Results of reviews
5. Conduct a procurement audit to review the entire procurement process for this contractor.
6. See if there are any outstanding issues or change requests and resolve them.
7. Review the program's budget to see if sufficient funds remain that may be needed to pay the contractor's final invoice. If other funds are required, prepare a change request to obtain the needed funding.
8. Conduct a final performance review with the contractor/supplier for lessons learned.
9. Determine whether there are any follow-up activities because of any variations in the deliverables that were completed and provide a list of these activities to the contractor.
10. Agree upon a mutual date in which any follow-up activities will be completed.
11. Document any warranties or guarantees that are to be provided by the contractor.

The Program Closure Phase ■ 257

12. Assess the contract's terms and conditions to determine whether there are any outstanding intellectual property issues that require resolution; if there are outstanding issues, agree upon a plan and a date by which they will be resolved.
13. Pay the contractor's final invoice.
14. Prepare a written document that is signed by the appropriate people in the organization that states the contract is closed, and all deliverables have been accepted or rejected. Ensure this document is consistent with the contract's terms and conditions. Provide this document to the contractor. Include any required follow-up activities or warranties.
15. Inform stakeholders that the contract has been closed.
16. Review and document lessons learned regarding this contract, the contractor's performance, and the processes and procedures that are used.
17. Determine whether any updates are recommended to various processes that are used in the organization, such as to the:
    a. Procurement management plan
    b. Contracts management plan
    c. Evaluation criteria
    d. Performance and status report templates
    e. Contract terms and conditions
    f. Contract change control system
    g. Issue resolution process
    h. Claims resolution process
    i. Contract payment system
18. Prepare and submit a recommendation to the contracts/procurement department to retain this contractor on the qualified supplier list, drop this contractor from the list, or add the contractor if it is new to the organization and is not on the list.
19. Prepare a complete set of all the relevant documents about this contract, including the following:
    a. Contracts management plan
    b. Contract
    c. Status and performance reports
    d. Minutes from performance reviews
    e. Invoices and payment records
    f. Technical documents prepared
    g. Audit results
    h. Inspection results
    i. Lessons learned document
    j. Final closeout document
20. Index these documents with appropriate metadata tags so they can be easily retrieved for use on other projects in this program, by other programs and projects under way in the organization, or for future programs and projects.

Program Final Report

At the end of any program, a final report should be prepared to document the work of the program and to be part of the program's archives. This template for the final report is prepared in the close program process in the *Standard for Program Management*—Second Edition (2008).

Program Final Report Instructions

The program final report includes the following:

> **Purpose:** A brief introductory statement defining the purpose of the program final report, such as:
>
> The program final report contains the key information about the program, which will be useful to other programs and projects under way in the organization and for future programs and projects.
>
> In the Project Management Institute's *Standard for Program Management*—Second Edition (2008), the program final report is an output of the close program process.
>
> Although it is finalized during the closing process, it should be prepared throughout the program so key information is not forgotten. One best practice to follow is to work on this report at the end of each of the lessons learned reviews and governance reviews that are held. Information from the governance decision register, program decision log, risk register, program issues register, and lessons learned register is reviewed as the report is prepared. Audit, benefit, status, and performance reports also should be reviewed. Reasons for terminating a contract or a component early should be analyzed. Often, program managers will hold a knowledge transition meeting with team members before the program is officially closed; if this type of information is held, it may provide other data to include in the final report.
>
> Suggested items to include in the report are the following:
>
> > **Program strategic objectives:** The program's strategic objectives were described initially in the business case and program brief. This section states whether or not these objectives were met. If the objectives changed or were not met, this section describes the circumstances for future use by other programs and projects.
> >
> > **Program benefits delivered:** Using the benefits realization plan and the benefits reports, prepared throughout the program, this section states whether the intended benefits were met. If they were not, or if other benefits were added as the program ensued, it describes the specific circumstances involved.

Program participants: Since programs often are long, this section lists the people who performed key roles in the program, and the times they held the various positions: program manager, program sponsor, component managers, members of the program office and program management office, as applicable, and members of the governance board.

Stakeholder management: This section describes the stakeholders who were involved in, had an interest in, or influenced the program. It uses the stakeholder identification list, stakeholder inventory, stakeholder management plan, stakeholder register, and stakeholder strategy to summarize how stakeholders were identified, how involved they were in the program, and their importance to the program. It also describes the approaches used by the program management team to work with the key stakeholders in the program.

Summary of program metrics: Throughout the program, a variety of metrics were collected to see whether preventive or corrective actions were required. This section provides a summary of these metrics.

- **Earned value:** Recognizing that the schedule performance index will be 1, this section lists the other EV metrics, such as cost performance index, budget at completion, estimate to complete, estimate at completion, earned schedule, and total cost performance index.
- **Financial management:** This section lists the various financial management metrics collected in the program, such as return on investment, shareholder value added, net present value, payback period, time to break even, internal rate of return, and benefit-cost ratio.
- **Resources:** This section provides information on the planned versus actual resources used in the program, noting that resources are more than only people using the program resource plan as a reference.
- **Team management:** As team members leave the program, an excellent approach to follow is to survey them on areas for improvement. Other surveys can be used periodically to assess the needed competencies for people to the program, the managerial style used, the use of collaborative leadership on the team, and overall team maturity. This section describes the type of team management metrics that were used and makes recommendations for improvement as appropriate. It also describes whether a team-based reward and recognition system was used and its effectiveness.
- **Charters:** This section discusses the effectiveness of the program and team charters and contains recommendations for their improvement.
- **Organizational:** This section discusses any organizational-type metrics that were used in the program, such as the probability of success of the program deliverables, the strategic importance of the program and whether it changed over the course of the program, and the dura-

tion of the program as compared to the urgency of the need for its deliverables and benefits.

Program risks: This section describes program risks that were identified and the appropriateness of the risk response that was selected. It includes both opportunities and threats to the program. This section also includes any risks that were not identified but occurred and affected the program. It states the contingency plans that were used. It uses the risk management plan, the risk register, and risk reviews and audits as references.

Program issues: This section describes the key issues that affected the program, using the program issues register as a reference.

Escalated risks and issues: This section lists those risks and issues that the program manager escalated to the governance board for resolution and describes the decisions that were made and approaches that were used.

Baseline changes: This section describes the changes over the life of the program to the scope, schedule, cost, and quality baselines.

Interfaces: This section summarizes the interfaces in terms of interrelationships within the program, with other projects and programs under way in the organization, and organizational, technical, interpersonal, logistical, and political interfaces that occurred.

Communications: This section describes the communications methods used in the program to keep stakeholders informed. It notes any approaches that were added that were not in the program communications management plan and the communications strategy. It uses the communications log as a reference. It describes the appropriateness of the meetings that were held and notes whether changes were needed to the agendas for meetings of the governance board for phase gate and program reviews as well as the agendas for the risk management planning process and risk reviews. It lists the people who will receive copies of this final report.

Supplier performance: This section summarizes the performance of the various program suppliers and presents recommendations in terms of updating or changing the qualified supplier list as appropriate. It uses the contracts management plan as a reference.

Program decisions: This section describes the key decisions made during the program's life cycle using the decision log and the governance decision register as a reference.

Terminations: This section summarizes any terminations that occurred during the program.

    Contract: This section summarizes any contracts that were terminated prematurely, to focus on why they were terminated using the procurement program reports as a reference.

    Component: This section summarizes any components that were terminated prematurely, to focus on why they were terminated using the component termination requests as a reference.

Program acceptance: This section lists the formal acceptance of the program's scope to show that each deliverable was completed satisfactorily by the customers and the program sponsor.

Benefits transitioned: This section describes specific benefits that were transitioned to the customer or to a functional unit in the organization, such as a product support group or customer support group, and describes how they will be sustained. It uses the component transition decisions and the transition management plan as references.

Lessons learned: This section summarizes the lessons learned in the program, focusing on successes, failures, and areas of improvement using the lessons learned register as a reference.

> **Program:** This section summarizes technical lessons learned. It uses the program requirements document as a reference.
>
> **Program management process:** This section summarizes the lessons learned in terms of the processes, procedures, and guidelines that were used in the program. It uses the program road map as a reference.

Knowledge repository: To best contribute to the organization's knowledge management system and repository, this section contains the metadata tags to locate information about this program in an easy-to-use way as its archives become part of the organization's knowledge repository.

Approvals: This section contains the written approval of the program final report by the program sponsor, program manager, program management office, members of the governance board, and any other key stakeholders as appropriate.

Program Final Report Template

<Insert Program Name>
Final Report

Program name:	
Program manager:	PM's email address here as a hyperlink
Program sponsor:	
Actual start date:	
Approved end date:	
Actual end date:	
Program no.:	
Revision history:	
Business unit:	

A. PURPOSE

A brief introductory statement defining the purpose of the program final report, such as:

> The program final report contains the key information about the program, which will be useful to other programs and projects under way in the organization and for future programs and projects.

_____
_____

B. PROGRAM STRATEGIC OBJECTIVES

This section states whether the initially defined strategic objectives for the program were met. If the objectives changed, it describes the reasons for the changes for future use by other programs and projects.

_____
_____

C. PROGRAM BENEFITS DELIVERED

This section states whether the intended benefits were met. If they were not, or if other benefits were added over the program's life cycle, it describes the specific circumstances involved.

_____
_____

D. PROGRAM PARTICIPANTS

This section lists the people who performed key roles in the program and the times they held the various positions.

_____
_____

E. STAKEHOLDER MANAGEMENT

This section describes the stakeholders who were involved in, had an interest in, or influenced the program. It also describes the approaches used by the program management team to work with the key program stakeholders.

_____
_____

F. SUMMARY OF PROGRAM METRICS

This section summarizes the program metrics that were collected.

G. PROGRAM RISKS

This section describes the risks that were identified and the appropriateness of the risk responses that were selected. It also includes any risks that were not identified but occurred and affected the program. It states contingency plans that were used.

H. PROGRAM ISSUES

This section describes the key issues that affected the program.

I. ESCALATED RISKS AND ISSUES

This section lists those risks and issues the program manager escalated to the governance board for resolution and describes the decisions that were made and approaches used.

J. BASELINE CHANGES

This section describes changes over the life of the program to the technical, schedule, cost, and quality baselines.

K. INTERFACES

This section summarizes the interfaces in terms of interrelationships within the program and with other programs and projects under way in the organization, and the organizational, technical, interpersonal, logistical, and political interfaces that occurred.

L. COMMUNICATIONS

This section describes the communications methods used in the program to keep stakeholders informed, the approaches that were added, the appropriateness of the meetings that were held, and the agendas that were used, and lists those stakeholders who will receive copies of the final report.

M. SUPPLIER PERFORMANCE

This section summarizes supplier performance and presents recommendations to update or change the qualified supplier list as appropriate.

N. PROGRAM DECISIONS

This section lists the key decisions made during the program's life cycle.

O. TERMINATIONS

This section describes any contracts and components that were terminated prematurely and the reasons they were terminated.

P. PROGRAM ACCEPTANCE

This section lists the formal acceptance of the program's scope by the customers and the program sponsor.

Q. BENEFITS TRANSITIONED

This section describes specific benefits transitioned to the customer or to a functional unit in the organization and describes how they will be sustained.

R. LESSONS LEARNED

This section summarizes lessons learned, focusing on successes, failures, and areas of improvement in terms of the program and the program management processes used.

S. KNOWLEDGE REPOSITORY

This section contains the metadata tags to locate information about this program in an easy-to-use way as its archives become part of the organization's knowledge repository.

T. APPROVALS

This section contains the approval of the program final report by the program sponsor, program manager, program management office, members of the governance board, and other key stakeholders as required.

SIGNATURES AND DATE APPROVAL OBTAINED

Program manager _____

Program sponsor _____

Program management office director _____

Governance board chairperson _____

Governance board member 1   _____

Governance board member 2   _____

Governance board member N   _____

Stakeholder 1   _____

Stakeholder 2   _____

Stakeholder N   _____

Knowledge Transition

Knowledge management is especially important in program management. As part of the close program process in the *Standard for Program Management*—Second Edition (2008), a knowledge transition report is used to evaluate overall program performance.

Knowledge Transition Report Instructions

The knowledge transition report includes the following:

> **Purpose:** A brief introductory statement defining the purpose of the knowledge transition report, such as:
>
> The knowledge transition report is an assessment of the program's performance and is used so the program manager can share lessons learned with the team and others in the organization.
>
> In the Project Management Institute's *Standard for Program Management*—Second Edition (2008), the knowledge transition report is an output of the close program process. In preparing it, the program manager should review the knowledge management plan, the component transition decisions, the lessons learned database, and the results of lessons learned reviews. When this report is complete, it may lead to the need to update some of the organization's existing policies, procedures, and processes in program management. The program manager may wish to prepare this report in a meeting with the program management team to formally discuss lessons learned. This review may lead to a need to update some of the information in the final program report.
>
> **Knowledge management goals and objectives:** This section lists the goals and objectives for knowledge management based on the knowledge management plan and assesses whether or not they were met. Recommendations for changes are noted. It notes whether people in the program contributed content that was useful to others.

Program management plans: This section discusses the various plans that the program management team prepared to evaluate their usefulness. It also reviews whether changes were required to these plans and the improvements as a result of these changes. It evaluates the format of the plans, and the people who were involved in the preparation of each plan for future improvements.

Meetings and reviews: This section discusses the effectiveness of the program management team meetings that were held and the performance reviews that were conducted by the team, by the governance board, and by auditors. It notes whether the recommendations from the reviews were implemented. The program's decision log is reviewed.

Monitoring and controlling processes: This section describes the various monitoring and controlling processes the program team used to evaluate overall program performance and that of the various program components. It reviews the risk register, program issues register, metrics that were collected, status reports, and the lessons learned database.

Team performance: A motivated team is essential to program success. This section reviews team performance to determine whether other approaches could have enhanced overall team motivation. It evaluates the usefulness of the team charter, exit interviews with members of the team when they left the program, and rewards and recognition systems in place for program team members.

Contractors and suppliers: Since most programs use a variety of contractors/ suppliers, this section discusses the performance of the various contractors and suppliers with a focus on the effectiveness of the procurement management plan, the contracts management plan, the procurement performance reports, and the contract closure procedure.

Stakeholder management: Effective stakeholder management is a key to overall program success and benefits realization. This section assesses the stakeholder management strategy that was used. It reviews the initial stakeholder identification, the stakeholder inventory, the stakeholder management plan, and the stakeholder register. It notes changes in the various stakeholders throughout the life of the program and reviews the communications log to see the usefulness of the regular reports that stakeholders received, especially if additional reports were required.

Governance reviews: The importance of an effective governance board to overall program success cannot be overstated. This section describes the interaction between the program management team and the members of the governance board. It evaluates the usefulness of the meetings of the governance review board both at stage gates and for overall program performance reviews. It also assesses the governance management plan and reviews the governance decision register.

Customer involvement: Customers are active participants in many programs. This section discusses customer involvement apart from stakeholder management to see how the program management team interacted with the customers. It also assesses how benefits were transitioned to the customers and how customer satisfaction was measured.

Approvals: This section contains the written approval of the knowledge transition report by the program sponsor, program manager, program management office, members of the governance board, and any other key stakeholders as appropriate.

Knowledge Transition Report Template

<Insert Program Name>
Knowledge Transition Report

Program name:	
Program manager:	PM's email address here as a hyperlink
Program sponsor:	
Actual start date:	
Approved end date:	
Program no.:	
Revision history:	
Business unit:	

A. PURPOSE

A brief introductory statement defining the purpose of the knowledge transition report, such as:

> The knowledge transition report is an assessment of the program's performance and is used so the program manager can share lessons learned with the team and others in the organization.

_____

_____

_____

B. KNOWLEDGE MANAGEMENT GOALS AND OBJECTIVES

This section lists the goals and objectives for knowledge management and assesses whether or not they were met.

_____

_____

C. PROGRAM MANAGEMENT PLANS

This section discusses the various plans the program management team prepared and their usefulness.

_____

_____

_____

D. MEETINGS AND REVIEWS

This section discusses the effectiveness of the program management team meetings that were held and the performance reviews that were conducted by the team, the governance board, and auditors.

_____

_____

_____

E. MONITORING AND CONTROLLING PROCESSES

This section describes the various monitoring and controlling processes the program management team used to evaluate overall program performance and that of the program components.

_____

_____

_____

F. TEAM PERFORMANCE

This section reviews program team performance to determine whether other approaches could have enhanced team motivation.

_____

_____

_____

G. CONTRACTORS AND SUPPLIERS

This section discusses the performance of the various contractors and suppliers with an emphasis on the effectiveness of the procurement management plan, the contracts management plan, procurement performance reports, and contract closure procedures.

_____

_____

_____

H. STAKEHOLDER MANAGEMENT

This section assesses the stakeholder management strategy that was used in the program.

_____
_____
_____

I. GOVERNANCE REVIEWS

This section discusses the interaction between the program management team and the governance board.

_____
_____
_____

J. CUSTOMER INVOLVEMENT

This section discusses customer involvement apart from stakeholder management to see how effectively the program management team interacted with its customers.

_____
_____
_____

K. APPROVALS

This section contains the approval of the knowledge transition report by the program sponsor, program manager, program management office, members of the governance board, and other key stakeholders as required.

SIGNATURES AND DATE APPROVAL OBTAINED

Program manager	_____
Program sponsor	_____
Program management office director	_____
Governance board chairperson	_____
Governance board member 1	_____
Governance board member 2	_____
Governance board member N	_____
Stakeholder 1	_____
Stakeholder 2	_____
Stakeholder N	_____

Supplier Performance Review

When finalizing a program contract, care must be taken to ensure that everything the program needs has been satisfactorily obtained or at least resolved as an issue. For future purposes, we also need to understand how well the supplier performed during this engagement. Here we present a format to help ensure a successful review of supplier performance as noted in the close program procurements process in the *Standard for Program Management*—Second Edition (2008).

Supplier Performance Review Agenda Instructions

As part of the contract closure process, the member of the program management team who is serving as the contract administrator for each supplier should conduct a final review of the supplier's overall performance. These reviews provide a number of advantages, both for the performing organization and for the supplier.

The program management team discusses overall performance in terms of objectives that were met, benefits that were achieved, and progress according to plans. This review may be the last time to formally discuss any deficiencies with the supplier. The program management team member then summarizes the results of the review and makes recommendations to the organization's procurement or contracts department concerning adding this supplier to the qualified supplier list if it was a new supplier, or continuing to keep the supplier on the list if the supplier has worked for the organization in the past.

The supplier can use the review to discuss any problems that occurred that affected overall performance and any opportunities should the supplier be selected to work on a similar type of contract in the future.

In the *Standard for Program Management*—Second Edition (2008), this review is a tool and technique in the close program procurement process. It does not substitute for other reviews that may be held as described in the contracts management plan.

An agenda for these reviews is as follows:

PARTICIPANTS (NAMES/ORGANIZATION)

Date: _____

Time: _____

Place: _____

Contract overview: A member of the program management team, ideally the person who prepared the contracts management plan and who worked with the supplier throughout the contract as the program's contract administrator, presents a brief overview of the contract. He or she describes why it was needed, its deliverables, and impact to the program. He or she also describes why the contract now is complete.

Specific performance requirements: The next part of the review discusses the specific performance requirements to be met by the contract. The program management team reviews each deliverable and describes whether it was completed according to plan. If the planned delivery date was missed, the supplier representatives can explain needed preventive actions. The program management team can discuss the impact of a missed delivery date on the overall success of the program, especially if a missed delivery date affected other parts of the program adversely. Lessons learned can be shared by both parties to improve future performance on similar contracts.

Monitoring and control processes used: During this part of the review, the program management team discusses the various monitoring and control processes used on this contract, such as meetings and status reports. The format for the reports and the frequency in which they were submitted can be discussed. The supplier representatives discuss whether they found these meetings and reports to be useful and present any ideas for change. The program management team can discuss whether change requests were required because of the status reports that were submitted or the meetings that were held. Both groups can discuss whether there was an atmosphere of trust between the two parties and ways in which trust could be enhanced in the future.

Change control: Although changes may be needed as a result of the reports and reviews, suppliers often submit change requests. During this part of the review, the change control system can be discussed to see if there are any recommended changes to improve its effectiveness. The supplier representatives can discuss why they needed to submit change requests, if this was done during the program. They can comment on items such as the length of time it took to submit a request and how they were notified whether the request was approved, deferred, or rejected, and also whether they needed to submit additional information to the program management team to analyze the impact of the change request on the program.

Claims process: If there were a number of contract claims, the claims process should be reviewed to see why many claims were submitted. Both groups can discuss the effectiveness of this process to see if any changes would have facilitated the resolution of claims that were submitted.

Invoicing and payment process: The invoicing and payment processes also can be discussed. Both groups can determine whether any changes could have led to a smoother process.

Additional comments: The program management team provides any additional comments about the supplier performance, and the supplier representatives also provide comments as appropriate.

SIGNATURES OF PARTICIPANTS

Program manager   _____

Project manager   _____

Program management team member 1   _____

Program management team member 2   _____

Program management team member N   _____

Supplier representative 1   _____

Supplier representative 2   _____

Supplier representative N   _____

Procurement Performance Report

During your program, you inevitably learn lessons about your program procurement processes and about your suppliers. This report structure helps you record those procurement-specific lessons learned. They will be useful in future procurements, and this report is prepared in the close program procurements process in the *Standard for Program Management*—Second Edition (2008).

Procurement Performance Report Instructions

Purpose: Contractors/suppliers prepare procurement performance reports throughout the life of the contract according to the contractual terms and conditions. The program management team also outlines status reporting requirements in the contracts management plan. The team and other stakeholders use these reports for contract monitoring and control, to ensure that any issues that are raised are resolved in a timely way, and for general information as appropriate. The procurement performance reports are an input to the close procurement process in order that the program management team can ensure that all issues raised in these reports are resolved in a satisfactory way.

In the *Standard for Program Management*—Second Edition (2008), a procurement performance report also is an output of this close procurement process to show the results of the supplier performance review and to record any issues as needed in the program issues register. Additionally, any lessons learned are included in this report. A separate format is provided for this final procurement performance report.

The following describes the recommended items to be part of the Final Procurement Performance Report.

1. **Contract Number:** List the contract number.
2. **Prepared By:** List the name of the person who prepared the report and his or her contact information.
3. **Date:** List the date the report was prepared.
4. **Report Recipients:** State the recipients of the report.

5. **Contract Overview:** Provide a brief summary of the contract and its purpose.
6. **Deliverable Status:** Provide summary information about the various contractual deliverables. Consider the following:
   a. **Deliverable:** List the deliverable and any corresponding number used for tracking purposes.
   b. **Description:** Provide a description of the deliverable.
   c. **Completion Date:** State the actual date the deliverable was completed.
   d. **Notes:** Use this field for any notes or comments about the deliverable.
7. **Schedule Status:** Provide information for lessons learned concerning the schedule for the deliverables. State any schedule revisions that were required and why they were needed.
8. **Budget Status:** Provide information on the total budget for the contract. Note whether any additional funding was needed to complete the contract.
9. **Change Request Status:** Use this section for a summary of any contract change requests.
   a. **Description of the Change Request:** Provide a brief description of the change request.
   b. **Submitted Date:** State the date the change request was submitted.
   c. **Status and Date:** List whether the change request was approved, deferred, or rejected and the date.
   d. **Implementation Date:** State the date the change request was implemented, if appropriate.
   e. **Notes:** Use this field for any notes or comments about the change request.
10. **Issue Resolution Status:** Use this section to summarize how issues were resolved during the contract. Consider including the following:
    a. **Issue:** Provide a brief description of the issue.
    b. **Assigned To:** State the person who was responsible for resolving the issue and provide contact information.
    c. **Actual Resolution and Date:** State the actual resolution and the date the issue was resolved.
    d. **Notes:** Use this field for any notes or comments about the issue.
11. **Risk Resolution Status:** Use this section to summarize how risks were resolved during the contract. Consider including the following:
    a. **Risk:** Provide a brief description of the risk.
    b. **Assigned To:** State the person who was responsible for resolving the risk and provide contact information.

c. **Actual Resolution and Date:** State the actual resolution for the risk and the date.
   d. **Notes:** Use this field for any notes or comments about the risk.
12. **Resource Issues:** Describe any resource issues that affected the contractual deliverables. Consider including the following:
   a. **Description:** Provide a description of the resource requirement.
   b. **Assigned To:** State the person who resolve the resource issue and provide contact information.
   c. **Actual Resolution Date:** State the actual resolution and date.
   d. **Notes:** Use this field for any notes or comments about the resource issue.
13. **Earned Value Metrics:** Use this section to report final earned value metrics, as appropriate.
   a. **Cost Variance (CV):** Use this field for the Cost Variance.
   b. **Cost Performance Index:** Use this field for the Cost Performance Index.
   c. **Estimate at Complete (EAC):** Use this field for the Estimate at Completion.
   d. **Estimate to Complete (ETC):** Use this field for the Estimate to Complete.
14. **Results of the Contractor Final Performance Review:** Provide a summary of the final contractor/supplier performance review. Include the date of the review and the people who were present with their contact information.
15. **Procurement Process Recommendations:** Use this section for recommendations regarding updates to the program procurement process. Consider items such as the following:
   a. Make-or-buy analysis
   b. Procurement management plan
   c. Contracts management plan
   d. Criteria for inclusion on the qualified seller list
   e. Evaluation criteria for source selection
   f. Contractual terms and conditions
   g. Contractor performance report format, information included, and frequency
   h. Contractor performance reviews agenda information, items covered, and frequency
   i. Interaction between the program management team and the contractor staff
   j. Other lessons learned specific to program procurement management
16. **Additional Comments:** Use this field for any additional comments to include in the report.

Final Procurement Performance Report Template

<Insert Program Name>
Final Procurement Performance Report

Contract Number	Prepared by	Date	Report Recipients

Contract Overview

Deliverable Status

Deliverable	Description	Completion Date	Notes

Schedule Status

Lessons Learned	Schedule Revisions	Notes

Budget Status

Total Budget	Description of Additional Funding Requirements	Notes

Change Request Status

Description of the Change	Submitted Date	Status and Date	Implementation Date	Notes

Issue Resolution Status

Issue	Assigned To	Actual Resolution and Date	Follow-Up Items	Notes

Risk Resolution Status

Risk	Assigned to	Actual Resolution and Date	Notes

Resource Issues

Description	Assigned To	Actual Resolution and Date	Notes

Earned Value Metrics			
CV	CPI	EAC	ETC

Results of the Final Performance Review		
Summary	Attendees	Date

Procurement Process Recommendations

Additional Comments

Component Termination Request

Components can be terminated before completion because of the lack of adequate progress or a change in the strategic direction of the program. When a component is to be terminated, it is important to document why; make clear the follow-up tasks that must be accomplished by the program, such as personnel reassignments; communicate the event to stakeholders; and more. This form helps you cover all those bases when requesting component termination from your governance board.

Component Termination Request Instructions

The component termination request includes the following:

> **Purpose:** A brief introductory statement defining the purpose of the component termination request, such as:

The component termination request shows that the component should be closed, as it is no longer contributing to the overall program benefits.

Components include both projects and nonproject or operations work that is part of the program. It may be necessary, however, to terminate a component before it is scheduled to be completed.

In most cases, the project manager or operations manager prepares the component termination request with input from other key stakeholders and the program manager. It may be provided by the client or the funding organization. The governance board typically approves this request. It serves as the mandate to close the component and document its current state.

In the Project Management Institute's *Standard for Program Management*—Second Edition (2008), this request supports the close program and approve component transition processes.

Reasons for request: This section describes the reasons for the termination request. For example, the component may not have completed its deliverables on time, and therefore, the deliverables will be obsolete when they finally are completed; suppliers working on the component may have defaulted, and new suppliers cannot be located in sufficient time; or perhaps the anticipated benefits to be realized by the component cannot be met.

Resources released: Once the component termination request is approved, resources can be reallocated to other parts of the program or to the performing organization. This section states the available resources for planning purposes by the program manager, program sponsor, and portfolio manager, as appropriate.

Closure requirements: Even though the component is terminated, the program's closing policies and procedures must be met. This section states that all closure activities are complete, such as archiving records, returning customer property, and documenting lessons learned, as defined by the program management plan and governance plan.

Stakeholder communications: Each component will have its own stakeholders, in addition to stakeholders at the program level. This section describes how the affected or interested stakeholders will learn that the component has been terminated.

Change requests: Once a component's termination request is approved, change requests will be required. This section states the various change requests that will be needed as a result of approval of the termination request.

Program documentation changes: This section states the requirements to update program-level documentation because of a component termination request, such as the program management plan, program resource plan, decision log, interface management plan, and the program road map. It describes the program management team member who is responsible for updating the artifacts and the planned date the updates will be completed.

Component termination closure certificate: This section describes who will prepare the certificate noting that termination has occurred and who must sign off on it once the request is approved.

Approvals: This section contains the written approval of the component termination request by the program manager, program sponsor, members of the program's governance board, and any other key stakeholders as appropriate.

Component Termination Request Template

<Insert Program Name>
Component Termination Request

Program name:	
Program manager:	PM's email address here as a hyperlink
Project or operations manager:	
Program sponsor:	
Component start date:	
Proposed component end date:	
Date prepared:	
Prepared by:	

A. PURPOSE

A brief introductory statement defining the purpose of the component termination request, such as:

> The component termination request shows that the component should be closed, as it is no longer contributing to the overall program benefits.

_____
_____
_____

B. REASONS FOR REQUEST

This section describes the reasons for the termination request.

_____
_____
_____

C. RESOURCES RELEASED

This section states the resources that will be released once the termination request is approved in order that they may be used on other program components or elsewhere in the organization.

_____
_____
_____

D. CLOSURE REQUIREMENTS

This section describes the program's closure requirements for its components to ensure all of them have been completed.

_____
_____
_____

E. STAKEHOLDER COMMUNICATIONS

This section states those stakeholders who will be notified when the component termination request is approved.

_____
_____
_____

F. CHANGE REQUESTS

This section describes the change requests that will be needed once the termination request is approved.

_____
_____
_____

G. PROGRAM DOCUMENTATION CHANGES

This section describes each of the program documents that will be updated when the component termination request is approved, the program management team member who is responsible for the update, and when it is expected to be completed.

_____
_____
_____

H. COMPONENT TERMINATION CLOSURE CERTIFICATE

This section states who will prepare the certificate and who will sign off on it.

_____
_____
_____

I. APPROVALS

This section contains the approval of the component termination request by the program manager, program sponsor, members of the program's governance board, and other key stakeholders as required.

Signatures and Date Approval Obtained

Program manager	_____
Program sponsor	_____
Governance board member 1	_____
Governance board member 2	_____
Governance board member N	_____
Stakeholder 1	_____
Stakeholder 2	_____
Stakeholder N	_____

References

1. United States Department of Defense, *Defense Acquisition Guidebook*, 2004.
2. United States Department of Defense. *Integrated Master Plan and Integrated Master Schedule Preparation and Use Guide*, 2005.
3. Project Management Institute. *The Standard for Program Management* - Second Edition. Newtown Square, PA., 2008.
4. Dr. Seuss, *Oh, the Places You'll Go!* New York: Random House, 1993.
5. *Analyze This*, Village Road Show Pictures, 1999.

Index

A

Acronyms, xvii
American National Standards Institute (ANSI), xiii
Assumptions, 15–16, 18, 22–23
  program benefits, 6
Audit plan
  approvals, 55, 57
  audit results, 55, 56–57
  goals, 54, 56
  instructions, 53–55
  monitoring and tracking, 55, 57
  roles and responsibilities, 54, 56
  schedule, 53, 54–55, 56
  template, 55–56
Audit report, 198
  appendices, 200, 202
  approvals, 200, 202
  audit rationale, 199
  audit type, 199
  background information, 199, 201
  findings, 200, 202
  instructions, 198–200
  methodology, 199, 201
  participants, 199
  place, 199
  program areas affected, 199
  recommendations, 200, 202
  template, 201
  time period, 199

B

Benefits realization plan, 33
  approvals, 36, 39
  benefit impacts on outcomes, 35, 37
  benefits delivery schedule, 36, 38
  benefits-related risks, 36, 39
  communications plan, 36, 38
  instructions, 34–36
  metrics and procedures, 35, 38
  program benefit definitions, 35, 37
  required changes to processes and systems, 36, 39
  roles and responsibilities, 35–36, 38
  template, 37
  transitions, 36, 39
Benefits realization report, 231
  approvals, 233
  background information, 232
  benefits realized during reporting period, 232
  instructions, 231–233
  new benefits, 233
  preparer, 232
  program overview, 232
  qualitative benefits, 232–233
  quantitative benefits, 232
  reporting period, 232
  template, 233–235
  unrealized benefits, 233

285

C

Change management plan
    approvals, 57, 60, 62
    change control, 59, 62
    change evaluation and approval process, 59, 61
    change process definition, 58, 61
    change status accounting and control, 59–60, 62
    change type, 58–59, 61
    change verification and audits, 60, 62
    identification and controlled configuration items, 59, 61
    instructions, 58–60
    template, 60
Change request form, 140
    change description, 141
    change identification number, 141
    instructions, 140–141
    PWBS number, 141
    request date, 141
    requestor identification, 141
    template, 141
Change request log, 218
    change description, 220
    change ID number, 220
    change impact, 220
    change owner, 220
    change type, 220
    closed date, 221
    cost, 220
    date, 220, 221
    decision, 220
    decision maker and actual resolution, 221
    feasibility, 220
    input/output processes, 219
    instructions, 218–221
    level of effort, 220
    priority/severity, 220
    proposed resolution, 220
    PWBS number, 220
    requested by, 220
    risk/opportunity, 220
    subsequent impacts, 221
    template, 222
Change type, 141
Communications log, 97
    instructions, 98–99
Communications strategy, 99
    approvals, 101, 103
    assumptions, 100, 102
    constraints, 100, 102
    information transfer, 100, 102
    instructions, 99–101
    organizational, 100, 101
    potential communications channels assessment, 100, 102
    resolution of stakeholder issues and concerns, 100, 102
    template, 101
Component charter, 223
    approvals, 224, 226
    component constraints, 224, 226
    component deliverables, 223–224, 225
    component expected benefits, 223, 225
    component manager's authority, 224, 226
    component objective, 223, 225
    component stakeholders, 224, 225
    instructions, 223–2224
    related program assumptions, 224, 226
    template, 224
Component initiation request, 205
    approvals, 206–207, 209
    business case, 205–206, 207
    change requests, 206, 208
    component governance structure, 206, 208
    component sponsor, 206, 208
    instructions, 205–207
    program documentation changes, 206, 209
    project/operations manager, 206, 208
    resource requirements, 206, 208
    stakeholder communication, 206, 208
    template, 207
Component stakeholder management guidelines, 78
    instructions, 78–80
Component termination request, 278
    approvals, 280, 282
    change requests, 279, 281
    closure certification, 280, 281
    closure requirements, 279, 281
    instructions, 278–280
    program documentation changes, 279, 282
    reasons for, 279, 280
    resources released, 279, 281
    stakeholder communication, 279, 281
    template, 280
Component transition request, 209
    approvals, 211, 213
    change requests, 211, 213
    closure requirements, 211, 212
    instructions, 210–211

program completion closure certificate, 211, 213
program documentation changes, 211, 213
project completion closure certificate, 211
reasons for request, 210, 212
resources released, 210, 212
stakeholder communications, 211, 212
template, 211
Constraints, 15–16, 18, 22
program benefits, 6
Contingency plan, 137
approvals, 138, 139
cost impact, 138, 139
instructions, 137–138
required resources, 138, 139
responsibilities, 138, 139
schedule impact, 138, 139
template, 138
trigger conditions, 137, 139
Contract closure procedure, 255
instructions, 256–257
Contracts management plan, 156
approvals, 160, 163
buyer-seller performance requirements, 158, 161
change control, 159, 162
contract closure, 159–160, 163
contract performance review meetings, 159, 162
instructions, 156–160
meetings to be held with contractors, 159, 162
monitoring and control, 158, 161
payment control, 159, 162–163
roles and responsibilities, 158, 160–161
schedules, 158–159, 161
status reporting, 159, 162
subcontract selection process criteria, 158, 161
template, 160

D

Decision log, 202–203
instructions, 203
template, 204
Defense Acquisition Guidebook, xiv

E

Eisenhower, Dwight D., 3
Execution phase, 191

audit report, 198–202
change request log, 218–222
component charter, 223–226
component initiation request, 205–209
component transition request, 209–213
decision log, 202–204
program issues register, 214–216
team charter, 191–198
External influences, 13

F

Financial analysis, 11, 13
Financial metrics, 150
First steps, 4

G

Governance decision register, 235
actual implementation date, 236
assigned to, 236
background information, 236
decision number, 236
implementation date, 236
instructions, 235–236
life cycle phase, 236
meeting purpose, 236
PWBS number, 236
Governance requirements, 16, 19
Green, Allen, xvi
Guide to the Project Management Body of Knowledge (PMBOK), xiii, 1

I

Impact analysis, 227
approvals, 229, 231
approving authority, 228–229, 230
change decision, 228, 230
change requests, 229, 231
communication of change decision, 229, 230
effect on common objectives, 228, 230
factors involved in change, 228, 230
instructions, 228–231
template, 229
type of change, 228, 230
Initial stakeholder identification, 6
approvals, 9
instructions, 7–9
program life cycle phases, 9
stakeholder communications methods, 9

stakeholder definition, 8–9
stakeholder roles, 9
template, 8
Interface management plan, 163–164
    approvals, 165, 168
    governance board management interface, 165, 167
    instructions, 164–165
    interpersonal interface identification, 164, 166
    logistical interface identification, 164, 166
    management approach for component interfaces, 165, 167
    organizational interface identification, 164, 166
    political interface identification, 164–165, 167
    roles and responsibilities for, 165, 168
    technical interface instruction, 164, 166
    template, 165
Internal influences, 13
Issue escalation process, 50
    instructions, 50–52

J

Justification, 22

K

Knowledge management plan, 185
    approvals, 187, 189–190
    goals and objectives, 186, 188
    instructions, 185–187
    metrics, 187, 189
    rewards and recognition, 187, 189
    roles and responsibilities, 186–187, 188–189
    template, 188
    tools and techniques, 187, 189
    training and orientation sessions, 187, 189
Knowledge transition, 266
    approvals, 268, 270
    contractors and suppliers, 267, 269
    customer involvement, 267–268, 270
    governance reviews, 267, 270
    knowledge management goals and objectives, 266, 268
    meetings and review, 267, 269
    monitoring and controlling processes, 267, 269
    program management plan, 267, 269
    report instructions, 266–268
    report template, 268
    stakeholder management, 267, 270
    team performance, 267, 269

L

Lessons learned database, 124
    affected program processes, 126
    archives submission date, 128
    date submitted to knowledge repository, 128
    description, 125–126
    instructions, 125–127
    key words, 126
    lesson learned number, 125
    program documents affected, 128
    program life cycle phase, 126
    PWBS number, 125
    submission date, 126
    submittor, 126
    supporting details, 126
    use in program, 128
Lessons learned review agenda, 123
    decisions, 124
    instructions, 123–124
    risk management processes, 124
    suggestions and recommendations, 124
Levin, Ginger, xv

M

Monitoring and controlling phase, 227
    benefits realization report, 231–235
    governance decision register, 235–236
    impact analysis, 227–231
    program closure recommendation, 244–248
    program performance report, 237–244
    risk audit report, 249–253

O

Organizational process assets, 3

P

Paralysis by analysis, 3
Phase gate review agenda, 46
    instructions, 46–47
Planning
    indispensability of, 3
    rationale, 3–4
Pre-Program Preparations Phase, 5

alternative analysis, 13
approvals, 9, 14, 19
assumptions and constraints, 18
business case, 10–14
financial analysis, 13
governance requirements, 19
initial stakeholder identification, 6–9
initial stakeholder identification template, 8
internal and external influences, 13
program benefits statement, 5–6, 13, 17
program brief, 14–19
program brief template, 16
program business case template, 12
program complexity, 14
program importance, 17
program life cycle phases, 9
program schedule, 18
program scope and components, 18
program strategic objectives, 17
program vision, 17
purpose statement, 8
required resources, 13
resource requirements, 18
risks and issues, 18
stakeholder communications methods, 9
stakeholder considerations, 19
stakeholder definition, 8–9
stakeholder roles, 9
Procurement management plan, 150–151
approvals, 153, 156
contract types, 153, 155
instructions, 151–153
procurement documents, 152–153, 155
procurement planning approach, 152, 154
proposals, 153, 156
qualified seller lists, 153, 155
required and available resources, 152, 154
required procurements, 152, 155
sourcing decisions, 152
statements of work, 152, 155
template, 153–154
Procurement performance report, 273
budget status, 274
change request status, 274
contract number, 273
contract overview, 274
date, 273
deliverable status, 274
earned value metrics, 275
instructions, 273–275
issue resolution status, 274
preparer, 273
procurement process recommendations, 275
report recipients, 273
resource issues, 275
results of final contractor performance review, 275
risk resolution status, 274
schedule status, 274
template, 276–278
Program architecture plan (baseline), 112
approvals, 114, 115
change management, 114, 115
instructions, 112–114
management approach, 114, 115
program structure, 113, 115
template, 114
Program benefits statement, 5, 11, 13, 15, 17, 22
instructions, 6
Program brief, 14
approvals, 19
assumptions and constraints, 18
governance requirements, 19
instructions, 14–19
program benefits, 17
program importance, 17
program schedule, 18
program scope and components, 18
program strategic objectives, 17
program vision, 17
resource requirements, 18
risks and issues, 18
stakeholder considerations, 19
template, 16
Program business case, 10
alternative analysis, 13
approvals, 14
financial analysis, 13
instructions, 10–14
internal and external influences, 13
program benefits, 13
program complexity, 14
program strategic objectives, 12
required resources, 13
Program charter, 21–22
approvals, 23, 27
assumptions, 22–23, 25
benefits, 22, 24
constraints, 22, 25
governance, 23, 26
high-level road map, 23, 26
instructions, 22–27
justification, 22, 24
known risks and issues, 23, 25

manager authority, 23, 25
resource requirements, 23, 26
schedule, 25
scope, 23, 25
stakeholder issues, 23, 26
template, 23–28
vision, 22, 24
Program closure phase, 255
component termination request, 278–282
contract closure procedure, 255–257
knowledge transition, 266–270
procurement performance report, 273–278
program final report, 258–266
supplier performance review, 271–273
Program closure recommendation, 244
approvals, 246, 248
closure certificate, 246, 248
continued benefits realization, 246, 248
disposition of property, 246, 247
instructions, 245–246
reasons for request, 245, 247
recommended changes, 246, 247
resources released, 245, 247
stakeholder communications, 246, 248
template, 246
Program communications management plan, 91
approvals, 94, 97
escalation process for communications issues, 93, 96
frequency of information, 93, 96
glossary of common terminology, 93, 96
information recipients, 93, 95
information to be communicated, 92, 95
instructions, 91–94
meeting and e-mail guidelines, 93, 97
stakeholder communications requirements, 92, 95
team member responsibilities, 93, 95
technologies to convey information, 93, 95
template, 94
update methods, 93, 96
Program complexity, 12, 14
Program final report, 258
approvals, 261, 265
baseline changes, 260, 263
benefits transitioned, 261, 265
charters, 259
communications, 260, 264
earned value, 259
escalated risks and issues, 260, 263
financial management, 259
instructions, 258–261
interfaces, 260, 263
knowledge repository, 261, 265
lessons learned, 261, 265
organizational, 259–260
program acceptance, 261, 264–265
program benefits delivered, 258, 262
program decisions, 260, 264
program issues, 260, 263
program metrics summary, 259, 263
program participants, 259, 262
program risks, 260, 263
program strategic objectives, 258, 262
resources, 259
stakeholder management, 259, 262
supplier performance, 260, 264
team management, 259
template, 261
terminations, 260, 264
Program financial plan, 145
approvals, 147, 150
financial framework and goals, 146, 148
format and criteria for cost estimating, 146, 149
funding constraints, 146, 148
instructions, 145–147
methods for financial monitoring and control, 147, 149
program financial metrics, 147, 149
program operational costs, 146, 148
program payment schedule, 147, 149
remaining budget allocation, 147, 150
template, 147–148
Program governance plan, 40
approvals, 43, 47
assessment of effectiveness, 43, 46
gate review requirements, 42–43, 45
goals, 41, 44
governance decisions, 42, 45
initiation, transition, and termination processes, 42, 45
instructions, 40–43
meeting schedule, 42, 45
organizational structure, 41–42, 44
performance review requirements, 43, 45
roles and responsibilities, 42, 44
template, 43
Program importance, 15, 17
Program initiation stage, 21
program charter, 21–27
program road map, 27–31
Program issues register, 214

date, 215, 216
date closed, 216
decision, 216
identifier, 215
instructions, 214–216
issue identification number, 215
issue impact, 215
issue owner, 215
issue type, 215
proposed resolution, 215
PWBS number, 215
resolved by, 216
root cause, 215
subsequent impacts, 216
template, 217
Program life cycle, phases, 7, 9
Program management, 1–2
Program management life cycle, 34
Program management plan, 176–177
    approvals, 181, 184
    budget and cash flow requirements, 179, 182
    end result and schedule, 179, 181
    instructions, 178–181
    management approach, 179–180, 183
    program assumptions, 179, 182
    program constraints, 179, 182
    program dependencies, 179, 182
    program management information system, 180, 183
    program organization, 180, 183
    risks and issues, 179, 182
    schedule milestones and budget goals by component, 180, 183–184
    template, 181
    tolerance ranges and decision making, 180, 184
    updates, 180–181, 184
Program Management Professional credential, xi
Program performance report, 237
    benefit status, 238
    business case, 238
    change request status, 239
    date, 238
    deliverable status, 239
    earned value metrics, 240
    escalated risks and issues, 240
    funds expended, 238
    instructions, 237–241
    issue resolution status, 239
    planned accomplishments, 241
    preparer, 238
    program budget, 238
    program name, 238
    reporting period accomplishments, 241
    resource issues, 240
    risk resolution status, 240
    schedule status, 239
    template, 241–244
Program requirements document, 107
    approvals, 109, 111
    instructions, 107–109
    requirements analysis process, 109, 110
    requirements gathering tools, 109, 110
    requirements management process, 108, 110
    requirements review process, 109, 111
    requirements validation and verification, 109, 111
    template, 109–110
Program resource plan, 103
    approvals, 105, 107
    instructions, 103–105
    internal and external required resources, 104, 106
    methods for meeting resource requirements, 104, 106
    organizational influences, 104, 106
    resource calendars, 105, 106
    template, 105
    tracking and monitoring, 105, 106
Program review agenda, 48
    benefits status, 49
    budget status, 49
    change request status, 49
    component status, 49
    contract status, 49–50
    decisions, 50
    instructions, 48–50
    issue status, 49
    lessons learned, 50
    milestones and deliverables, 48–49
    program overview, 48
    resource status, 49
    risks, 49
    stakeholder communications, 49
Program risk management plan, 127
    approvals, 130, 132
    instructions, 127–130
    probability and impact matrix, 129
    risk categories, 128, 131
    risk management approach, 128, 130
    risk management budget, 129, 131
    risk management schedule, 129, 131
    risk reporting, 129, 132

risk tracking, 130, 132
roles and responsibilities, 128–129, 131
stakeholder risk tolerances, 129, 132
template, 130
Program risk register, 133
actual response, 135
approvals, 135
close date, 136
date of identification, 134
identified by, 134
instructions, 133–136
probability/impact, 135
probability/impact matrix, 136
proposed response, 135
PWBS numbers, 134
risk ID number, 134
risk owner, 135
risk type, 134
root cause, 135
subsequent impacts, 135
symptoms and warning signs, 135
Program road map, 27–28
approvals, 26, 31
endpoint objectives, 28, 30
instructions, 28–31
key challenges and risks, 28, 30
key milestones and decision points, 28, 30
program organization, 29, 30
supporting infrastructure, 29, 30
template, 29
Program schedule, 16
Program scope and components, 15, 18
Program scope management plan
approvals, 65, 66
expected stability of scope, 63, 64, 66
instructions, 63–65
product and program scope, 63–64, 65
scope change control process, 65, 66
scope statement development process, 64, 66
template, 65
work breakdown structure development process, 64, 66
Program scope statement, 67–68
acceptance criteria, 69, 71
approvals, 69, 71
assumptions, 69, 70
constraints, 69, 70
definitive cost estimate, 69, 71
deliverables and milestones, 69, 71
instructions, 68–69
objectives and success criteria, 68, 70
program scope, 68, 70

resources, 69, 71
risks, 69, 71
template, 69
Program setup phase
audit plan, 53–57
benefits realization plan, 34–39
change management plan, 57–63
change request form, 140–141
communications log, 97–99
communications strategy, 99–103
component stakeholder management guidelines, 78–80
contingency plan, 137–140
contracts management plan, 156–163
financial metrics, 150
interface management plan, 163–168
issue escalation process, 50–52
knowledge management plan, 185–190
lessons learned database, 124–127
lessons learned review agenda, 123–124
phase gate review agenda, 46–47
procurement management plan, 150–156
program architecture plan—baseline, 112–116
program communications management plan, 91–97
program financial plan, 145–150
program governance plan, 40–46
program management plan, 176–185
program requirements document, 107–111
program resource plan, 103–107
program review agenda, 48–50
program risk management plan, 127–133
program risk register, 133–137
program scope management plan, 63–67
program scope statement, 67–72
program stakeholder management plan, 72–78
program transition plan, 173–176
programs WBS, 116
quality management plan, 117–121
risk management planning meeting agenda, 121–123
schedule management plan, 141–145
staffing management plan, 168–173
stakeholder inventory, 82–87
stakeholder management strategy, 87–90
stakeholder register, 80–82
task responsibility matrix, 116
work breakdown structure matrix, 116–117
Program stakeholder management plan, 72

approvals, 74, 75
considerations, 77
instructions, 72–74
plan preparation steps, 77–78
stakeholder analysis chart, 74, 75
stakeholder commitment, 74, 75
stakeholder communications approach, 74, 75
stakeholder management matrix, 76
template, 74
Program transition plan, 173
approvals, 174, 176
component transition requests, 173–174, 175
documentation requirements, 174, 175
instructions, 173–174
roles and responsibilities, 174, 175–176
template, 174
transition critical success factors, 174, 176
transition process, 173, 175
Program vision, 15, 17, 22
Program work breakdown structure (WBS), 116
Project interdependence, 6
Project Management Body of Knowledge (PMBOK), xi
Project Management Institute (PMI), xi, 1, 3
Projects, as assets, 2

Q

Quality management plan, 117
approvals, 118, 120–121
instructions, 117–118
organizational quality standards, 117, 119
program benefits overview, 117–118, 119
program-level roles and responsibilities, 118, 120
quality metrics, 118, 120
quality planning, assurance, and control requirements, 118, 120
quality planning tools and techniques, 118, 119
template, 118–119

R

Resources required, 11, 13, 16, 18
Risk audit report
appendices, 251, 253
approvals, 251, 253
audit participants, 250
background information, 250, 252
findings, 250–251, 252
instructions, 249–251
methodology, 250, 252
place, 250
program areas affected, 250
reason for audit, 250
recommendations, 251, 253
template, 251–252
time period, 250
Risk management planning meeting agenda, 121
decisions, 122
instructions, 121–122
risk management activities, 122
risk management plan, 122
risk management responsibilities, 122
Risks, 18
Rohn, Jim, 1

S

Schedule management plan, 141
approvals, 143, 145
incremental benefits delivery, 143, 144
instructions, 142–143
program funding schedule, 142, 144
program schedule constraints, 142, 144
schedule management software, 143, 144
schedule metrics, 143, 145
schedule tracking and monitoring methods, 143, 144
template, 143
Staffing management plan, 168
approvals, 170, 172
compliance requirements, 170, 172
instructions, 168–170
internal and external required resources, 169, 171
methods to meet human resource requirements, 169, 171
organizational influences, 169, 171
program team roles and responsibilities, 169, 171
resource calendars, 169, 171
rewards and recognition, 170, 172
staffing release, 160–170, 172
template, 170
Stakeholder communication methods, 8, 9
Stakeholder definition, 7, 8–9
Stakeholder inventory, 82
approvals, 85, 86
instructions, 83–85

matrix example, 87
possible stakeholder responses, 84, 86
potential mitigation strategies, 84, 86
stakeholder categories, 84, 85
stakeholder influence, 84, 86
template, 85
Stakeholder management strategy, 87
    approvals, 89, 90
    instructions, 87–89
    stakeholder engagement, 88, 89
    stakeholder feedback, 88, 90
    stakeholder mitigation strategies, 88, 90
    template, 89
Stakeholder register, 80
    areas of influence, 81
    contact information, 81
    information requirements, 82
    instructions, 80–82
    issues identified, 82
    management strategy, 82
    name and position, 80
    program impact, 82
    program opinion, 81
    resolution and date, 82
    responsible team member, 82
Stakeholder roles, 7, 9
Standard for Program Management—Second Edition (2008), xiii, xiv, 1
Strategic objectives, 11, 12, 15, 17
Success criteria, 6
Supplier performance review, 271
    agenda instructions, 271–273
    change control, 272
    claims process, 272
    contract overview, 271
    invoicing and payment processes, 272
    monitoring and control processes, 272
    signatures, 272–273
    specific performance requirements, 272

T

Task responsibility matrix, 116
Team charter, 191
    administrative activities, 194, 197
    approvals, 194, 198
    charter updates, 194, 198
    client's role, 193, 196
    conflict management process, 193, 197
    decision-making process, 193–194, 197
    deliverables, 193, 197
    instructions, 192–194
    issue calculation process, 194, 197–198
    other stakeholders, 193, 196
    program commitment statement, 193, 195
    program manager's role, 193, 195
    program sponsor's role, 193, 195
    scope/boundaries of work, 193, 196
    success measures, 193, 196
    team performance objectives, 193, 196
    template, 194–195
Templates, 4

U

Unmanaged change, 3
U.S. Department of Defense, xiv

W

Work breakdown structure matrix, 116–117